Lynn M Burlbaw

Search and Re-Search
What the Inquiring Teacher
Needs to Know

Falmer Press Teachers' Library Series: 2

Search and Re-Search
What the Inquiring Teacher
Needs to Know

Edited by

Rita S. Brause and John S. Mayher

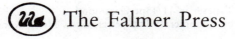 The Falmer Press

(A member of the Taylor & Francis Group)
London • New York • Philadelphia

UK   The Falmer Press, Rankine Road, Basingstoke, Hamsphire, RG24 0PR

USA   The Falmer Press, Taylor & Francis Inc., 1900 Frost Road, Suite 101, Bristol, PA 19007

First published 1991

We appreciate Carl Rakosi's permission to reproduce on p. 60 "The Experiment with a Rat" from his *Collected Poems* (1986) The National Poetry Foundation, University of Maine Press.

British Library Cataloguing in Publication Data
Search and re-search: what the inquiring teacher needs to know.
  1. Education. Research
  I. Brause, Rita S. II. Mayher, John S.
  370.78

  ISBN 1–85000–855–8
  ISBN 1–85000–856–6

Library of Congress Cataloging-in-Publication Data
Search and re-search: what the inquiring teacher needs to know/
  editors, Rita S. Brause and John S. Mayher.
      p.   cm.
    Includes bibliographical references and index.
    ISBN 1–85000–855–8: —ISBN 1–85000–856–6 (pbk.):
    1. Education—Research—United States. I. Brause, Rita S.
  II. Mayher, John Sawyer. III Title: Search and research.
  LB1028.25.U6S43   1991
  370'.7'8073—dc20   90-48863
                                                                CIP

Jacket design by Caroline Archer

Typeset in 11/13pt Garamond
by Graphicraft Typesetters Ltd., Hong Kong

Printed in Great Britain by Burgess Science Press, Basingstoke on paper which has a specified pH value on final paper manufacture of not less than 7.5 and is therefore 'acid free'.

Contents

List of Tables   vii

List of Figures   viii

Series Editor's Preface   ix

Introduction   x

Part I — An Inquiring/Learning Perspective   1

Chapter 1   New Lenses for Old Problems: What We Believe   3
            is What We See
            John S. Mayher

Chapter 2   The Never-ending Cycle of Teacher Growth   23
            John S. Mayher and Rita S. Brause

**Part II — Interpreting Published Research on Classroom   43
            Practice**

Chapter 3   Research Objectives: Generating Hypotheses,   45
            Testing Hypotheses and Critiquing Educational
            Practice
            Rita S. Brause and John S. Mayher

Chapter 4   Reading and Understanding Hypothesis Testing   63
            Research
            William L. Smith

Chapter 5   Reading Hypothesis Generating Research   91
            Ken Kantor

Contents

Part III — Designing and Conducting Classroom Research   113

Chapter 6   Finding and Framing Questions   115
             John S. Mayher and Rita S. Brause

Chapter 7   Collecting and Analyzing Classroom Data in   131
             Theory and in Practice
             Rita S. Brause and John S. Mayher

Chapter 8   Testing Hypotheses in Your Classroom   157
             James L. Collins

Chapter 9   Hypothesis Generating Studies in Your Classroom   181
             Rita S. Brause

Chapter 10   Concluding and Beginning   207
             John S. Mayher and Rita S. Brause

Notes on Contributors   211

Index   213

List of Tables

Table 3.1: A comparison of hypothesis generating and hypothesis testing research procedures — 57

Table 4.1: Mean spoken and written information scores for groups A and B — 83

Table 6.1: Framing research questions from our practice — 123

Table 7.1: Relative frequency of appearance of defined words — 140

Table 7.2: Frequency of appearance of the world *synonym* — 150

Table 7.3: Number of turns to match synonyms — 150

Table 8.1: Matrix pattern for presenting sample studied — 175

Table 8.2: Comparing length of essay — 176

Table 8.3: Comparing error rates — 176

Table 8.4: Two-way ANOVA for length of essays — 177

Table 8.5: Two-way ANOVA for rate of error — 177

Table 9.1: Examples of hypothesis generating research design — 184

Table 9.2: Example of a writing episode — 197

List of Figures

Figure 2.1:   The never-ending cycle of teacher growth   26

Figure 2.2:   The Teaching Act Model   27

Figure 3.1:   Sources of professional knowledge   50

Figure 3.2:   A schematic presentation of hypothesis generating   56
and hypothesis testing research procedures

Figure 4.1:   Oral and written syntactic complexity across   84
grades

Figure 4.2:   Pre- to post-test change in two groups   84

Figure 4.3:   Change in two groups across five points   84

Figure 4.4:   Comparison of two plots of pre- and post-test   86
change

Figure 5.1:   Data sources cited in selected research reports   104

Figure 7.1:   Transcript of a three-minute excerpt of a word-   149
study lesson

Figure 8.1:   Scatter diagram of number of errors on two drafts   162
for twenty-six writers

Figure 8.2:   Outlining clustered error scores   162

Figure 9.1:   Components of the analysis process   189

Figure 9.2:   Processes involved in generating hypotheses   190

Figure 9.3:   Study phases and procedures   198

Figure 9.4:   The functions of writing in room 12   201

Figure 10.1:   Benefits of teacher-research   208

Preface

This book constitutes the second volume in the new *Falmer Press Teachers' Library*. In its approach and tone the volume resonates with the major objective of this new series of books. Above all the concern is to inform schools-based practitioners of research findings and research concepts which are of use to them as they go about their daily work.

The tone of optimism which can be found throughout the book is represented at a number of levels. Firstly, the editors judge that schools-based studies will conceivably lead to the development of more appropriate educational policies, ones which are, to use their words, 'sensitive to the needs of individuals who live in classrooms'. Alongside this idealistic commitment to more sensitive educational policy making, there is the commitment to make research 'accessible and attractive' to schools-based practitioners whether they be teachers, administrators, interns or curriculum developers. Throughout the volume is their belief that the provision of research studies and the involvement of practitioners in that research is the way to improve practice. At root the book echoes an old theme, which is nonetheless true for being long established, namely that the best way to improve schooling and the school curriculum, and the best way to develop students is through teacher development. Teacher development happens best when we have reflective teachers who act out their daily lives as learning individuals. It is not by chance that they begin the volume with the quote from Garth Boomer that 'to learn deliberately is to research'. This is true for all individuals, but perhaps most importantly for teachers, who in the very nature of their work act as mediators and facilitators in the learning process. For a new library of books dedicated to a notion of teachers as researchers this book makes a very eloquent and powerful testimony.

Ivor Goodson
Series Editor

Introduction

To learn deliberately is to research. (Garth Boomer)

If research is seen primarily as a process of discovery, then the day-to-day work of a teacher comes under the term *teachers as researchers*. It cannot be said too often that effective teaching depends upon the concern of every teacher for the *rationale* by which he or she works. (James N. Britton)

Living necessitates learning — and most of that learning occurs through personal inquiry, another term for research. Garth Boomer and Jimmy Britton see research both in our everyday lives and our professional lives. Professional educators make thousands of decisions about organizing instruction and assessing student learning. These decisions are based on personal hunches, assumptions, established traditions, textbook contents, teachers' guides, research reports, and explicit theories. Contemporary educators, enacting our professional responsibilities as reflective practitioners must study, search, and re-search to form and inform our decisions. We read published research critically in addition to conducting research to reflect on and enhance the effectiveness of our practice.

We are determined to demystify research so that all educators will be equally empowered to interpret the past and guide the future. This perspective contrasts with previous traditions which separated educational researchers from those who work in schools. By explaining research traditions, the authors hope to open the world of research to a larger pool of people, particularly those who will be the focus of much of this research, and therefore need to play a much more influential role in the process and interpretation of findings.

We recognize that research in school settings enlightens us by identifying numerous influential factors concealed in laboratory-based studies. From school-based studies the complexity of school achievement becomes apparent, which can influence the development of more appropriate educational policies, sensitive to the needs of individuals who live in classrooms. There are extensive references to specific classroom practices. These examples are intended to make the concepts and processes accessible to people who work with students at all grade levels. The goal is to make research as inviting as possible to all school-based practitioners — teachers, administrators, interns, and curriculum developers. Let's join the research community and utilize the findings of school-based research to improve educational practice for all students, enabling schooling to more consistently result in the mental liberation inherent in the term 'education'.

When we do research we call on our professional expertise to both explore the consistency between our theories and our practices and to design strategies which will more effectively implement good educational practice. A researching stance requires us to 'leave all our assumptions at the door' so we can explore familiar territories as though they were uncharted: our schools, our classrooms, our students. We invite all committed professional educators to join our never-ending search.

The chapters address the clarion call for teacher empowerment and accountability through understanding and conducting research. Acknowledging the importance of educators' dual roles as critical consumers of research and as teacher-researchers, *Search and Re-search* provides extensive guidance in both how to read research and how to conduct research particularly in classroom settings. It focusses on the concerns of classroom educators at all educational levels. *Search and Re-search* tries to initiate educational practitioners with little conscious research experience into the early steps of this exciting professional activity, thereby sustaining the torch of idealism which initially attracted us all to education, and making burn-out impossible.

The original inspiration for this book can be traced to Tony Petrosky of the University of Pittsburgh who as Chair of the National Council of Teachers of English Standing Committee on Research asked the authors to consider writing a very different book. Through meetings in a series of bars at the sites of various NCTE conventions, this book's progress waxed and waned with the seasonal tides. While we're not at all sure how Tony will feel about his long delayed offspring, we have to acknowledge his initial impetus.

Similarly, David Dillon of McGill University, as Editor of *Language Arts*, inadvertently gave the collection a further push by asking the editors to write a column on teaching-as-learning for his journal. Many of the ideas which take final form here began as columns for *Language Arts*.

We are also grateful to those students and colleagues whose classroom data and insights have contributed to our general understanding of teaching and learning, and more specifically to particular aspects of this collection. Special thanks in this connection to Jo Bruno, Dorothy Feola, Adele Fiderer, Fran Boren Gilkenson, Denise Levine, Harold Vine, Patty Sue Williams and anonymous teachers whose classrooms we explored during the last decade.

Other people including our students in research courses have responded to and helped us revise these efforts along the way. We are grateful to all of them, but let's make special mention of Ruth Brause, Ana Fuentes, Lou Guinta, Sandra Lanzone, Nancy Lester, Denise Levine one more time; Carmen Mercado, Arlene Moliterno, Barbara Smuckler and Maxine Weiss.

Final thanks go to Bill Smith, Jim Collins and Ken Kantor for their collaborative efforts in the early stages and for their patience throughout the book's long gestation.

Rita S. Brause and John S. Mayher
New York
July 1990

Part One
An Inquiring/Learning Perspective

Professional educators are constantly learning, searching and re-searching for increased understanding despite the fact that most schools do not support the professional growth and intellectual stimulation which are outcomes of such activities. Nevertheless, professional educators adopt an inquiring, uncommonsense stance. The chapters in this section provide lenses for understanding research as the key to improving educational theory and educational practice. Engagement in this process is essential for our own sustenance as well as for the enhancement of our profession. The contributors set the stage for subsequent chapters which guide our reading of published research and our designing research within our classrooms.

Chapter 1

New Lenses for Old Problems: What We Believe is What We See

John S. Mayher

As we begin our journey into the world of research we often find, like Alice when she first went through the looking-glass, a world where our previously established mental constructs don't work very well to account for the new ideas which new theoretical lenses are revealing to us.[1] When Alice first meets the Red Queen, for example, she suddenly finds herself running as fast as she can, but 'The most curious part of the thing is, that the trees and the other things around' never changed places at all (Lewis Carroll, 1981, p. 126). However fast they went, they never seemed to pass anything. And when the Queen finally lets her rest, she observes

> 'In *our* country . . . you'd generally get to somewhere else — if you ran very fast for a long time as we've been doing.'

> 'A slow sort of country!' said the Queen, 'Now, *here*, you see, it takes all the running *you* can do, to keep in the same place. If you want to get somewhere else, you must run at least twice as fast as that.' (p. 127)

While it is true that most of us in teaching ofte feel that every time we open the school door we are in a looking-glass world where we are running fast to stay in place — particularly when we regard the stacks of student papers which seem to magically replenish themselves no matter how many we read – my reason for mentioning Alice's confusion is not to bemoan our fate. It is, instead, to point out that all of us view the world on the basis of our experiences in it, that we use these experience-based mental constructs to make predictions about the future course of events and further, that these constructs always influence and frequently distort our ability to perceive the nature of reality which surrounds us. We can't help but do so, of course, any more than Alice can help expecting to be under a different tree after running so fast and so long, but it is important both to be aware that we do so and to be prepared to change our mental constructs when experience doesn't conform to our predictions.

Theories and Teaching

Although I used the term 'constructs' to describe our knowledge, belief, and perceptual structures, derived from the work of George Kelly (1955), I could just as easily have used 'theories' or 'hypotheses'. My major purpose in this chapter is to try to explode one of the prevalent misconceptions that severely limits the possibilities of change in schools: the belief that theory, and research based on theory, have no direct relevance to pedagogical problems and that what is really needed are practical answers to the question: What can I do on Monday? I am going to argue that: What can I do on Monday? is always answered on the basis of theory. The problem, I will argue, is not that theory and research are not practical, but that we have built our practice on *unexamined* theories and inapplicable research.

This may seem paradoxical, but this time the White Queen has the answer. When Alice complains that: 'One *can't* believe impossible things' the Queen replies:

> I daresay you haven't had much practice ... When I was your age, I always did it for half-an-hour a day. Why, sometimes I've believed as many as six impossible things before breakfast. (p. 157)

The impossibility or impracticality disappears like the Cheshire Cat — maybe leaving a smile behind — when we see that all of our teaching decisions are based on our view of the world. This is the source of the subtitle of this chapter: what we see is what we believe. How we view our subject determines what we see as problems and what we will accept as solutions to those problems. While many teachers may not recognize that these perceptions are theory based, they are no less so for being unrecognized. Unless one has a theory of spelling, there are no spelling problems; without a theory of grammar, no participles can dangle; in the absence of a theory of literature, there are no plots or themes.

Theory itself often seems like a fearful word to teachers for whom a scientific view of the world may be alien. There are undoubtedly many aspects of teaching which will continue to resist scientific explanation, and many of which depend upon the idiosyncratic relations of a particular teacher and a particular class. But for many areas of our teaching, scientific inquiry is not only possible but essential if we are to most effectively help our students to learn. *Theories* are attempts to explain phenomena in a particular domain by formulating explicit principles and laws that account for what happens.

The distinction that I make here between common and uncommon sense theories is based on the view that all of us operate in our daily lives on the basis of personal explanations about why things happen which can be called theories. But it is more important to distinguish between intuitive theories (*common sense*) and more scientific ones (*uncommon sense*), since only the latter have been built on explicit inquiry and are susceptible to change through further research.

Science is necessary, in fact, because things are not always as they seem. If appearance and reality always coincided, there would be no need for science. We could, for example, go on believing that the sun circles the earth since that is what it appears to do. But scientific theories have taught us that, despite how it appears to our common-sense, the earth is not flat, and the sun does not circle the earth. The thrust of this chapter is that, like Alice, we can never be certain about the conceptual lenses we are using to look at our problems since what seems to be most real or basic or to be taken for granted may, after scientific inquiry, prove to be as illusory as the 'reality' of a flat earth.

If our common sense assumptions or beliefs about effective teaching were always accurate, there would be no need to worry about any of this at all. But since every teaching activity is designed to solve a problem, it becomes crucially important to understand that every time we perceive a problem we do so on the basis of a lens provided by a theory or set of theories. I will exemplify how this works shortly, but first I must admit that many of the theories that have been urged on us as teachers as panaceas for our difficulties, certainly aren't, or at least aren't directly so, teaching transformational-generative grammar to students being the most obvious case that I am familiar with. And second, that even the most relevant theoretical insights or research findings need to be transformed through serious intellectual endeavor in the process of applying them to teaching activities.

Donald Schön (1983) has gone further and argued that theories and knowledge developed in the laboratory are frequently misleading guides to practice and to solving practical problems like those facing teachers. He argues that the kinds of controls imposed, and the abstraction from the context of the real world necessary in what he calls 'technical rationality' research, makes it inevitable that the knowledge generated by that research will not neatly fit the swampy and messy problems of the real world of professional practice. He urges practitioners to become researchers of their own practice — the major theme of this book — and attempts to show that the kind of knowledge generated by such teacher research, which he calls reflection-in-action, is of a different, but no less important sort than that generated by theorists working in the traditions of technical rationality.

Whether the knowledge that is needed to improve practice is to be based on the transformation of a technical rational theory into a form which is usable or whether it is derived directly from practice through reflection-in-action research, the crucial issue is that we cannot assume that the lenses through which we initially define teaching problems are the appropriate ones. In my *Uncommon Sense* (Mayher, 1990) I argue that the failure to really make improvements in practice has derived from our failure to reconceptualize our unconsciously built common-sense theories of teaching and learning. Part of what is necessary, therefore, for teacher research and reflection-in-action to be effective, is to learn to recognize and critique our unexamined beliefs and assumptions. The process may not be as dramatic as that which Alice experienced in the looking-glass world, but seeing that many of the things we have always taken for granted may be hurting us as much as they help, is a crucial first step toward becoming what Schön calls a reflective practitioner.

Commonsense Versus Uncommonsense Theories

Part of the reason this process is difficult, is that most of us operate most of the time, even in our professional lives, on the basis of what I am calling commonsense theories. These are the theories which we have largely built on the basis of our personal experiences and the violations of which are so troubling to Alice. Our memories, like Alice's don't permit us to 'remember things before they happen', and since we tend to agree with the White Queen that 'It's a poor sort of memory that only works backwards', we compensate by assuming on the basis of our commonsense theories that the future will be much like the past. While that is both normal and essential, theories of this sort usually have the weakness of being largely unconscious, unreflected upon, and relatively impermeable in the sense that we tend to try to have our reality fit our theory, rather than adjusting our theory to be better in harmony with our changing sense of reality.

Commonsense theories in education are particularly difficult to penetrate because they tend to have been built on the experiences of teachers when they were students of the age they are teaching, rather than on any later learning. When Alice discusses education with the Mock Turtle, he allows that he only took:

... the regular course.

What was that? inquired Alice.

'Reeling and Writhing, of course, to begin with', the Mock Turtle replied, 'and then the different branches of Arithmetic, Ambition, Distraction, Uglification and Derision'. (p. 73)

For many teachers the kinds of Reeling and Writhing we teach and the way we teach them are more affected by our experiences as students than by any teacher preparation courses, district curricula, or in-service extravaganzas. This is true, in part, because we were usually relatively good Reelers and Writhers or we wouldn't be teaching these subjects. But mostly it is true because our own student experience defined the way education is 'spozed to be. Perhaps because we have never been through the looking-glass, nothing that has happened to us since has had much effect on our most basic assumptions about what kids are supposed to learn and how they are to learn it.

The problem with commonsense theories in education is that they lead us to identify the wrong problems, to ask the wrong questions, and to come up with inadequate answers. This is principally true because they assume that the basic principles underlying our work are all unchallengeably true and the only important questions remaining are of the *What* do I do Monday? (and *How* do I do it?) sort. This would be tolerable, I guess, if everyone were convinced that we were doing an effective job, but ...

Uncommonsense theories, on the other hand, while connected to personal experience, are more based on collective, public, and shared experiences, not idiosyncratic ones. They are more likely to be both conscious and to have been consciously learned. They are more reflected upon, more explicitly worked out, and perhaps most importantly, more open to change and modification on the basis of our own experience and that of others. Although uncommonsense theories may be as strongly held and as fervently argued for as commonsense theories, uncommonsense theories contain a commitment to both empirical verification and to revision or even abandonment on the basis of counter-examples.

We don't have any fully worked out uncommonsense theories which explain all the issues and phenomena we are concerned with as educators. But that strengthens our need to shift the source of our curricular decisions from commonsense to uncommonsense theories. It is only by attempting to develop and implement new theory-based curricula with an uncommonsense spirit of experimentation and revision that we can begin to close the gap between what we wish to achieve (our goals) and what we are actually accomplishing (our results).

One of the reasons we don't have very many adequate uncommonsense theories in education is that the complexities of the human mind, its language system, as well as all the other influences on human development, are so difficult to explain. Ironically, one of the advantages of uncommonsense theories is that they explicitly recognize and have specific mechanisms for gradually filling in the gaps both for what they can and cannot explain. They offer only hypotheses, not certainties, but it is only through formulating and testing hypotheses and reformulating new ones that we are likely to ever understand more than we do about why our pedagogical practices are likely (or unlikely) to lead to our desired goals.

To adopt an uncommonsense approach to education requires a tolerance for ambiguity and uncertainty, however, which many teachers (and indeed most people) find highly uncomfortable. We do, to be sure, have to make teaching decisions, plan lessons, evaluate student learning on the basis of the best approximation we have of the way things work. But unless we recognize that we are employing *tentative* strategies rather than eternal verities, the prospects for change and improvement are dim indeed. And until all teachers become partners in the research enterprise leading to better answers to our questions, stagnation is the most likely outcome.

When Alice discovers 'Jabberwocky' her first problem is merely to decode it. She solves the problem by holding it up to a mirror, a logical step in a looking-glass world. Once she has done so, however, she is still in a quandary, for what is she to make of:

> 'Twas brillig and the slithy toves
>   Did gyre and gimble in the wabe:
> All mimsy were the borogoves,
>   And the mome raths outgrabe. (p. 117)

'It seems rather pretty', she said when she had finished it, 'but it's *rather* hard to understand'. (You see she didn't like to confess, even to herself, that she couldn't make it out at all.) (p. 119)

She is still puzzled by it when she runs across one of the world's most self-important literary critics (and teachers?), Humpty Dumpty. Professor Dumpty, with little tolerance for ambiguity and full confidence in his own commonsense certainty, is prepared to definitively pronounce on any text. (He has earlier pointed out to Alice: 'When I use a word, ... it means just what I choose it to mean — neither more nor less.... The question is which is to be master — that's all' (p. 169).

When Alice, playing the dutiful if somewhat skeptical student, asks him to 'tell me the meaning of the poem called "Jabberwocky"', he is fully prepared to reply.

> '*Brillig* means four o'clock in the afternoon — the time when you begin *broiling* things for dinner.'
>
> 'That'll do very well', said Alice. 'And "slithy"?'
>
> 'Well, "*slithy*" means 'lithe and slimy'. '*Lithe*' is the same as 'active'. You see it's a portmanteau — there are two meanings packed up into one word. (p. 170)

As a good student, Alice rapidly gets into the game, providing her own definition for *wabe*, but the danger here is that Professor Dumpty seems so sure of himself and so arbitrary. (He is equally sure that he will be all right if he falls off the wall, and even Alice knows how wrong he is on that account.) It is precisely this impression of certainty which lets students allow teachers to interpret literature for them (if they don't get it from Cliff's notes). This impression of arbitrariness nurtures the view that only English teachers have the key to the poetic code and that students needn't even bother.

This attitude of certainty is bad enough in teaching students — particularly about literature which is notoriously 'slithy' stuff — but even worse when it comes to thinking about the whys of our teaching. I'd like to spend the rest of this chapter, therefore, briefly sketching four problems confronting teachers, contrasting commonsense and uncommonsense analyses of them and solutions for them. The requirements of brevity will make some of the positions more caricatured than I'd like, but I'll invoke the noble tradition of Lewis Carroll to ask your forgiveness for that.

Vocabulary Development

The first problem I want to address is the frequently voiced complaint that students have inadequate vocabularies. This correlates in complaints about low scores on ACT or SAT verbal tests, poor reading ability and limited diction in writing. (This complaint is usually addressed to English language arts teachers, but is considered to be an important problem because it has impact across the curriculum.) Part of the difficulty here, to be sure, is that the commonsense definition of what counts as a large vocabulary takes very little account of the areas of student lives, such as sports, fashion and music, where students may indeed have large and productively useful vocabularies. What they are less likely to have, hence the 'problem', is productive control of the *academic* vocabulary. This is a problem for students who wish to continue and succeed in education. But in so identifying it, we should help students recognize they do have a large vocabulary already, and what we are trying to do is enrich and enlarge it without replacing or denigrating the words they already know.

One traditional (i.e. commonsense) way of trying to solve this problem is to teach vocabulary directly. Methods of doing so usually involve giving students lists of words on which they are then tested weekly in a variety of ways: picking out synonyms, using the word in a sentence, writing a definition and so on. Some lip-service is paid to reading as a source of vocabulary enrichment, but ironically, the controlled vocabulary used by publishers to ensure 'readability' has meant that most school books retard rather than stretch student vocabularies. (This has really been seen as a way of avoiding the 'problem', but its actual effect has been to exacerbate it, since if students never encounter new words in meaningful contexts, they have no opportunity to learn them.) The direct teaching approach is usually based on a variety of commonsense theories and research which compares one commonsense method with another. The most fundamental is a kind of unexamined behaviorism which holds that kids learn words through direct instruction and practice, building the appropriate stimulus-response associations. A related commonsense assumption involves the idea that a diagnosed problem needs a direct instructional remedy. Most people who have tried such approaches recognize their limited utility (such teaching/testing is one of the best examples I know of the kind of 'learning' which is mastered for the quiz and forgotten by the time school is over for the day), yet they are continued because they help convince everyone involved (teachers, students, administrators, and parents) that the school is 'doing something' about the problem. They also provide a neat and precise record of grades which allegedly show whether or not the learning has occurred.

An uncommonsense theory approach to the problem, on the other hand, would be based both on our recognition of the failure of current approaches, and our emerging knowledge of the mental lexicon we build as we acquire a language. Recent psycholinguistic research has shown how fast we naturally learn words when we have a context for using them productively (see for example, Carey, 1978.) The full possession of a word means controlling its grammar, phonology, and morphology as well as its meaning and a variety of subtle restrictions on its appropriate use (Chomsky, 1969). The development of such a full command is reached through a gradual process of refinement of successively close approximations of meaning and is arrived at only through an active process of language use in which the word is needed to fit the situation rather than creating a situation (or a sentence) to fit the word (Clark, 1973). This process begins at the earliest stages of language acquisition as when children learn to stop overgeneralizing *daddy*, which often first seems to mean *adult male* (a potential source of some embarrassment for mom and dad alike) and continues through the process of gradually refining the meanings of technical terms like *atom* and *cell*.

The crucial pedagogical implication for vocabulary development based on current uncommonsense theories and research, is that words are learned *indirectly*, in the context of a rich environment of active language use when the words are needed for some other purpose. The challenge for us as teachers is to find teaching activities that indirectly promote vocabulary development. These include reading and listening, of course, but most crucially they center on the production of language in talk and writing. Since the goal of vocabulary development is the enrichment of a student's repertoire of words which can be used appropriately, we must recognize that unless they are acquired in a context where the concepts they express are needed, the words will never become part of the student's permanent lexicon because they are never needed. If the ideas become important, and are talked about and written about, the words will be learned.

We must, of course, help students (and parents and administrators) see how this process works. And we must develop better, probably indirect, means of assessing vocabulary development so that all parties can see that it is happening. And we must look to our uncommonsense theoretical frames to help us evaluate our efforts. Both the process — of developing better assessments of student vocabulary growth, and using these to assess the success of our teaching — depend upon research of the sort described later in this volume.

One role that seems amenable to direct vocabulary instruction is teaching derivational morphology (by connecting word meanings as in nation and national, for example). To be consistent with psycholinguistic research, however, such an approach should not be directed to teaching new words as such, but to showing students that the lexicon they already know has given them a flexible system for creating and understanding words related to those they already know. And that when they learn a new word they are, in a sense, learning a whole family of related words as well. Helping students recognize the power of the language system they already possess and giving them confidence in their ability to use it productively, is one of the few areas where direct language teaching seems likely to pay off. Whether or not it will actually do so, however, is an empirical question which only uncommonsense theory research can effectively answer.

Reading and Reading Literature

A second problem I'd like to address is the frequently expressed concern that students don't read very well, and specifically they don't read literature well. The recent national assessment shows that students can read well for facts, but can't make inferences or interpretations well at all (Mullis and Jenkins, 1990). Related to this, of course, is the fact that students don't read enough literature either in school or, even more importantly, on their own. The analysis also shows that students actually read less as they go through school. Clearly something is seriously amiss with our approaches to teaching reading and literature which have the effect of turning students (and adults) off reading. Like vocabulary, part of the problem is that our commonsense approaches don't exploit children's and adolescents' knowledge of the world (and of literacy) and part of the problem is that our attempts often seem to be counter-productive.

Part of the difficulty with this 'problem' is that of the theoretical lens through which it is defined. Although there are many sources for the current definition of this problem, the two most significant, although somewhat conflicting practices, are the kinds of reading tests that are used to assess student reading achievement and the ways literature is taught to teachers in many graduate English departments. The first, resulting in part from the failure of English teachers to understand and confront our colleagues in 'reading', has led to an overemphasis on teaching and testing for literal comprehension. This isn't even justified in the reading of non-fictional prose since even there, inference and the ability to see the forest rather than just the trees, are important goals. In the testing of literature, for example, concentration on 'facts', like where Silas buried the money or who whitewashed Tom Sawyer's fence, is too often overemphasized at the expense of helping students understand *why* Silas felt he had to bury the money or *how* Tom got his friend to do the work.

Parallel problems often develop in other disciplines as well. If teachers in the social sciences, for example, give multiple choice exams on the textbook, they are teaching future teachers (and parents) that there is a determinate meaning and set of facts contained in the text. This denies, and crucially conceals the importance of the interpretation that lies behind the apparent 'objectivity' of *any* multiple choice test. In this case it conceals the teacher's personal role in selecting the text(s) to be read, his/her role in choosing what aspects of the text to ask questions about, and most crucially, what the 'right' answer will be. (The choices made by the writer(s) of the text(s) are even more deeply hidden and it is a rare class which even brings up the possibility that any selection process is involved at all.)

This is often compounded by the student perception that only teachers have the keys to unlock the secret meanings of literature (or of non-literary texts). This second source of the problem often results from teachers doing to their students what their teachers had done to them; that is, insisting on a single 'correct' interpretation of each text. The student is often confronted, therefore, with the recognition of an orthodox, impermeable interpretation derived from the teacher. The effect is usually both to implicitly tell students that they are incapable of determining the meaning of texts through individual effort and that they should concentrate on the 'facts' and wait for the teacher to provide the interpretation. Two misleading, commonsense theories have created the problems: the centrality of literal meaning is derived in part from the 'decoding' emphasis of the reading teacher, and the orthodox approach to interpreting texts derived in literary circles mostly from the now old school of literary interpretation called 'new criticism'.

A different theoretical basis for the reading of literature may provide a better approach to teaching it. The uncommonsense theoretical stance, called the transactional theory of literature by Louise Rosenblatt (1938 and 1978), one of its pioneers, is built around the observation that each reader's 'transaction' with a text is somewhat idiosyncratic. As we read literature, or any text, we are engaged in a process of meaning-making in which the words on the page are interpreted on the basis of our individual experiences which are colored by our sociocultural status, our personalities, our beliefs, and our linguistic capacities. This process is clear to everyone in the theater, where it is obvious that directors and actors must have their own vision of the text and its meaning. Olivier's *Hamlet* is not Burton's or Gielgud's or Williamson's or Kevin Kline's. But its reality and validity are less often recognized and exploited in the classroom, although most teachers know that the Huck Finn that eighth graders read is not the same as that of eleventh graders or our own.

The reality of reading is that the experience of a text is a private, personal transaction between reader and text. It is the private nature of that experience that has led Northrop Frye (1957) to argue that literature cannot be taught directly. What teachers can do, however, is to help students extend and enrich their capacities to make meaning from texts, but they must do so initially by sincerely recognizing the personal validity of the meaning that each student has made from the text. Sharing such reader responses, exploring their sources both in the text and the reader, and moving toward the achievement of a loose consensus recognize the inevitability of diverse interpretations which are consistent with the text. It directly involves the student's meaning-making powers by requiring the articulation of his/her response in talk or in writing. And by legitimizing the student's central role in the process of interpretation, it can provide a basis for growing student confidence in their ability to read on their own, a necessary prerequisite for doing so.

The teacher's role is crucial but essentially indirect in the sense that the teacher no longer serves as the ultimate judge of interpretation, but rather serves as questioner, prober, skeptic, and discussion leader, whose goal is to help students deepen their own responses without imposing his/her response upon them. To achieve this kind of classroom requires considerable re-education and practice for students and teachers alike, because all parties are likely to be quite comfortable with the traditional, more clear-cut assignment of interpretive power.

Treating texts as the objects of uncommonsense theoretical inquiry in which hypotheses are proposed and tested, ambiguities are welcomed and explored, and all readings are viewed as the tentative products of fallible readers is hard for many to accept. But until we accept this uncommonsense perspective, texts, and especially literary texts, will remain the exclusive preserve of elite priests and acolytes who will continue to deny access to all but their most devoted followers. And this approach undoubtedly contributes to the kind of diminishing quality and quantity of reading reported by the national assessment. Jack Thomson's study of teenagers' reading (1987) makes it clear that students taught in commonsense ways blame themselves whenever they have a problem with a text, develop few strategies for coping with any but the simplest texts, and rapidly abandon reading as a potential source of either pleasure or enlightenment.

What an uncommonsense approach means in practice is that every time we teach a text, it becomes a kind of hypothesis generating research project in which each reader generates hypotheses about an interpretation based on his or her individual transaction with the text. These hypotheses are then shared and reflected upon in light of others' responses with a goal of building a mutually satisfying set of hypotheses which recognize both the individual differences among the readers and whatever interpretive consensus the class or group has achieved. This may not be as comfortable as having one definitive meaning on which all can be tested, but it is both truer to the individual nature of the reading process and more likely to achieve what ought to be the ultimate goal of instruction: creating lifelong readers.

The parallels between literary and non-literary texts are not exact in the sense that the rhetoric of what we call non-fiction invoves a different set of truth conditions than those required for literary texts. (It's not always a straightforward matter to determine which texts are 'literary'. Satire provides an obvious example as in the case of Swift's 'A Modest Proposal' which reads like a political tract. I once sat with an audience watching General Jack D. Ripper in *Dr. Strangelove* deliver his warning on the evils of fluoridation with an audience which reacted as though they thought they were hearing a serious lecture.) But just as there are multiple readings possible in literary texts, so too are there with almost any other. I expect, for example, that different readers will make different meanings from this chapter depending on the extent to which they have begun to question the commonsense beliefs of the culture. There are certainly texts which intend to be less open to multiple readings: warning labels on medicines, directions on fire extinguishers, etc. — but even these must be interpreted within the constraints of a culture and the wise course seems to me to leave room in all reading processes for the reality that multiple interpretations will happen and that they are an essential part of the process we call reading.

Correctness in Writing

Still a third problem confronting teachers is the complaint that students don't write well, by which is meant that they spell poorly, punctuate badly, and have poor command of grammar and usage. In the last several years this complaint has developed greater urgency as students (and by implication, schools and teachers) have been tested on their knowledge of these matters.

While the reality of such 'problems' is indisputable for some students, the traditional solution of attempting to directly confront the problem by means of extensive drills and exercises in grammar just doesn't work to change the way kids write, as research study after research study has demonstrated since the turn of the century. (For a review and discussion of this research, see Hartwell, 1985.) And, sadly, for those teachers who have spent endless hours circling and annotating every error they can find on student papers, such extensive correcting of student work doesn't have much effect either. (For a review of this research, see Knoblauch and Brannon, 1984.)

The urge for a direct attack on such problems is understandable. The tenacity of grammar teaching in the face of both experiential and research-based counter-evidence seems to spring from several sources: a confusion of correlation with causation, partly from the same kind of unconscious behaviorism which underlies much of commonsense education, and most importantly, from the genuine conviction of parents and teachers (and students, too) that their own personal successes (or even more commonly their failures) as writers have depended upon their knowledge (or lack of knowledge) of grammar. The commonsense theory based on the confusion between correlation and causation usually springs from the fact that grammar came relatively easily to most teachers. Since they were often learning grammar as they were learning to write, they have built a commonsense theory that it was a causative factor in their success. Conversely, those who have had problems with writing have often constructed their own commonsense theory that where they went wrong was in not learning enough grammar.

Uncommonsense theories of the processes of composing and of language development bear directly on this problem and give promise of a more adequate solution to these problems. One of the most striking findings of recent composing process research was Perl's (1979) discovery that the basic ('unskilled') writers she studied were excessively worried about correctness. On average, by the time they reached the third word of the texts they were writing, they were stopping to wonder whether or not they were spelling words correctly, where the commas were supposed to be, and the like. They were hampered throughout their writing by trying to remember rules and maxims which in most cases they had either learned incompletely or were trying to apply incorrectly. The net effect was that they produced tortured texts without adequate development, clarity, or organization, which were also, ironically, still filled with exactly the sorts of 'errors' that the rules they were trying to recall were supposed to remedy.

When we look at the human language system, at how it is developed and used from an uncommonsense perspective, two other striking realities emerge. The first is that all speakers of a language have control over an incredibly complex and powerful linguistic system which enables them to speak and listen. Secondly, the 'grammar' that enables us to do this, however, is a system which we use unconsciously as we write or speak. Neither any reader of this chapter, nor I as its writer, has any conscious knowledge at this moment of what grammar rules are being followed as I produce and you understand this sentence. To try to be conscious of them would make it impossible for the meaning exchange which is being attempted to take place. And that is just the point: control of a grammatical system is developed as a means to the end: being able to express one's own ideas and comprehend the ideas of others. It develops naturally and unconsciously as (or if) we find ourselves in increasingly complex and purposeful linguistic environments.

The first solution to the grammar problem, therefore, is to provide students with the richest language environment possible; one filled with multiple opportunities for purposeful talk and writing, as well as reading and listening. As a correlate to this, it is crucially important to help student writers see that proper use of the formal features of the written language is important because it facilitates communication. Their first priority (and ours) should be in shaping meanings. There is little point for either writer or reader to create an impeccably error-free paper that says nothing.

The first solution — that of a rich language environment — is essential for developing the 'ear' for the written language which is the primary basis for making appropriate language choices and catching errors after they have been made in an early draft. Composing process research like Perl's shows that editing can be separated from the process of drafting and revising which make up the primary meaning-making and shaping aspects of writing. Students can learn to develop and trust their own sense of language through reading their own work aloud, sharing it with peers, and looking to the teacher as a supporter of their attempts to improve a paper while it is still in process rather than wait for judgment when it is finished.

This solution recognizes that extensive teacher annotations of error have been largely ineffective: they come long after the paper has been finished and the problems the student may have recognized while composing the text, have long since disappeared from consciousness. If editing annotations are to be useful, they must be made *during* rather than after the process of composing. They will be most helpful of all if they can be framed in terms of assisting the writer's effort to communicate to a reader rather than as a set of arbitrary and irrelevant demands which only teachers really care about.

The second uncommonsense solution to the 'grammar problem' therefore, is to seek to develop metalinguistic awareness within the context of helping the student writer more effectively express and communicate his or her ideas. This is only likely to happen, of course, if students are writing to audiences who show more interest in what they are saying than how they are saying it. And that is the ultimate source for solving all sorts of writing problems.

This area of inquiry is, unfortunately, the best example we have of the failure of research to affect classroom practice. The power of the commonsense theories that people hold in this area supported from text publishers and testing industries have made the findings of nearly a century of research impotent in changing educational practice. While it would be naive to expect change to occur soon, one of the goals of this book is to help teachers control our own pedagogical destinies by understanding and using the products of research to enlighten our teaching, and to do additional research ourselves which will bring further light to bear on those problems which remain. If teaching is to become a truly professional enterprise, then as practitioners we must learn to build our practice on the basis of research and uncommonsense theory rather than on the basis of commonsense assumptions and beliefs.

Power in Writing

Indeed much of what I've just said relates equally to the solution of the other major types of complaints about student writing: that they don't write clearly, coherently, powerfully, persuasively, and so on. While this, too, is often true, one important causative factor in this regard is that students simply don't write enough in school. The responsibility for this rests on the whole faculty of the school, which is why we must encourage the use of writing-for-learning throughout the curriculum. There is no way that students will learn to write in all the modes of writing they need, unless the whole faculty of a school makes them write frequently. It isn't easy to get that to happen, as I know very well, but try we must.

This is also an area where more research and theory development are sorely needed. We need to work with our colleagues from other disciplines to determine what kinds of learning they are trying to promote in their classes, and then do research which would help to discover how writing can promote the kind of learning they are seeking. Too often writing across the curriculum programs have foundered because teachers in other fields saw writing as a new and additional burden which was being placed on them. The intent of writing-to-learn, however, is quite different: it is to support and facilitate the learning that mathematics, social studies, and science teachers are trying to achieve, and doing so using some new means. It will take careful research, however, to show how this can happen, and doing so should be an important priority for teaching and learning. This will require collaborative expertise: subject matter experts must determine the ends to be sought, language experts can collaboratively help develop a variety of means to achieve them.

The particular aspect in the development of effective writers that I want to focus on as the last problem is the commonsense view that writing 'skills' develop from small units to large ones. This approach, which I have sometimes called the bottom-up strategy, operates on the basis of a commonsense theory which maintains that one must be able to write a good sentence before one can write a good paragraph, a good paragraph before three paragraphs, three before five, and so on. A frequent pedagogical corollary to the bottom-up approach is the insistence that students can't write good paragraphs, for example, unless they know how to identify and explicitly write topic sentences, and know several paradigms for paragraph development such as the use of supporting details, and of comparison/contrast. The analytical theories of rhetoric upon which such pedagogies have been built are not what I am criticizing here, nor am I suggesting that they never have a place in writing instruction. My criticism is really of the informal, commonsense psychological theories of learning which have influenced the process of instruction. These theories have implied that writers first have a form in mind before they have determined what they have to say, and, that the best way to achieve rhetorical control is to have a set of rules or principles in mind while you are composing.

While I do believe that some aspects of rhetorical analysis can be helpful in the revision process — particularly with relatively proficient writers who are attempting to meet a variety of rhetorical demands — burdening beginning writers with prescriptions about sentence types, where topic sentences belong, and how arguments are built, puts the structural cart before the meaning-making horse and encourages student writers to believe, once again, that no one much cares what they say as long as their form is appropriate. Until school writing becomes meaningful enough to the writer that he/she cares about its rhetorical effectiveness, there is little point in trying to have students master various rhetorical strategies.

My main criticism of the bottom-up approach, however, is based on those uncommonsense theories of language which show that when language is used for communication, what we produce are whole ideas. These may be short or long, but they always have some sense of completeness even if they are not grammatically complete. Even in writing, people rarely try to write a single paragraph, as a paragraph, except in school. Limitations of space may sometimes require us to limit ourselves to a paragraph, but the point is that in real communication situations, it is the meaning being transmitted that determines the form and the extent of the piece rather than the reverse. It is usually the case that younger writers write shorter pieces than older ones, but even then, this is more the result of limits on the complexity of their messages, than on their capacities to write longer pieces. Recent classroom research has shown elementary school children writing long stories, even novels (Atwell, 1987).

The sentence errors produced by inexperienced writers are more often than not errors of omission (producing fragments, which can usually be corrected by reading one's work aloud), or of punctuation (which can only be mastered through discovering the kinds of message confusions they cause). Research has shown that punctuation exercises with others' work, or limiting writers to producing perfect single sentences before allowing them longer pieces, have been continuously ineffective (Bissex, 1980). In fact the only times we read, use and therefore learn to control more complex sentence forms are when we have complex ideas to express. Providing the occasion for complex thought to be communicated will be far more valuable than any other means for students to advance their control of complex structures.

This area is one in which teachers can run their own informal experiments of the sort described in Jim Collins' chapter to help determine the relative efficacy of these practices. Careful observation of what actually works (and doesn't work) in our own classrooms is the beginning of the shift from commonsense teaching to uncommonsense teaching. Questioning our practices and the assumptions on which they are based is the essential first step that must be taken to join the ranks of teacher-researchers. And if that growing band can become an army, teaching may finally receive the respect it deserves as one of the most complex endeavors anyone can undertake.

Conclusion

The large generalizations that I would hope you would ponder as a result of this chapter spring directly from uncommonsense theories of language which have emphasized (i) meaning-making is the driving force for mastering structures, and structure is used to express meaning; and (ii) the most significant occasions for language development and learning are those where language is a means rather than the end of learning. The pedagogical implications of these views, stated most simply, are that direct teaching has very limited impact and what seems like the long way around is often the only way to get to where we want to go.

Further, I hope I have shown that since teaching decisions are directly rooted in theory, the problems facing teachers have been caused by the fact that we have too many unexamined, commonsense theories at the root of our teaching, not that we have too much theory and not enough practical pedagogy. We don't need fewer theories; we need better applications of the best theories and research. As Nancy Martin has said: 'There is nothing as practical as a good theory', by which she means, of course, that genuine solutions to the problem of What can I do on Monday? must be based on uncommonsense theories.

As teachers, curriculum leaders, and teacher educators, we must all learn to adopt an uncommonsense theoretical attitude toward our own teaching. We must strive to adapt and apply the best available theories to our pedagogical problems. And, most important, we must further the development of new theories by articulating more clearly the problems we face so that solutions to them can be found through research. Only by becoming consumers and practitioners of theory and research can we escape the looking-glass world.

Note

1 An earlier version of this chapter was delivered as a speech to the Arizona English Teachers Association and appeared in the *Arizona English Bulletin* in April 1982.

References

ATWELL, N. (1987) *In the Middle*, Portsmouth, NH, Heinemann.

BISSEX, G. (1980) *GNYS at WRK*, Cambridge, MA, Harvard University Press.

CAREY, S. (1978) 'The child as word learner', in HALLE, M., BRESNAN, J. and MILLER, G.A. (Eds) *Linguistic Theory and Psychological Reality*, Cambridge, MA, MIT Press.

CARROLL, L. (1981) *Alice's Adventures in Wonderland and Through the Looking Glass*, New York, Bantam.

CHOMSKY, C. (1969) *The Acquisition of Syntax in Children from 5 to 10*, Cambridge, MA, MIT Press.

CLARK, E. (1973) 'What's in a word? On the child's acquisition of semantics in his first language', in MOORE, T.E. (Ed.) *Cognitive Development and the Acquisition of Language*, New York, Academic.

FRYE, N. (1957) *The Anatomy of Criticism*, Princeton, NJ, Princeton University Press.

HARTWELL, P. (1985) 'Grammar, grammars, and the teaching of grammar', *College English*, 47, 2.

KELLY, G. (1955) *The Psychology of Personal Constructs*, New York, Norton.

KNOBLAUCH, C.H. and BRANNON, L. (1984) *Rhetorical Traditions and the Teaching of Writing*, Portsmouth, NH, Boynton/Cook.

MAYHER, J.S. (1990) *Uncommon Sense: Theoretical Practice in Language Education*, Portsmouth, NH, Boynton/Cook.

MULLIS, I.V.S. and JENKINS, L.B. (1990) *The Reading Report Card, 1971–1988: Trends from the Nation's Report Card*, Princeton, NJ, ETS.

PERL, S. (1979) 'The composing processes of unskilled college writers', *Research in the Teaching of English*, 18, 3, pp. 317–36.

ROSENBLATT, L.M. (1938) *Literature as Exploration*, NY, Noble & Noble.

ROSENBLATT, L.M. (1978) *The Reader, The Text, The Poem*. Carbondale, IL, Southern Illinois University Press.

SCHÖN, D. (1983) *The Reflective Practitioner*, New York, Basic Books.

THOMSON, J. (1987) *Understanding Teenagers Reading: Reading Processes and the Teaching of Literature*, New York, Nichols.

Chapter 2

The Never-ending Cycle of Teacher Growth

John S. Mayher and Rita S. Brause

Several basic hypotheses form the core of this book:

- that teaching is so complex it is impossible to ever get it perfect;

- that teaching practice directly stems from teacher beliefs (implicit or explicit theories);

- that change in practice depends on change in belief (theory);

- that the best sources of change in belief (theory) are:

  reflection-in-action on one's current practice;

  understanding and transforming research findings and theories so they can form the basis of practice; and

  sharing problems and reflections with colleagues both locally and nationally.

All of these ideas, collectively, form the basis for the title of this chapter: that teachers must be involved in a never-ending cycle of professional growth.

This may or may not be good news for teachers. We would all like to be able to feel that we have finally mastered our chosen profession. But uncommonsense teachers (Mayher, 1990) recognize that while we can master many aspects of what we do, and while we can and do steadily improve through reflection on our practice, every new class, indeed every new student, presents new challenges which, if we recognize them, force us to stretch and grow.

Part of the key, of course, is recognizing them. The essential argument of the first chapter was that our commonsense lenses may restrict our vision so that we fail to see problems appropriately, and therefore, our inadequate analysis will inevitably lead to inadequate solutions. Commonsense teachers who see this year's class as a duplicate of last year's or even today's as a duplicate of yesterday's waste enormous amounts of pedagogical energy trying to make the old familiar shoe fit rather than considering the possibility that a new pair is needed. These perceptions of overlap are not completely erroneous, of course, since we can and must learn from our experience with third graders or sophomores; the danger lies in assuming identity and building our curricula and our teaching strategies on that all too common, and hence commonsensical, assumption.

It is just this assumption that has been embodied in many of our most consistently unexamined commonsense beliefs about schooling. It lies behind the notion in secondary schools that teaching will be more manageable if teachers have 'a smaller number of preps'. That is, they will, for example, have three sections of freshman English and two of junior English rather than five different levels. (In schools where students are tracked — which is to say in most schools — this attempt to reduce the number of preps is fine-tuned to ability level: the three freshman sections and the two junior ones must all be the 'same' — developmental, college prep, or the like.) In elementary school the idea lies behind both inter- and intra-class ability grouping and the nearly ubiquitous scope and sequence charts.

And perhaps most fundamental of all it helps to justify the basic pattern of American teaching which remains whole class instruction (Goodlad, 1983; Sizer, 1984; Powell *et al.*, 1985). And with that pattern comes the practice so dear to educational publishers: that all students will be reading the same things, writing the same things, using the same workbooks and texts, and taking the same tests.

It is not the purpose of this chapter to explore the strengths and weaknesses of such commonsense beliefs and the practices which embody them. Some of them were looked at in the last chapter and more can be found in Mayher (1990). What is essential here is to see that such beliefs are finally stultifying to both effective instruction and teacher growth. By attempting to paper over even those differences which teachers notice and by building curricular and scheduling structures whose goal is to minimize them, we delude ourselves into hoping that we can define sophomore English or third grade once and for all and that our teaching needs to vary only minimally from day to day and from year to year.

Even those of us who teach in schools that are so organized must learn to recognize the real heterogeneity that lurks beneath the surface of every class and to use that recognition to provide the basis for a more accurate understanding of who our students are, what they already know and can do, and what they need to work on in order to continue to learn. Evolving toward individualization and student-centered modes of teaching is not an easy process, but the constant challenges it presents make teaching continually fascinating and a genuine profession. As we move from what Schön (1983) calls the 'expert' stance to that of the 'reflective practitioner' we have to abandon those sources of satisfaction that come from certainty for the more ambiguous satisfactions that come from a combination of actually being more effective in the real situations we work in and of seeing ourselves as never-ending learners.

A Never-ending Cycle: Using the Teaching Act Model

When we start with the uncommonsense assumption that however good we are at teaching in September, we hope and expect to be better by the next September, we need a process which will help us to accomplish this growth. Figure 2.1 shows one such process based on the assumption that systematic reflection on, and inquiry into, our teaching situation can provide the impetus for and the means of learning which can help assure such change. The figure is based on a process of inquiry which can vary greatly in formality and explicitness. It can range from our observing how Susie tackles the book she is reading and then using that as the basis for guiding her next choice, to the development of a fully worked out research study. What unites all these types of inquiries are their mutually complementary goals: improving instruction for this student or this class and improving the competence of the teacher to help next year's students.

The process begins with a self-assessment: a reflection on who we are, what we are trying to accomplish, and where we see problems in our teaching. Doing such a self-reflection can be facilitated by looking at a variety of aspects of our teaching. One way to do so is through what Mayher and Vine (1974) called the Teaching Act Model. This model, schematically illustrated in figure 2.2, attempts to reveal the connection between a teacher's beliefs (theories) and a teacher's practice. While such a self-assessment does not guarantee change by itself, it does provide the basis for it which is the identification of a problem, a question, or an issue which can be further explored. The expectation is that such explorations can and will provide the basis for change. But a further assumption being made here is that genuine change — like all kinds of genuine learning — must spring from the learner's defining

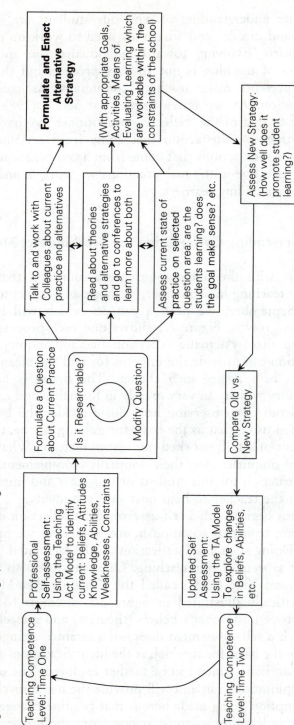

Figure 2.1: The never-ending cycle of teacher growth

Figure 2.2: The Teaching Act Model

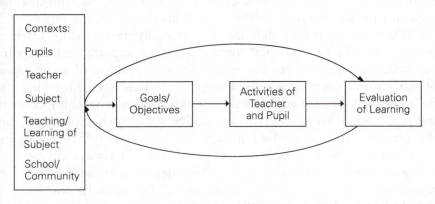

Note: These contexts are the *teacher's* construal/image/perception/mental model of the teaching situation. (After Mayher and Vine, 1974.)
Source: Mayher (1990).

the question to be answered and/or the problem to be solved. No one else can tell us what our teaching problems are; we have to identify them ourselves.

Other people can, of course, play a role by sharing their problems and questions and even their solutions to them, but the ones we select to work on will define the areas in which we can change. If we are satisfied with the way we do something, we don't have much motive either to inquire further into it or to change it. So the first step in the process must be problem identification, and that's one way the Teaching Act Model can be used.

The Teaching Act Model's major strength is that it stresses the fact that each of us, as teachers, builds on our own interpretation of the contexts in which we work, on the basis of our theories/beliefs/constructs of our students, and of learning and teaching. As emphasized in the last chapter, what we believe is what we see. Our construal of the context in which we work, therefore, will largely determine how we plan, that is: what our goals and objectives are; what our classroom activities will be like: what we do; what we ask our students to do; and perhaps most important, how we assess the effect of what happens in the class on our students' learning. It is, of course, true that just as our interpretations of a literary text depend in part on the text itself, so too, our interpretation of the nature of our classrooms is constrained by reality: Sue and Juan are in the class, Masahiro and Gloria are not; the class meets in a cramped classroom, but it is light and sunny; there are plenty of books available in the bookroom; the principal is largely indifferent to what I am trying to do, but it seems as though he won't bother me as long as the noise doesn't get too loud; etc. (Notice that even in this 'description', interpretation inevitably creeps in.)

The first source of defining a potentially researchable teaching problem usually comes when some dissonance appears between what our belief system predicts and what our interpretation of some aspect of our current practice reveals. Given the complexity of teaching and the multiple variables which make up any particular teaching context, the reflective observer will always notice some such dissonance, but the creative trick is to find productive issues to reflect upon and inquire into. This inevitably means that we won't always choose correctly — some problems may be so big they need to be chopped into segments, others may be too small or related to only one child to be worth a full-blown inquiry, and others may not yet be answerable given our current state of knowledge and may, for the moment at least, have to remain mysteries.

The primary source of the dissonance giving rise to such inquiries according to the Teaching Act Model, derives from our assessment of student learning. This assessment provides the primary feedback from the classroom activities to our construal of the teaching context. Therefore, reflective teachers don't blame the students when they don't learn some aspect of the curriculum, but instead we try to use our recognition of their difficulties to pose a question. If we're trying to help our students to become better writers, for example, then whatever difficulties they may be having in learning to do so will be potential sources for inquiry. When we have also noticed that they seem to be having trouble getting started on their texts, then we have the beginning of a problem we can inquire into. Looking into writing development as a totality is probably too big to be the basis of a productive question, so some aspect of writing development, like how can students become better at getting started in writing, will be likely to work better as the basis of our inquiry.

Formulating and Reformulating Our Questions

This process of question selection and modification is illustrated schematically by the loop in the third box in figure 2.1. Because we are reflecting on, and inquiring into, our own practice, this process of modifying our question can go on many times through our inquiry as we remain in conversation with our situation. In this case the further specification of our question can take several forms depending on our beliefs. A commonsense teacher (Mayher, 1990 and chapter 1) might believe that the 'getting started' problem derived from a failure to plan adequately and so might, for example, decide to see whether or not teaching students to outline their papers would help. An uncommon-sense teacher, in contrast, might decide to have as few preconceptions as possible about what was causing the problem, but to first think about what could be causing it, and to second and most important, watch and listen to the students to see what their perceptions of the problem were. (To be fair, this last strategy would be open to a commonsense teacher, but the teacher-centered nature of such instruction and the consequent search for teacher-directed solutions usually precludes much listening to and/or open-ended observing of learners in action.)

Seeking Out Colleagues

Whatever assumptions we have and whatever choices of problems we make initially, one crucial feature of the cycle in figure 2.1 is that it recognizes the crucial importance of each teacher's breaking out of his/her isolated classroom and becoming part of the larger professional community. One of the drawbacks of diagrams is that they inevitably linearize what are actually a more fuzzy and interactive set of processes. After the question has been formulated — and, indeed even while it is being formulated and/or modified, the cycle encourages us to seek out colleagues, articles, conferences, books, etc.: in short to become aware of what is happening in the field and to use it to explore alternatives to our current beliefs and practices.

The crucial importance of these steps out of professional isolation cannot be overemphasized. Teachers will never become fully recognized as professionals until those of us who teach at all levels assert our professional competence and demand the kind of autonomy now only granted to those of us who teach in higher education. (Such autonomy is by no means complete, but it looks like paradise compared to that accorded elementary and secondary teachers.) And such assertions of competence cannot be done alone but demand collective action. It may be possible that teachers' unions will be able to help in this matter, but their history to date in the USA has been that their exclusive focus on economic issues has led them to either downplay or ignore most aspects of teacher professional development. Nor have they given any serious attention to bargaining on those aspects of teachers' working conditions which might make professional development easier.

Recent statements by some union leaders suggest this may be changing, but teachers looking for collective voices to help provide support for professional autonomy and collegiality might look first to those organizations devoted to the learning (and teaching) of a subject (English, science, reading, etc.). Such organizations are by no means flawless, but they do provide forums wherein various approaches to teaching and learning can be explored, journals which propagate a variety of teaching strategies and research findings, and a potential network of colleagues both locally and nationally who are facing similar problems. Even teachers who find lots of opportunity for productive collegial interaction in the school and/or district they work in can profit from the larger context of a regional or national set of colleagues, but teachers who find themselves in isolating contexts need and can learn from them most of all.

The greatest impediment to teachers becoming never-ending growers is undoubtedly teacher isolation and all it implies. Such isolation is, of course, built into the structure of most schools where teachers are cut off from the contact of other adults for most of their working day. Even the 'prep' periods allocated — almost never enough in quantity — are rarely seen as opportunities for collegial interaction. Teachers who teach the same grades or subjects are rarely scheduled for common prep times, and there are few schools with productive work spaces for teachers to work together even if they had the time. Most teachers' 'lounges', dining rooms, and the like, are inhospitable places in general, and in too many schools go further to foster an atmosphere which is anti-professional and worse, often anti-pupil.

It is beyond the scope of this chapter to explore the reasons why schools are so structured and teachers so treated: the fact that schools are run by men and staffed by women has played a part, so too has the general effort to control the quantity and quality of instruction from outside the classroom. The principal's office, the district office, state department of education, and even textbook publishers all deserve a share of the blame. So too do those of us in teacher education who have been too often content to 'train' future teachers to fit into the square pegs of the status quo. (And those of us who have tried to urge uncommonsense alternatives have too often not been willing to do more than pontificate about the way it ought to be. It's a lot easier to give advice than it is to do the work necessary to help bring real change.)

But assessing blame is not really the point — as Ted Sizer has pointed out in another context (1984), the men who did the basic designing of our elementary and secondary schools did so in the nineteenth century and they are all dead. The depressing reality is that as Larry Cuban (1984) has shown, today's schools are extraordinarily similar to those of 100 years ago. So the important questions to be asked concern how we can help make the contexts of schools more supportive of evergrowing teachers.

Financial support continues to be important. The unions are right on that. But this derives not only from the fact that teachers need and deserve to live with reasonable material comfort, but even more importantly from the fact that financial support directly reflects community and societal respect. So one of the interesting questions financial support inevitably raises is the question of differential pay. Should teachers who are striving to grow professionally be rewarded more than those who aren't? To some extent this idea is a standard part of teacher's salary scales which reward differentially those teachers who have accumulated particular numbers of graduate credits. While this is a well-intentioned attempt to encourage teacher professional growth, in practice it has become so mechanistically applied. Like most of the rest of the commonsense schooling of both children and teachers — no effort is made to differentiate among those teachers who are actually seeking to improve and those who are just meeting the credit requirements.

Like any kind of genuine assessment of learning, making the appropriate distinctions will be hard to do and will, inevitably, involve collective subjective human judgment. There is just no blinking the fact that the complexity of human learning resists reductive and mechanistic measurement. Counting credits tells us something — mostly about the persistence of the learner — but it rarely distinguishes the strong performers from the weaker ones in the case of either students or teachers. The necessity of relying on human judgment, however, doesn't mean that all is lost, that bias and favoritism and politics will inevitably corrupt the system. These are dangers, to be sure, but the strategy which could evolve would be far less biased than most current systems turn out to be despite their apparent 'objectivity'.

The cycle in figure 2.1 provides an important structure here emphasizing process rather than product alone. The cycle does demand that a new strategy be enacted and assessed, but it doesn't demand that the strategy itself be successful. That is, what the cycle focusses on is the reflective process:

self-assessment →
   question formulation and modification →
      professional sharing →
         formulating and enacting an alternative strategy →
        assessing the effectiveness of the
        new strategy in solving the
        problem →
   new self-assessment →
      etc.

In such a learning/growth process, the important documentation required would not be limited to testing pupil learning, but would involve instead illustrating the whole process from beginning to end. (Care would have to be taken to resist the commonsensification of such a process should it ever become 'required'. The power of schools to commonsensify their systems by making them mechanical can never be overstressed and must be constantly guarded against.)

The reason for stressing the institutionalization of these processes is that while individual teachers can and have managed to build such networks and involve themselves in a larger professional life, few are encouraged to do so and the stories of teachers denied professional time off to attend conferences are legion. And the chances of getting actual financial support is so rare as to be noteworthy when it occurs. Until states and local districts begin institutionalizing the support of genuine paths to professional growth, there will be little incentive for it to occur.

And this is most serious, of course, for those teachers who are not self-starters, who don't perceive their problems as learning problems for themselves or their pupils, or who simply don't care. It is easy enough to say such teachers should be removed, but reality dictates that they can't or won't be, and so the best we can hope for are management systems which encourage genuine growth by providing a wide range of support for it. Such changes won't be easy to achieve — especially since growing teachers are not docile teachers and therefore threaten many administrators — without them we will continue to lose the best and most adventurous of our new teachers to other fields. Such potential leaders just don't stay in a system which consistently rewards and therefore seems to encourage mediocrity, laziness and minimal professional growth.

A Growing Teacher in Action

But what happens when a teacher tries to change? What's in it for her? Let's listen to one in order to get a better idea of what the benefits of enacting the cycle can be.

> I cannot recall ever feeling as powerful as a result of any other thing I've ever done in the twenty-odd years that I've been teaching elementary children. It's a remarkable feeling.

Adele Fiderer, a fifth grade teacher-researcher shared some of her experiences of learning through teaching. She provided us with an insightful report on a project involving collaborative partnerships in which fifth graders wrote books for first graders. Ms. Fiderer was concerned with accomplishing several tasks simultaneously, namely: enriching the concepts of the fifth graders about stories and the writing process; introducing first graders into the process of story writing; and most important, learning both about her students and her teaching.

Self-Assessment and Reflection

Before she decided on this specific project, Ms. Fiderer was involved in a collegial process of developing a teacher-research center in her school district. She and her colleagues had realized through their reading, their conversation, and their seeking out of each other and others in the area that their teaching patterns needed to be examined and potentially changed. In the process of working together, of attending professional conferences, and seeking out appropriate graduate courses, they developed a pattern of self-assessment and reflection which led each of them to see problems in their own classrooms.

In part these problems were newly visible because they were deliberately seeking them out and in part they became visible because they had acquired new theoretical lenses through which to view them (see chapter 1). In her case these new lenses derived primarily from new insights into the teaching of writing of which she, like many teachers, had very little understanding as part of her earlier teacher education. In addition to the insights about writing itself, she had also acquired new understandings about her role as a teacher through experiencing and reading about writing workshops. The question she selected, therefore, derived from both a new understanding of the development of writing abilities and a new stance as a teacher.

In order to implement this project, Ms. Fiderer adopted a stance different from what she called the 'teacher-controller'. She focussed on learning what her students needed to know by carefully observing her students' participation in activities. This perspective contrasted sharply with her previous commonsense stance in which she set all the tasks for students to perform and then assessed how well students performed them. This newly-adopted position has reignited Ms. Fiderer's enthusiasm for teaching because she has become a learner in her classroom.

We emphasize here her reflective learning, much of which occurred as Ms. Fiderer wrote in her research journal. One of the important things she learned is that the process of reflective/interpretive writing is itself a learning process. Based on these insights, she revised plans, speculated on alternate results and refined procedures. For example, her research question was enlarged to include the effects that this project would have on the attitudes and writing of fifth-grade students in the partner project in addition to her initial focus on what the first graders would learn. The fifth graders themselves became fellow teacher/learner/researchers and used their own reflective writing as a means of learning, much as their teacher did.

Using the Literature and Her Colleagues

The writing project was similar in some ways to that described by Frances Van Tassell (1983). Each fifth grader was assigned a first-grade partner to write a story for and about. The first of their meetings began with an interview to collect details about 'their' first grader that could be included in the story. In the library, her class read picture books to get a 'feel' for literature written for an audience of 6-year-olds. Then each fifth grader began a draft of a fictional story featuring their first grade partner in fictional disguise.

Her initial modes of observation and assessment of what was going on in her class also derived from her reading of such writing teacher/researchers as Donald Murray (1982) and Donald Graves (1983). Although she later found she had to modify some of their approaches to fit her own inquiries and her own situation, they provided a crucial beginning point for structuring her inquiry.

And throughout the process of inquiry, she was able to share her developing insights and get feedback on her questions and problems with a collegial support group in her district. The members of this group were each pursuing their individual inquiries into their own classrooms, but they also met regularly to share progress and frustrations. This support community made it less risky to try out new approaches and provided a forum through which she could continue to learn collaboratively.

Learning Through Observation and Reflection

Once the project was underway, the fifth-grade writers had opportunities to read their stories-in-progress to their partners. The writers involved the younger students in their writing choices. For example, Matthew wrote a story of a runaway school bus for 6-year-old Roger. Roger read the draft aloud.

Matthew: Do you understand all the words? What words don't you understand?

Roger: Control.

Matthew: When you're out of control, you're going crazy. Like a car going back and forth out of lanes. (He takes out the first draft.) Do you think this is better than the first draft? See?

Roger: (Pointing to a part with lines drawn through it.) Why did you cross that out?

Matthew: 'Cause I didn't like it. Tell me which title I should use: 'A Close Call', 'The School Bus', or 'A Close Crash'.

Roger: A close Crash.

Matthew: O.K. I'll use it. Mrs. Fiderer, what shall we do now?

Ms. Fiderer: Think of what other partners did last week.

Matthew: Oh. O.K. Roger, do you want to make pictures for the book?

Roger: O.K. (Goes for crayons)

Matthew: Can you make a bus? Draw like this. (Roger draws directly on the last draft in yellow crayon. Matthew adds details to the yellow bus in orange crayon. Matthew turns the page and they continue to alternate illustrating.)

Ms. Fiderer reflected,

Matthew's and Roger's conference particularly interested me because Matthew, immature emotionally and academically, received help with his own writing and reading skills. I had never seen in our normal classroom environment the confidence and maturity he exhibited here.

Matthew is certainly not acting as an 'immature' young man in taking the teacher/writer role with Roger. Ironically, however, his questioning techniques and the focus of the questions, imitate the 'teacher-controller' role that Ms. Fiderer is trying to abandon. Ms. Fiderer refuses to continue to play that role. (She tells M. here, 'think'.) But Matthew has learned well the rules of the traditional commonsense school game. When it's his turn to play teacher, he knows what to do. While this kind of experience is immensely valuable for all concerned, it could be even more so if as a next step, we help Matthew and his classmates reflect on the role they played when they were 'teaching'.

Ms. Fiderer gathered her data from a variety of sources:

(i)   logs and journals in which student-researchers and the teacher-researcher recorded observations and reflections systematically;

(ii)   activity checklists derived from a list of partnership activities;

(iii)   recordings (audiotape and videotape) of writing conferences; and

(iv)   an interview by the fifth graders to find out the first graders' views about writing.

As Adele Fiderer discovered while she was doing her research, even the most carefully designed set of procedures and questions may not yield the most useful data. This is particularly true in exploring a real setting from a naturalistic/ethnographic perspective. Therefore, she recognized the need for other kinds of data. In her reflections after completing the project, she pointed out,

The logs, begun a month after the project was underway, yielded richer information than did the activity checklist. Next time we will use the logs over a longer period of time. I think the checklist may have served to make the students more aware of the necessity of including specific details in their logs.

After the completed stories had been read to the first graders, the students interviewed their partners to find out what they had learned from the project. Each fifth grader asked his or her partner questions such as these: What are the things a writer has to do to write a story? What do you think makes a story good? What did I do to make my story about you better? What did you do to help me to make my story better?

Analysis

In order to help the fifth graders consistently interpret their partner interviews, the whole class discussed a taped interview using three categories: Donald Murray's (1982, pp. 40–1) principal elements which make readers read (information, significance, people, order, and voice); mechanics; and conventions. In small groups of threes and fours students listened to the interviews and discussed how to interpret them. Again, Ms. Fiderer reflects on the process of data gathering and interpretation.

We soon realized that some qualities on our checklist were inappropriate and had to be deleted (for example, 'paragraph sense') and that the checklist had to be expanded to include characteristics of good stories (good characters; make-believe characters; if you take your time the story will be good) and steps in the writing process (concentrate; it feels good to write). The physical act of writing made it difficult for the students to capture all of the first graders' responses; luckily we've recorded ten interviews. Next time we'll record all interviews.

What Was Learned: By the First Graders

The children's awareness of writing processes increased. They learned that the process and content of writing are more important in good writing than are the mechanics of writing. These students became aware of the importance of focussing on an interesting topic, describing details, and creating exciting beginnings and endings. This should pay off as they become their own storytellers.

What Was Learned: By the Fifth Graders

While acting as researchers, students learned much about writing and about people. Amy ends her research paper with this conclusion:

> I think this project was a good experience. We learned more about Mrs. Johnson's first graders and we also learned different ways to write.

Kim noted,

> While (Jeff) read, I noticed he did not stop at periods and didn't pause at paragraphs. I also realized he did not read dialogue the right way. When he finished reading I taught him what paragraphs meant and what quotes meant. I am not sure if he learned anything, but it was worth a try. Jeff seemed to like to learn.

Rose's summary is insightful:

> Our final interview with our partners was to find out what our partners knew about writing. Meredith knew much more about writing than she did at the first meeting. To write a story she said you have to write a rough draft; change things; make a new copy ...

What Was Learned: By the Teacher-Researcher

When I reflect on the gains to the participants in this study, I realize I was a major learner focussing on two major issues: learning about my students and learning about my role as teacher. As a result of observing my students closely I came to better understand and appreciate the qualities that I had viewed in less than positive lights. Matthew, whose talkativeness during many classroom lessons had driven me wild, now commanded my respect for his skillful use of talk in writing conferences with his 6-year-old subject. Amy, who I had identified in pre-research days as a relentless perfectionist, impressed me as a remarkably persistent person when I read her log entries describing her attempts to work with a distractible young partner.

I learned more about teaching, too. I cannot revert back to myself, ever, as a teacher-controller, after seeing myself as teacher-researcher. In the past, I assigned what I assumed the children should be learning. Children passed or failed depending on how they met my expectations. I never knew how much real learning was going on beyond the narrow focus I peered through. I repeated the same lessons, the same units, even the same dittos and assignments, year after year!

Now, a spirit of inquiry affects my teaching. When I try a new approach, I wonder whether and what my students are actually learning. Their journals reveal their understandings and misunderstandings more clearly than did the dittos and workbooks. From their writing I learn what my lessons must be. I recognize the need to discover what the children know before I try to teach them.

Finally, my research has caused me to revise my perceptions of my role as teacher-researcher. I have documented information that contributes to a broad base of knowledge about writing. I think I now know something about the effects on young children who participate in the writing process of older students that could be useful to other teachers.

Ms. Fiderer has continued to be a teacher-learner and, as her last sentence suggests, she has become an active sharer of her insights about both the processes and the results of her inquiries with her colleagues both locally and nationally. She has participated in, and led workshops, on becoming a teacher-researcher and has been active in her district in encouraging and supporting the development of other teacher-researchers. One of the nice features of the cycle described here is that it can and should become self-sustaining for teachers who manage to build a network of professional support for ourselves in our local context and to join those others that are emerging regionally and nationally.

What Was Learned: By Us (the Teacher-Educators)

Teachers, teacher-educators, and curriculum developers have long recognized that good teaching must begin where the learners are. Our practice, however, consistently contradicts this proposition because we assume we know where the learners are. We don't really look at what they do and don't understand. We teach 'fifth graders' or 'graduate students' as though all students in the class had the same knowledge. This fiction makes our planning process easier, but it frequently leaves some or all of our students unconnected to the concepts and processes we hope they are learning.

It is only by abandoning our 'teacher-controller' role, as Ms. Fiderer has done, and becoming the kind of teacher-learner/teacher-researcher she exemplifies that we can really know where each individual student is on the learning continuum. We can see new strength in our students and view weaknesses in terms of their need for strategies to solve real problems and perform real tasks.

And perhaps most important of all, we have learned anew that when students join us in the role of teacher-researchers, they intensify their own learning as well. Being a 'teacher-controller' is not necessarily a teaching role. When we and our students reflect on our teaching and our learning, the process of learning itself becomes a legitimate focus of the curriculum. Since above all else, the school's role is to create learners rather than knowers, students and teachers who engage in this kind of project will be building a solid foundation for lifelong learning.

Everyone involved in this project gained a new sense of power and accomplishment through their achievements. Ms. Fiderer had freed her students to learn. Thereby she freed herself to learn by reflecting on what was happening as her students were learning. All participants enjoyed the project and each has grown through the experience . . . the true essence of learning through teaching: becoming a learning-teacher.

An Invitation

The various chapters in this book are, in essence, an invitation to join in this process of growing. But beyond inviting professionals to join us in this process we hope, as well, to be providing some of the insights and answers necessary to make the processes of inquiry less forbidding and more rewarding. The chapters in Part II are designed to help us all learn how to read and understand the strengths and weaknesses of published research studies by understanding the assumptions on which they are based and the procedures they employ. The chapters in Part III are intended to help growing teachers learn some useful methods, techniques and approaches for designing and carrying out an inquiry into their own classrooms.

Teaching can, and should be, a profession that sustains and nourishes a lifetime of enrichment. It only achieves this level of sustenance for those who find a way to keep growing and changing throughout their careers. As noted briefly here, some of the conditions under which teachers work make it difficult to build and sustain the kind of inquiring spirit and collegial, supportive relationships so essential for professional growth. These conditions must be changed. But the best way to help that happen is for teachers to work together toward that end. For an example of how that can begin to happen, see Lester and Onore (1990) where they show how the teachers of one school district combined classroom research and collaborative action to restructure the in-service program in their district, to change some of their working conditions, and to begin to change the nature and conception of the curriculum.

While individuals can and do grow on their own, they grow best in a supportive and collegial environment. What is true of our students in our classrooms is just as true for us. The cycle described in this chapter and indeed all of the processes suggested in this book depend crucially on teacher-learners becoming part of the community of inquirers. There are growing circles of such colleagues already forming and each of us can help ourselves grow by joining them and starting new ones in our own local context. Doing so is both the best recipe for our own professional and personal growth and the essential ingredient in the process of changing the experiences of the people for whom the whole enterprise exists: our students.

References

Cuban, L. (1984) *How Teachers Taught: Constancy and Change in American Classrooms, 1890–1980*, New York, Longman.

Goodlad, J. (1983) *A Place Called School*, New York, McGraw-Hill.

Graves, D.H. (1983) *Writing: Teachers and Children at Work*, Portsmouth, NH, Heinemann.

Lester, N.B. and Onore, C.S. (1990) *Learning Change: One School District Meets Writing Across the Curriculum*, Portsmouth, NH, Boynton/Cook.

Mayher, J.S. (1990) *Uncommon Sense: Theoretical Practice in Language Education*. Portsmouth, NH, Boynton/Cook.

Mayher, J.S. and Brause, R.S. (1985) 'Learning through teaching: Adele Fiderer reflects with her fifth graders', *Language Arts*, 62, 3.

Mayher, J.S. and Vine, H.A., Jr. (1974). 'The Teaching Act Model', *NYU Education Quarterly*, 6, 1.

Murray, D.M. (1982) *Learning by Teaching*, Portsmouth, NH, Boynton/Cook.

Powell, A.G., Farrar, E. and Cohen, D.K. (1985) *The Shopping Mall High School*, Boston, Houghton-Mifflin.

Schön, D.A. (1983) *The Reflective Practitioner*, New York, Basic Books.

Sizer, T. (1984) *Horace's Compromise*, Boston, MA, Houghton-Mifflin.

Van Tassell, F. (1983) 'A writing assignment with a different flair', *Language Arts*, 60, 7.

Part Two
Interpreting Published Research on Classroom Practice

This section discusses the purposes for which research studies are conducted, namely: to test hypotheses, to generate hypotheses and to critique educational practice. The authors provide systematic guidance in how to go about reading studies which are categorized as hypothesis testing or hypothesis generating, referring to and analyzing specific, landmark studies. They also discuss differences and similarities among these research purposes and provide criteria for evaluating both the credibility of research findings and the validity of recommendations included in published studies.

Chapter 3

Research Objectives: Generating Hypotheses, Testing Hypotheses and Critiquing Educational Practice

Rita S. Brause and John S. Mayher

Historically classroom educators were expected to read and use the research which educational researchers conducted through large-scale testing programs in isolated laboratory settings. Predictably classroom teachers found little in the decontextualized, laboratory-based research to inform practice with specific students. Therefore it carried little, if any weight in our professional decision-making.

As professional educators, we constantly seek to improve practice acknowledging that perfection has not been (and never will be) realized. Ideally, when we have the time, we reflect on published research and our own personal experiences. In practice few of us do systematic research and even a smaller number of us reflect on its implications for our own teaching. Although we might be studying how student language use contributes to that student's learning, we may continue to lecture in our own classes. But much of this is changing. Teachers are sharing reflections, becoming practicing researchers, sustaining our excitement about teaching and learning.

Contemporary teachers consciously study real classrooms (frequently our own classes and practices). We engage in long-term participant-observer studies in classrooms, our native land. Moving educational research from laboratories to classrooms is occurring at the same time that education is being labelled a 'true' profession, with participation in research a professional responsibility (Brause and Mayher, 1983; Giroux, 1988; Schön, 1983 and 1987; The Holmes Report, 1983). This development renewed the excitement and idealism of many experienced teachers who were 'burning out'. As a prelude to encourage more participation in this professional activity we consider the objectives of such professional practice.

What is Research?

We personally do research as we go about our daily lives, finding out which sherbet our taste buds prefer, or what sights we will pass as the train takes us to our intended destination. This inquiry process makes living exciting. We constantly question and explore our options. In this context, research refers to finding out — searching for answers to influence our daily, personal decisions. Kelly (1955) suggests that we act as scientists when we engage in this type of activity. While these daily 'researches' may have few specific long-term effects, they do characterize an open-minded inquiring stance, essential traits of active learners. There are other contexts in which we engage in research with more far-reaching consequences.

Professional research is a highly structured, public activity in which we reflect on specific practices (either planned by the researcher or naturally occurring in the setting). One outcome of such studies evaluates the validity of the principles or theories on which we formulate our practice. From this perspective, teaching and learning are not viewed as a 'bag of tricks'. Rather, we subject our specific classroom practice to scrutiny — to bring to a level of consciousness the implicit theory which is influencing our decision-making. Research involves either identifying or evaluating the theory(ies) undergirding our practices. Classroom research then focusses on identifying or evaluating the 'method in our madness' as it effects our students' learning. As researchers we seek to reflect on our rational beliefs, for example, students need to be quiet to learn. Schön (1983) labels this belief system 'technical rationality'. In the reflective process we elevate our practice from what intuitively seems right to more explicit principles.

The major intent for conducting any educational research is to eventually improve practice. Research provides us with a lens to consider our practice from a more philosophical perspective. Research cannot tell us specifically what to do tomorrow. It does provide principles on which to plan strategies which are likely to be effective with our specific students. But not all research is of equal value to us. One of our professional responsibilities is to critically evaluate information, not to accept it on blind faith. To persuade us and our professional colleagues of its importance, we critically evaluate research reports considering such issues as its intensiveness, systematicity and ethics as we decide how much weight to give the findings.

Research which is *intensive* carefully scrutinizes minute elements and details. Intensive investigation can be mounted by knowledgeable, open-minded researchers. If we have predetermined what we expect to find, we usually find what we seek. True research involves *re-searching* — that is searching over and over again — not to confirm predispositions, but to get new insights — new perspectives. As researchers we need to have an open mind, and approach our questions deeply and extensively, to provide findings which are persuasive to ourselves and our colleagues. We also need to be able to draw on important studies and theories. It is this extensive knowledge base which enables us to pick good theories — and reject weak or unsupported ones. We integrate this information into a broader knowledge base, attempting to understand the complex concerns at the heart of educational practice such as the nature of the teaching-learning process, what is worth knowing, and how learning is promoted.

A second attribute of research is that it is *systematic*. Research is a carefully planned, 'scientific' activity. It does not happen spontaneously. Although an inspiration for *what* to research might be serendipitous, the collection and analysis of data are highly organized activities. Research is inquiry in its most rigorous form. It involves unrelenting collection, analysis and reflection. It clearly documents its processes and products to allow the researcher to understand and readers to evaluate the insightfulness of the researcher in conducting the study.

A third characteristic of research is that it is *ethical*. This domain is concerned not only with insuring each individual's privacy, but also with the ultimate goal of enhancing the quality of life for all. Educational research which is ethical, then, seeks to find ways for all to learn, not just the mythical average student. Such research is impartial and democratic. An educational researcher studying adolescents' self-esteem, for example, would study student-truants, as well as those who regularly attend public and non-public schools. The findings are used to inform decisions in a broad range of contexts. Ethical research involves our critical reflection on the social consequences of our professional practice. We seek to accommodate these three ideals across the range of purposes for which we engage in research.

What are the Purposes for Doing Research?

There are two complimentary purposes for conducting educational research: *to enhance the quality of life*, making our practices more democratic, more equitable, and more humane; and *to enlarge our understandings*, moving our practice from intuition, 'lore' and beliefs to more principled decision-making, as advocated by North (1987) in his discussion of composition research.

As we teach we make decisions which reflect our personal constructs of a particular situation, tapping our assumptions, beliefs and theories about teaching and learning. As professional educators, we constantly evaluate the impact of these decisions on our individual students and collectively on all students, carefully searching, questioning and deliberating about the impact of our choices on our students' lifelong learning. In education we seek answers to such diverse questions as those listed in (i)–(xv).

(i)   Would my pupils make fewer errors in punctuation and capitalization if they wrote three 100-word themes each week instead of one 300-word theme?

(ii)   Would my pupils' handwriting improve faster through five minutes of practice each morning or one thirty-minute period once a week?

(iii) Would my class do more independent reading if I read them portions of books than if I assigned them to read a book a month? (Singleton, Diederich and Hill, 1961, p. 4)

(iv)   How does penalizing for misspellings in compositions for example, influence students' spelling advancement?

(v)   Would my class make faster progress in spelling by mastering five words each day or by increasing their reading and writing activities throughout each day?

(vi)   What do students learn about social participation and people's values during whole class instruction?

(vii) Does Beth interpret stories differently from Billy?

(viii) How do I decide what my students need to know in a basic science course?

(ix)   How can I help intensify students' understandings of divergent perspectives on wars?

(x)   How do classroom discussions in small and large groups influence students' conceptual understandings of character motives?

(xi)   How does tracking students influence their developing writing proficiencies?

(xii) What distinguishes drop-outs from graduates?

(xiii) What are the goals of schooling?

(xiv) What do schools reward?

(xv)   How do standardized test scores predict 'success' in life (five, ten, twenty-five years after leaving/graduating from school)?

There are several striking characteristics which divide these questions into three groups: (i)–(v); (vi)–(x); and (xi)–(xv). Questions (i)–(v) are derived from implicit, commonsense assumptions which include:

— Spelling is basic to all other learnings.
— Isolated practice carries over to real uses.
— The specific form of an individual's handwriting is an important educational concern.
— The exclusive criterion for evaluating good writing is the quantity of errors.
— Allocating extended time to a task and repetitive drilling are effective instructional strategies.
— Speed is an important criterion in learning.
— Teacher assignment is the principal way students learn.
— Large quantities of pages read independently guarantee learning.

Questions (i)–(iii) were cited by Singleton, Diederich and Hill (1961) as questions typically posed in classroom studies. They clearly convey the common sense assumptions prevailing in education circles at the time of that publication, specifically focussing on the need to correct errors and the emphasis on quantity. These questions highlight two common sense beliefs:

(a) Learning is only evidenced by displaying discrete, predetermined 'correct' behaviors; and
(b) Learning results from the frequency of student exposure to direct, teacher-led instruction.

Both of these beliefs are at the heart of a learning theory labelled Behaviorism (Skinner, 1957). Researchers and educators accepted the theory, attributing differences in students' learning to the length of time and frequency of occurrence of programmable experiences. After countless studies of educational practice testing behaviorist theory, we are still at a loss to predict how or why each student learns or fails to learn in specific situations.

Realizing both the insufficiency of the behaviorist theory to predict how or when students learn, or to account for the complex processes and factors influencing learning, we are searching for more accurate theories. Answers to research questions (vi)–(x) exemplify this changed focus of our inquiry. These question are more open-ended, reflecting the need to generate a more predictable theory. These questions imply underlying uncommon sense beliefs including:

— Students may learn an unpredictable range of concepts in whole class instruction.
— Students may have unique learning styles.
— Some knowledge is of greater worth than other knowledge.
— Interpretation is somewhat an idiosyncratic process.
— Each individual learner's talk is essential in learning.

Questions (xi)–(xv), in contrast to (i)–(x) are more philosophical in nature, considering the impact of specific school practices on students' lives. Answers to these questions guide the evaluation and possible reformulation of educational settings and practices. The issues implicit in these questions have an ethical base:

— Tracking limits opportunities for educational achievement.
— School success does not guarantee success in later life.
— Stated School goals or purposes are frequently inconsistent with the credentialling and other reward systems.

Another way to group these questions is to consider the similarities among questions (i)–(x) in contrast to questions (xi)–(xv). Questions (i)–(x) study what *is* happening in highly specific settings. These research studies are considered *empirical* in contrast to those which take a more philosophical perspective (see figure 3.1).

Figure 3.1: Sources of professional knowledge

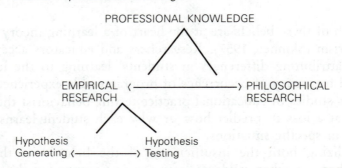

Philosophical research, in contrast to empirical research, takes a more comprehensive perspective across diverse settings and considers the implicit values, priorities and objectives as realized through specific practices. To arrive at this philosophical stance, numerous documents and points of view are considered, with extensive debate over definitions of terms and goals. The research results in an explicit philosophical perspective which can then be subjected to empirical testing to discover the mesh between the idealized goals and the realized outcomes. For example, philosophical research may conclude that educational institutions provide settings where many students' perspectives are not valued. These philosophical findings may influence assessment in many school districts including their procedures for evaluating the likelihood of success in mainstream American society as well as the importance of that goal.

Teacher researchers more frequently engage in empirical rather than philosophical research. We tend to seek immediate answers to specific classroom dilemmas, while philosophical research defers consideration of such concerns, preferring to focus on these dilemmas from a more generic perspective. Engaging in philosophical research suggests the possibility for accomplishing change from a broad perspective, reaching far beyond the individual classroom, and therefore frequently beyond the purview of us as classroom practitioners. Philosophical research requires critical reflection and detachment from our daily activities (Mayher, 1990; Brause, forthcoming; Lyons, 1990; Aronowitz and Giroux, 1985; McLaren, 1989; McNeil, 1986; Freire, 1973). Both types of research are essential for us to create more effective educational opportunities, and they are reciprocal in that both philosophical research and empirical research influence the knowledge base which is at the heart of our profession. Since we as teacher-researchers mainly conduct empirical research, we will elaborate on this source of knowledge in our discussions.

There are two major approaches to empirical research. One may be identified as hypothesis testing, the other as hypothesis generating. *Hypothesis testing* is the process of assessing or testing the validity of an existing, explicit instructional theory. All educational practice (in fact everything we do in our lives) enacts a theory as discussed by Mayher in chapter 1. Some of these theories are common sense theories (Mayher, 1990) or technical rationality (Schön, 1983) as exemplified in questions (i)–(iii), others develop from uncommon sense theories, such as Questions (iv)–(xv). The uncommon sense theory of spelling development would say in effect, children's spelling will

improve when they are encouraged to engage extensively in such practices as invented spelling, reading, being read to, writing, and having
their reading read and responded to by others. We could test the
effects of such an instructional program as exemplified in question (v).

We could design a basic hypothesis testing study to evaluate the
relative effectiveness of two different teaching strategies. We would use
a pre-test and post-test model in two different classrooms. In both
classrooms, both before and after the 'instructional treatment' there
would be specific evaluation of student spelling of predetermined
words as well as writing an extended, personally determined text from
which the researchers would analyze the range of strategies each student used to spell 'difficult' words. In one room, the teacher would
introduce five new words daily and have students use each in sentences. At the end of the month there would be a test on the total 100
words. During other times the regular instructional program would
prevail.

In the second classroom, the teacher would intentionally immerse
students in activities where they made extensive use of printed materials and created numerous written drafts which they shared with
peers. There would be no specific time for spelling instruction *per se*,
but the teacher would incidentally, as contextually appropriate, share
her own spelling strategies and encourage students to share and expand
their strategies in spelling infrequently used words. No other changes
would be made in the regular instructional program.

At the end of a month's time we analyze the 'correctness' and the
strategies students used in spelling the words on the original test and in
personally created text. The word test yields a quantitative result, a test
score say of 90 per cent correct. The analysis of strategies yields a
qualitative result in which the unique strategies each student uses in
spelling 'difficult' words are analyzed. Thus, in this hypothesis testing
study, we incorporate both qualitative and quantitative findings. We
compare the results for each student and the class average on the first
(pre-treatment) and final (post-treatment) assessments. The findings
from this research would help us to address our concern for students
learning such 'skills' as conventional spelling while in a whole
language/uncommon sense classroom. We already have some evidence
that whole language works (Graves and Calkins, 1980) but we need
studies which consider the impact on each of the students in the
classroom.

A critical issue to consider in designing hypothesis testing research is the selection of a 'good theory', that is a theory which has
been supported by credible research. If a growing body of research

does not support a theory, it is foolhardy to conduct research on an unsupportable theory, a theory which has been shown to be unhelpful in predicting student learning, as in the case of behaviorism.

Some people call hypothesis testing research 'experimental', focussing on the experimenter's or researcher's manipulation and control of activities. Others call it 'quantitative' research since it includes the compilation of numerical scores on specific tests. We believe 'hypothesis testing' is a more accurate designation since it clearly distinguishes this type of study from a second group we call hypothesis generating. Since hypothesis testing studies may include qualitative analysis in addition to quantitative analysis, as in the spelling strategies study discussed here, the analytical processes (qualitative vs. quantitative) do not distinguish one type of research from the other, supporting our labelling distinction in research types. [The terms 'qualitative' and 'quantitative' highlight the methods for analyzing the data rather than the goal of the project.]

Hypothesis Generating research examines a process as a basis for building or generating a theory. (Questions (vi)–(x) are samples of the research questions of hypothesis generating research studies.) If we want to determine strategies which are likely to help students to write persuasively we need to study how students who are proficient at this purpose for writing go about their task. Such inquiry would not only look at what each student does when picking up a pen or sitting down at a computer, but also would consider the range of materials and experiences the student is familiar with (editorials on TV and in newspapers; movie and book reviews; and advertisements, for example). Such study would, as an outcome, generate tentative hypotheses or predictions about factors which influence student writing.

In a hypothesis generating study, we would start with an initial, general premise, (such as students' writing proficiency reflects all of their experiences with print). During the process of conducting the study, this initial premise is subjected to scrutiny through observing and talking with students as they *naturally* go about gathering information, talking with peers, writing notes, highlighting texts, revising their drafts, and analyzing examples of published persuasive writing. The setting is one in which the students would be deciding what they do and when they do it. We would be participant-observers, taking in all the activities the students chose to do. If asked for assistance, we might share information about how we engage in these activities, and then continue to observe what the student does. We would not choose to manipulate the situation. We seek to determine what it is students do — as a way to understand their current state of knowledge about writing an effective persuasive letter, for example. We would initially consider all of their engagements (as they spoke with their neighbors, read friends' works, looked at previous drafts of their own work, started and discarded drafts, etc.). Slowly we would narrow our focus to those specific activities which seemed to contribute to their production of persuasive text. (We might pay greater attention to their chats with their friends, as they read each others' work — and as they try to formulate 'an opening'. Then we might see they eventually discard that initial opening which served to get them started, but in the end rewrote that opening in a more highly focused way, especially after reading their work aloud to their neighbor.) As we analyze our data, we consider the specific issue of how students get their thoughts on paper including sources which contribute to that thinking.

As we consider our findings, we focus both on quantitative and qualitative issues. When we focus on the quantitative aspects, we might count the number of words, the number of drafts created, the number of times they went to other sources. A qualitative analysis might study stylistic elements, similarities between published samples and student products, and the uses of humor and metaphors, for example, as a way to distinguish between students' writings.

We may compare hypothesis generating research to investigative reporting in journalism wherein the reporter checks out numerous leads, hoping one will lead to fruitful information. The reporter collects all available data, sifting through it to develop a theory which accounts for and predicts events. The experienced, reflective reporter becomes an expert at understanding people and therefore more likely to choose the 'best' or most viable theory (Dreyfus and Dreyfus, 1986). An expanded discussion of the processes involved in this type of research is presented in Brause and Mayher, 1982 and Brause, chapter 9.

Distinguishing Between Hypothesis Generating and Hypothesis Testing

Since the phrasing of the research question identifies the researcher's specific goal, we can tell from the research question whether the purpose of a study is either to generate or test hypotheses. The singular distinguishing characteristic between hypothesis testing and hypothesis generating studies is the outcome for each: *either* a hypothesis is tested *or* a theory is generated. Questions (xvi) and (xvii) are clear contrasts.

(xvi) Do students who are exposed to a direct instructional strategy in learning specific spelling words related to their experiences discussing literature, achieve statistically higher test scores than students experiencing no such direct instruction? How does this achievement predict their strategies in spelling infrequently used words, newly acquired words, and other words not specifically taught?

(xvii) How do students who participate in small group discussion about stories change their word choices (conventional spelling, precision in usage, choosing appropriate metaphors, etc.) over time?

There is a basic assumption, premise or theory underlying both questions, namely: Words are important indicators of learning. But the relative importance of such issues as the relationship of 'correct' or conventional spelling and the students' concepts about literature and life are unspecified; this is a philosophical issue in need of careful consideration by each educator as it tacitly influences our educational decisions.

Questions (xvi) and (xvii) focus on different issues, deriving from different philosophical priorities and theoretical bases. Question (xvi) implicitly draws on two theories, namely: direct instruction is beneficial in increasing students' knowledge of spelling and spelling knowledge can be assessed through explicit testing. The intent of a research study focussing on such a question would be to ascertain the predictability of such actions. Hypothesis testing studies assess the impact of theoretically driven instructional strategies typically through systematic collection of data on a large scale, sometimes combining data across the nation as in the case of the National Assessments of Educational Progress (Applebee *et al*, 1990, for example).

Question (xvii) derives from a different perspective. It does not start with a theory about how students reveal their understandings. It is intended to explore how individual student uses of specific vocabulary items (whether in written or spoken contexts) reveal current understandings of the literary concepts under discussion. This question grows from two theories (i) that we learn language through use — not dummy runs (Dixon, 1975; Wells, 1986; Romaine, 1984; Tannen, 1990); and (ii) that working in groups is beneficial because the shared,

Figure 3.2: *A schematic presentation of hypothesis generating and hypothesis testing research procedures*

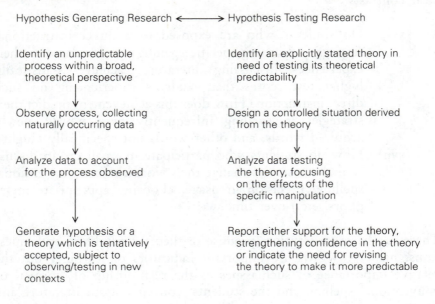

scaffolded support of each individual's knowledge encourages learners to experiment within areas monitored by those with greater expertise, or the zone of proximal development as Vygotsky (1978) called it.

Hypotheses are generated or formulated from tentatively held general principles, which are open to constant revision. As researchers from a hypothesis generating perspective, we are open to surprises, serendipitous findings, to individual differences, because we are actually looking at *real* situations and *real* learners — in naturally occurring, spontaneous situations. We admit the impossibility of controlling human actions but seek to make these more predictable through careful observation and systematic inquiry.

Hypothesis Testing and Hypothesis Generating research are complimentary and interdependent with each providing an essential perspective for increasing our knowledge. (See figure 3.2). Since each has a distinct goal or purpose, we will use this discrete characteristic to distinguish the two types of empirical studies. Thus we will use the terms Hypothesis Testing and Hypothesis Generating to denote their unique, and important differences. In later chapters we will discuss each in depth. At this point we want to establish a more holistic frame of reference. Despite the unique purposes of hypothesis testing and hypothesis generating research, they frequently share similar procedures in collecting and analyzing data.

Comparing Hypothesis Generating and Hypothesis Testing Research

Four characteristics distinguish hypothesis generating and hypothesis testing research, namely: their Origins, Processes, Contexts, and Outcomes (see table 3.1).

Table 3.1:   *A comparison of hypothesis generating and hypothesis testing research procedures*

| | **Research Type** | |
	Hypothesis Generating	*Hypothesis Testing*
Origin	The identification of a phenomenon which is unpredictable	An explicit theory or set of beliefs, facts or assumptions
Process	Inductive	Deductive
Context	Natural, spontaneous	Controlled, manipulated
Outcome	A tentative theory or hypothesis that is highly sensitive to the context or setting in which the phenomenon occurs	Either support for the theory, which is interpreted to generalize to much larger settings and populations, or a need to modify or revise the theory to be more consistent with the findings

Origins

Both hypothesis generating and hypothesis testing studies are scientific because, according to Kelly (1955) both are systematic inquiries. Hypothesis testing springs from reasonably impermeable, fixed constructs which are easily testable. The theory as presented is intended to be explicitly and extensively described, making it easy to test. Hypothesis testing research is derived from an explicitly stated prediction in the form of a theory. The research study formulated from the explicit theory, seeks to systematically examine the accuracy or validity of the general theory within one specific context. Hypothesis testing research seeks to establish the accuracy or predictability of the theory through an accumulation of data from many such highly focussed, repetitive studies.

Hypothesis generating studies, on the other hand, originate from the recognition that a wide range of things are happening, all seemingly unpredictable, and random. 'Rationalizations' are cropping up more and more to explain inconsistencies, making the constructs increasingly permeable, and subject to revision. Hypothesis generating studies are mounted when we find it impossible to either explain or predict what will happen due to a lack of a sufficient knowledge base. These studies represent an open-ended search for information. The researcher intends to consciously question implicitly held, basic assumptions, to discover systematically what *really* happens as people naturally go about their specific activities.

Processes

When we realize our instructional strategies are not working for some of our students, we seek to find out why the strategy is not working. Once we've established a question which we seek to find an answer to, we have set the wheels in motion for designing our research project. The likelihood of questioning depends to large measure on the strength of conviction we have in the theories we hold or our openness to serendipity. (Bissex, 1980, for example questioned her belief about the necessity for direct instruction in reading when her son wrote her a note (RUDF) causing her to realize he had learned to read and write without direct instruction).

Both hypothesis testing and hypothesis generating studies use rigorous, intensive and systematic approaches. Hypothesis testing studies *deduce* or generalize about the veracity of a theory using specific data or information from a small body of information. The findings are interpreted in two related ways:

— to support the larger theory of which the tested hypothesis is one small part; and
— to generalize to larger segments of our population.

Hypothesis testing studies systematically collect specific information. The researcher tests or experiments to determine if a particular theory can be supported by specific practice. The researcher deduces the general validity of the larger theory being tested from the aspect specifically tested. The findings are interpreted to be generalizable to large segments of society applying statistical theories of 'randomization' and 'normal curves' which are discussed in detail in later chapters.

Hypothesis generating studies *induce* generalizations and build theories by studying the recurring patterns of a phenomenon within a specific set of data. These generalizations are *tentative*. They are expressed as hypotheses which need to be subjected to more systematic data collection and intensive analysis. Hypothesis generating studies systematically collect a wide array of naturally occurring information from a very small number of people, seeking an intensive understanding of each individual's processes. Hypothesis generating research collects data which are then explored to identify repetitious, significant events. There is a cyclical process of data collection and analysis.

Once we as researchers have a theory, we test this out in new settings. Thus, hypothesis generating studies start with few individuals who are subjected to intensive study. From these preliminary explorations, hypotheses are induced which reflect the specific experiences in this small sample. Hypothesis generating studies construct theories about human interactions, recognizing human beings will never be as predictable as particles, molecules or metal machine parts. All theories are accepted tentatively, and subject to further revision, always seeking to get closer to TRUTH.

Context

Hypothesis generating research typically is conducted in the naturally occurring settings. The intent is to study what really happens, so the context is real and subject to the natural unpredictabilities of human beings.

In hypothesis testing studies, the researcher intentionally controls or manipulates the setting and the focus to test one specific facet of a theory. Frequently these studies occur in laboratories or utilize techniques constructed in laboratories, intentionally removing any connection with a familiar context or content.

Outcomes

Hypothesis generating studies present tentative hypotheses or models which seem to predict factors which influence the process studied. These hypotheses or models need to be subjected to continued research, seeking to get broader support for predictability while refining and clarifying all its elements. Ultimately hypothesis generating studies seek to contribute to theory building, providing more comprehensive and more valid theories than are currently available. Hypothesis generating research is highly contextualized, reflecting the unique impact of individuals and settings. On the one hand, it reveals the impossibility of generalizing beyond specific situations — suggesting the relative unpredictability of human activities. On the other hand, it does reveal activities which are fairly likely to occur, albeit not automatically predictable events. Hypothesis generating research ultimately reminds us of the complexity of our minds and our lives, emphasizing the excitement of that unpredictability.

As an outcome of hypothesis testing research either the tested theory is confirmed or is not confirmed. Studies which confirm a theory, strengthen the theory's ability to predict the outcomes in different settings with different individuals. This positive finding supports the theory, and increases the strength of our belief in its accuracy in predicting events. When the findings could happen by chance, the theory still stands, but has not been given increased support by the experiment. After many studies fail to achieve results which support the predicted theory, theorists conduct hypothesis generating studies to construct a theory more consistent with what actually happens.

Hypothesis Testing and Generating — A Matter of Personal Perspective

Carl Rakosi's poem, 'The Experiment with a Rat' cleverly contrasts hypothesis testing and hypothesis generating research by identifying the different perspectives of a rat and an experimenter. The elements of concern are a rat, a piece of cheese, a bell and a spring and who's doing what to whom?

The Experiment with a Rat
Carl Rakosi

> Every time I nudge that spring
>   a bell rings
> And a man walks out of a cage
> Assiduous and sharp
>   like one of us
> And brings me cheese.
>
> How did he fall
>   into my power?

We can see the conflict between two perspectives — the experimenter's and the rat's. If we take the experimenter's perspective, we are engaged in a hypothesis testing study. The experimenter places a rat in a cage with an apparatus including a spring, a bell, and cheese.

The experimenter, assuming that rats like cheese, seeks to use this knowledge to get the rat to ring a bell. The experimenter wants to get the rat to ring the bell — as an end itself. She/he believes s/he needs to teach the rat how to ring the bell and uses cheese to bait the rat. The experimenter replaces the cheese, in hopes the rat will repeat the sequence of events ... and fall into *his* (the experimenter's) control. The experimenter is seeking to test a hypothesis that through reward, s/he can orchestrate the rat's behavior to do what s/he wants — to control the rat's behavior. S/he interprets the rat's ringing the bell as an indication that the rat is under her/his (the experimenter's) control.

From the rat's perspective, we understand that the rat is trying to figure out how he was able to get the experimenter to do what the rat wants, which is to give more cheese. The rat, then, is engaged in hypothesis generating research. The rat is trying to figure out how s/he was able to cause the experimenter to respond to the bell ringing by bringing more cheese. The rat's inquiry is of the hypothesis generating variety in contrast to the experimenter's which is a hypothesis testing one. The two questions (one from the experimenter and one from the rat) represent two different interpretations of a situation, emphasizing the reality that there are multiple perspectives possible on a situation. Teacher researchers who seek to find TRUTH are open to all types of inquiry, ready to test hypotheses or to generate them.

The purpose of educational research is to bring our assumptions and perceptions about the teaching-learning process to a level of consciousness such that we can talk about them and use this knowledge for decision-making. Inevitably there are diverse perspectives on reality which influence the entire professional community. Research in its different forms provides strategies to improve our reality base from which to improve our educational practice. In the next chapters we consider how to interpret and design research studies to increase the effectiveness of our educational practice.

References

APPLEBEE, A.N., LANGER, J.A., MULLIS, I.V.S. and JENKINS, L.B. (1990) *The Writing Report Card, 1984–1988: Findings from the Nation's Report Card*, Princeton, NJ, ETS.

ARONOWITZ, S. and GIROUX, H.A. (1985) *Education Under Seige: The Conservative, Liberal and Radical Debate Over Schooling*, So. Hadley, MA, Bergin & Garvey.

BISSEX, G. (1980) *GNYS at WRK*, Cambridge, MA, Harvard University Press.

BRAUSE, R.S. (forthcoming) *Enduring Schools*, Lewes, Falmer Press.

BRAUSE, R.S. and MAYHER, J.S. (1982), 'Teachers, students and classroom organization', *Research in the Teaching of English*, 16, 2.

BRAUSE, R.S. and MAYHER, J.S. (1983) 'Classroom teacher as researcher', *Language Arts*, 60, 6.

DIXON, J. (1975) *Growth Through English*, 3rd edn, Urbana, IL, NCTE.

DREYFUS, H.L. and DREYFUS, S.E. (1986) *Mind Over Machine*, NY, Free Press.

FREIRE, P. (1973) *Pedagogy of the Oppressed*, New York, Seabury Press.

GIROUX, H.A. (1988) *Teachers as Intellectuals: Toward a Critical Pedagogy of Learning*, Granby, MA, Bergin & Garvey.

GRAVES, D.H. and CALKINS, L.M. (1980) 'Research update: When children want to punctuate: Basic skills belong in context', *Language Arts*, 57, 5.

HOLMES GROUP (1983) *Tomorrow's Teachers*, East Lansing, MI, The Holmes Group.

KELLY, G. (1955) *The Psychology of Personal Constructs*, New York, Norton.

LYONS, N. (1990) 'Dilemmas of knowing: Ethical and epistemological dimensions of teachers' work and development', *Harvard Educational Review*, 60, 2.

McLAREN, P. (1989) *Life in Schools*, New York, Longman.

McNEIL, L.M. (1986) *Contradictions of Control: School Structure and School Knowledge*, New York, Routledge.

MAYHER, J.S. (1990) *Uncommon Sense: Theoretical Practice in Language Education*, Portsmouth, NH, Boynton/Cook.

NORTH, S.M. (1987) *The Making of Knowledge in Composition: Portrait of an Emerging Field*, Portsmouth, NH, Boynton/Cook.

ROMAINE, S. (1984) *The Language of Children and Adolescents: The Acquisition of Communicative Competence*, New York, Basil Blackwell.

SCHÖN, D.A. (1983) *The Reflective Practitioner*, New York, Basic Books.

SCHÖN, D.A. (1987) *Educating the Reflective Practitioner*, San Francisco, CA, Jossey-Bass.

SINGLETON, C., DIDERICH, F. and HILL, J. (1961) *Research Methods in the Language Arts*, Urbana, IL, NCTE.

SKINNER, B.F. (1957) *Verbal Behavior*, New York, Appleton, Century and Crofts.

TANNEN, D. (1990) *You Just Don't Understand: Women and Men in Conversation*, New York, Morrow.

VYGOTSKY, L.S. (1978) *Mind in Society*, Cambridge, MA, Harvard University Press.

WELLS, G. (1986) *The Meaning Makers: Children Learning Language and Using Language to Learn*, Portsmouth, NH, Heinemann.

Chapter 4

Reading and Understanding Hypothesis Testing Research

William L. Smith

I once held the belief that speakers of other languages talked faster than speakers of English, but I couldn't understand why. Consequently, for a term project in a German course, I analyzed the speed with which Germans and Americans spoke. To my amazement, there was no difference. Some Germans spoke rapidly, but so did some Americans. I accepted this new truth, but it still didn't make sense until, a few years later, I discovered the reason. I had been trying to hear each German word, one word at a time. When listening to English, I listened selectively; I didn't try or need to hear all of the words. If I heard but a few, I could guess the rest because I had a mental grammar and a communicative competence system for English.

My problems in understanding German were most notable when speakers left out information, information any native speaker of German could supply, or used pronouns and other cohesion techniques to relate to previously stated information. Similar usage in English didn't bother me because I knew both the rules and the implied context. It was not until I had sufficient familiarity and experience with German to develop a mental grammar and communicative competence that I was able to keep up with a conversation.

Reading hypothesis testing research reports poses analogous problems for the 'non-native' reader. Until the reader learns the rules (the grammar) and the context (the communicative competence) for such reports, that reader will try to read too much, and by so doing, will not make full use of the appropriate pieces of information to create the inferences necessary for efficient reading and full comprehension. The intent of this chapter is to present and discuss some important aspects of the grammar and the context of a hypothesis testing research report so that a reader can read effectively and efficiently and make the appropriate inferences from the report.

William L. Smith

Characteristics of Hypothesis Testing Research Reports

When most people think of hypothesis testing research, they immediately think of numbers, statistical formulae, tables, and figures. However, these are but the tools of this type of research. The heart of all good hypothesis testing research lies elsewhere, for numbers, by themselves, mean nothing. All hypothesis testing research has three defining characteristics: theory, purpose, and measurement.

The first, and the most important (actually, it is the most important for any type of research) is a theory or motivating force. Hypothesis testing research is not just done; it is done for a particular reason, either to test an assumption or theory (for example, 'the teaching of grammar rules improves students' writing') or to provide a descriptive picture of the status of some group because we don't know how to characterize that group (for example, what are the characteristics of tenth graders' knowledge of poetry?). This theory or motivating force is crucial, for, as will be explained in detail later, it also provides the lens through which the data will be viewed and explained. Given one set of data and three theories, one can draw three totally different sets of conclusions. For an example, one need look no further than the economic projections made by different economists. They all use the same data, but they often draw totally different conclusions, especially in an election year. The different theories and motivating forces provide quite different lenses. Although one can find published research which lacks a theoretical framework or any apparent motivating force, such reports are rare because theory and motivating force form one of the primary criteria by which researchers decide to do the research in the first place.

The second characteristic is a clearly defined problem, a delimited statement of purpose. This, naturally, is closely related to the theory or motivating force. Hypothesis testing research must be controlled, precise, and cautious. If the researcher's purpose is fuzzy or ill-defined, no amount of high powered statistical testing will make the research valid, important, relevant, or useful. In the surest sense, garbage in will net garbage out.

The third characteristic is a consequence of the first two. Hypothesis testing research must have a meaningful way of measuring. The data, the numbers produced, must represent something about the people being tested and the topic being researched. If the measures are not valid, reliable, and relevant, no sensible conclusion can ever be drawn.

There is also a fourth characteristic, but it seldom is visible in published research, except to the trained eye. Good hypothesis testing research is based on a constant cycling between naturalistic, impressionistic research and empirical testing. Good researchers have a feel for the data because they have looked beyond those data, at the students themselves, at the classrooms and teachers, at the topic being tested. Without this 'feel', a researcher cannot understand the data; she or he can only report them, and that is of no real use to anyone. While conducting our hypothesis testing research, we commonly interview students and teachers, and anyone else who might give us relevant information.

In one of my recent projects, I discovered, through such interviews, that I actually was creating a rather powerful side-effect, one which I might never have discovered had I not taken the time to let the participants in the study give me their impressions. This information did not alter that study, but it did help me plan several new, and more important studies. This point cannot be stressed too much because the power of hypothesis testing research lies jointly in its precision and in the researcher's interpretation of the evidence. Therefore, one of the most essential features of hypothesis testing research is the questions the research provokes. The true value of any research does not reside in the research itself, but in the way it shapes both thought and future research. The true purpose of research is not just to answer questions but to provide better questions.

Hypothesis testing research is defined by these characteristics. Such research is never truly seminal, for before one can quantify, one must know what is worth quantitative investigation and how to adequately measure that entity. In most cases, the seminal work in any line of inquiry (i.e., a series of research projects, each building on its predecessor) is hypothesis generating research, which is discussed elsewhere in this book. In the few instances where a piece of hypothesis testing research is considered seminal, in actuality, that researcher did a considerable amount of hypothesis generating investigation before doing the quantitative research.

Types of Hypothesis Testing Research

Hypothesis testing research is not monolithic; rather, there are several types, each of which has distinct characteristics. Since numbers (statistics) are used in such research, the researcher must know, prior to starting the research, what to quantify and how to quantify it. Thus, hypothesis testing research is always based on some theory, even if it is but a tentative concept. There are two basic purposes for conducting hypothesis testing research: to describe what can be called natural or existing states, and to determine what happens if a new condition is introduced. The former can be called status or survey research; the latter experimental or intervention.

In status research, the researcher computes numerically, on one or more defined points (for example, spelling errors or novels read) to determine differences among groups or issues, to create a picture; what we call the 'lay of the land'. These data provide a base line which can be used in future comparisons.

In experimental research, specific hypotheses are tested, and thus it is usually thought of when referring to 'hypothesis testing' research. The primary purpose is to draw inferences about the tested theory. The research may be formal (i.e., highly controlled) or informal. Informal experimental research is used by all teachers when they teach a new unit or use a new method and notice, by using some means of measurement, that the new unit or method works differently than the old.

Both of these types can be further divided according to the group or groups being tested. If one does research on one group at one time (students or teachers, for example), that research is considered 'status' research. However, if that time frame is expanded, even slightly, experimental research is possible. For example, one could measure how a single comment affected the answers given by a group of students as compared with the expected answers; this expectation, of course, must be based on adequate previous status research. This type of one-group, one-time research is somewhat rare in education because we lack those precise normative descriptions. Therefore, almost all hypothesis-testing one-group experimental research involves an extended time frame, from a few days to a full semester or year.

One group can also be followed for an even longer period. This is called longitudinal research. Each student is tested, using the same methods, procedures, and tests, at prescribed times during the course of the research. Very little longitudinal research has been conducted for several reasons: (i) it is extremely time-consuming and, therefore, costly; (ii) it is difficult to find a school system which will allow such testing every year, or worse, every month; (iii) one must begin with a large number of students, for not all will remain in the same school system, and thus one could end up with a mere handful still left to take the last test; (iv) all decisions about methods of testing, the types of tests to be used, and the techniques for counting must be established prior to the project and must be maintained throughout the project.

Thus, because our knowledge is constantly changing, with more precise techniques and measures emerging every year, and newer, more adequate theories being produced, longitudinal research can become dated, or antiquated, before the project is finished. Yet that doesn't mean that longitudinal research shouldn't be conducted. We certainly need and value such studies.

The most common sub-division of both status and experimental research is cross-sectional. This involves subjects from more than one grade level or ability level, for example. By assuming that a group of tenth graders would perform in the same manner as a group of ninth graders would when in the tenth grade, cross-sectional research obtains some of the power of longitudinal research, and the descriptive evidence could be nearly as good. Furthermore, because cross-sectional research can be done in a short period of time, one can also conduct experimental research with less fear of unforeseen variables affecting the results.

Perhaps the most common research method is a comparison of an 'experimental' and a 'control' group. This method deserves special mention because it is often poorly described. The most common error is not describing what the 'control' group did or was taught. The experimental curriculum or task is described because it is new and therefore unknown to the reader. However, the 'control' is summarily described with a few words, for example, 'The control group was taught the usual curriculum.' If we had standardized curricula, that statement might suffice, but we don't. Thus, the reader has no precise picture of that control method.

The word 'control' is also misused. In reality, both methods are experimental. A true control method would be identical to the experimental except for one definable, describable difference. If there is more than one difference, the researcher cannot be certain which caused the different results, if there are differences. Thus the results cannot be clearly interpreted or generalized. Since it is exceedingly difficult to arrange such a precise difference between the methods, the wiser strategy is to carefully explain both methods. This avoids the problem, but it also eliminates the instinct to treat one method, the control, as a straw horse, something which is somehow wrong-headed or poorly conceived. Yet that is precisely the implication one gets when reading such research.

Furthermore, if the readers can't determine what the control method was, they cannot determine whether the experimental method would be better than theirs. Consequently, generalizability is lost. Of the hundreds, perhaps thousands, of such studies I have read, in only a handful was the experimental method not 'significantly' better. I don't doubt the results, but I have concluded that it was probably the case that the experimental methods were better because the researcher conceived and planned them, whereas the 'control' had not been given this attention.

Reading Hypothesis Testing Research

Learning to read hypothesis testing research can be compared to learning to read a sonnet. The content is closely tied to and is, in part, explained by the form and the use of formulaic expressions (what we typically call 'conventions').

Hypothesis testing research is written for a relatively limited audience, and the members of that audience share certain characteristics. They know the conventions, and they probably know some of the related research. But most of all, they don't have time to read every word. Therefore, research reports are not like other prose. They are fully descriptive, but they are also concise. Thus, they require the reader to interact in order to obtain all the information. They include information that a wide variety of different readers, with different interests, may want, yet are written so that the reader doesn't have to read the entire report to gain that information. That is precisely why hypothesis testing research reports follow a prescribed format: Title, Rationale and Related Literature, Statement of Purpose, Questions and/or Hypotheses, Procedure, Results, Discussion, Interpretation, and References.

Each of these sections will be discussed below, but first, a few comments about style are warranted. Researchers often use the passive voice, not because they necessarily prefer it, but rather, because it is both established tradition and allows inferences. Since, in most hypothesis testing research, the researcher did the research, using the active voice would lead to redundancy, for 'I' (or the abominable 'this researcher') would be the subject of most sentences. By using the passive, the 'I' is deleted, except where it is necessary to specify the researcher as the agent. Thus, if a sentence reads, 'Each student was tested in his or her own classroom', the reader can assume either that the researcher, not the classroom teacher, administered the tests or that this piece of information is of no consequence because pilot testing or other research has shown that the administrator has no effect on student performance. The use of the passive also makes any use of the active voice, with 'I' as the subject, more forceful; the researcher, by using 'I' is making him/herself personally accountable. Many researchers use this 'notable "I"' in the interpretation section where they personally interpret the meaning of the evidence. Were the active voice used throughout the report, this willingness to be accountable would go unnoticed. This is not a strategy which a researcher necessarily uses consciously; rather, it is an accepted convention in reporting on hypothesis testing research and becomes a natural way of thinking and writing. However, if the reader is not aware of the purposes of the passive, important inferences will be missed.

Research writers tend to use complex, heavily embedded sentences. Indeed, they are sometimes difficult to read. But this too is with reason. The average length of a research article in *Research in the Teaching of English* and other research journals is fifteen pages. Thus, the writer must condense what took a year or more to plan, execute, and interpret into a few pages of text plus a few tables and figures. Consequently, every word, every construction, must be meaningful and, thus, carefully selected. Furthermore, like the sonneteer, the writer expects the reader to know the style and conventions, and how to read them.

Part of this complexity is due to what can be called 'semantic abbreviation'. James Collins uses this term to refer to children's writing in which they make reference to people, places, and activities which have not been introduced and thus about which the reader has no knowledge. But the term can also be applied to research writing, for the writers make cryptic references to theories, other research, and procedures, expecting the reader to make all of the necessary associations.

The complexity is also encouraged by the sectioning of a research report. Each main point in a report has its own section. Since these are labelled with headings, transition sentences are not used. Indeed, if the headings were removed, the text might seem disjointed. This use of headed sections is important in the research style of writing, for few researchers write the text in a linear manner; that is, most write by section, but not in the final order of presentation of those sections.

Because hypothesis testing research demands that the procedures be established before the research is conducted, the Procedures section is commonly written first (before the research is actually conducted) and only slightly revised before submitting the report for publication, barring catastrophes during the research. Parts of the Rationale, particularly the Related Literature, can also be written before conducting the research. The Results, Discussion, and Interpretation sections cannot be written until after the research project is completed, but even these may not be written in the final order of the published document. It is not uncommon to write one part of the Results section and the related parts of the Discussion and Interpretation together, then write a second and third part of each. For most researchers, the last part written is the lead paragraph in the report which is frequently an abstract of the total project.

In the following pages, each section of the research report will be discussed separately to explain its purpose and function and to provide insight into references a reader can make from that section. Examples will be drawn from three hypothesis testing reports, each selected because it exemplifies certain types and sub-divisions of such research and because it has stood the test of time.

1 Barry Kroll (1978) 'Cognitive egocentrism and the problem of audience awareness in written discourse', *Research in the Teaching of English*, 12, pp. 269–281.

This is an article reporting experimental research on one aspect of children's speaking and writing. One group, fourth graders, is used.

2 Walter Loban (1976) *Language Development: Kindergarten through Grade Twelve*, Research Report No. 18, National Council of Teachers of English.

This is a monograph reporting descriptive results of a longitudinal study of the one group's oral and written language.

3 Ann Terry (1974) *Children's Poetry Preferences: A National Survey of Upper Elementary Grades*, Research Report No. 16, National Council of Teachers of English.

This is a monograph reporting survey results from a cross-sectional survey of the poetry preferences of students in grades four, five and six.

For the sake of simplicity and because it is one of researchers' conventions, these authors will be referred to by last name only.

The Title

In research reports, titles are extremely important, for they must capture the essence of the research. The title becomes a contract, a promise of the contents. A reader's decision to read an article is often based on just the title. Thus, nothing is more frustrating than a misleading title. Consequently, research reports seldom have contrived, fancy, or cute titles. In most cases, the title is a precis of the purpose of the research. One of its contemporary functions, in fact, is to facilitate appropriate retrieval of the study through such computerized data-bases as the ERIC system. In order for this to work effectively for researchers who are searching for other studies which may be relevant to the one they are planning, the title must contain as many key words as possible, since key words are the basis upon which such databases are organized.

Kroll promises to study cognitive egocentrism and audience awareness. But note that he uses the phrase 'the problem of audience awareness in written discourse'. Thus, the reader can infer that Kroll will not determine the problems or the causes of those problems; instead, he will focus on what the informed reader already knows is the problem: students have difficulty assuming or apprehending the role of the reader when they write.

Loban's title is broader because he studies more variables. Yet the title still captures the essence of the study, including the inference that it is a longitudinal study.

Terry's title is a near perfect contract. She will report fourth, fifth, and sixth grade children's poetry preferences as determined through a survey (thus the study is cross-sectional and descriptive), and the results, because her study is based on a 'national survey', can be generalized to all children in the nation.

The Author

As one reads more and more research, the names of authors become powerful devices for inferencing. This is not different from reading novels or poetry for experienced readers of literature. The name 'Mark Twain' evokes an expectation of content, style, tone, even of quality. Similarly, one can often infer the focus, the topic, and the general line of inquiry just from the author's name. Many researchers spend years, even their lives, studying one line of inquiry. Eventually, we become so familiar with not just research but researchers' research that we refer to a piece of research by citing only a name and a year. 'Loban '76' becomes a single term with a complex meaning, including not just the data and the general conclusions, but also the research which led to that study, the methods Loban used, and the research which his study spawned.

One of the difficulties facing us when we begin to read research in a field where we are unfamiliar, can be the lack of broad contextual resonance evoked by such names. The writer of the research report, who is essentially writing for an audience familiar wth these names, may not have space to explain them to beginners. The effect is often that of going to a family dinner party of someone else's family and not having the vaguest idea who Uncle Leo or Cousin Betty are. The only way to solve the problem is to hang around long enough, reading widely in the literature, so that the names become your family too.

The Rationale and Review of Literature

The purpose of this first section of the text is simple: to provide sufficient information and logic to substantiate the existence of the research. However, creating this section is more complex than the final product implies. The amount of rationalization and the extent of the literature review depend upon three factors: first, where the report will be published, how much can be assumed about the audience's knowledge, and how much space can be allocated to this section; second, how well established are the line of inquiry and the procedures to be used, and third, the purpose of the research.

Loban was working within a well-established field and had already published some of his findings. Furthermore, his primary purpose was to describe. Consequently, he has less need for an extensive rationale or for a long review of the literature. Instead, he cites references in other places in the report. For example, he refers to the works of A.F. Watts and K.W. Hunt when describing his principal measure, the communication unit.

Terry's report required more rationalization and literature review because she suspected that the current beliefs about children's poetry preferences might not be realistic. Therefore, she had to create an introduction which would establish both that those beliefs exist and that there is some cause to doubt them, and thus a reason for studying the issue. She sets up her study by citing three studies and logically relating them, thus leading the reader to her purpose and the question she intends to answer by conducting the research. In her review of literature, she summarizes the important studies and synthesizes all of them into two basic conclusions, conclusions she can later refer to when discussing her own findings.

Kroll was breaking new ground in his study, so he had to spend considerable time establishing his study. Because he was wedding two fields, he had to review both to show how they are related and together inform his research. This strategy is typical of reports which focus on new, emerging, or controversial topics. Kroll synthesizes the rival positions, resolving them in his general hypothesis that 'writing, because it created increased cognitive demands, lagged behind speaking in level of decentration'. In his review, he leads the reader, by both his statements and by the inferences he carefully establishes, to the conclusion that this study is important. He seals this conclusion by stating that little empirical research has been conducted on this topic. Note that this statement clearly implies that his research will be empirical. The reader is now primed for the next section.

These three reports typify the basic techniques for writing this introductory section. The author must first determine how much background the reader needs. That decision is based on the answers to two questions: Is the need for the research so clear and the knowledge about the topic so common that little needs to be said? Or, am I attempting to refute a widely held belief or a conclusion drawn in previous research?

For Loban, the answer to the first question was 'yes'. Therefore, he includes only a short review. For Kroll, however, the answer was 'no', so he carefully selected the important studies and theories and synthesized them. For Terry, the answer to the second question was 'yes'. Therefore, she carefully explained why the current belief might be wrong. Each of these authors could assume that the readers who knew the literature well would just scan this section, but they each provided enough information to allow those readers who did not know the literature to understand the basic issues involved.

Although the writer is not required to create reader interest in this section (the title and the desire to learn should have done this), carefully establishing the raison d'être for a study will enhance that interest. More to the point, it will specify the nature of the problem. And this section establishes the points to which the author can and should return in the discussion and interpretation sections to tie the report together. Finally, a well-conceived and well-written introductory section indicates the ability of the author to conceive and conduct research, thus giving the author credibility.

The Statement of Purpose

Although this is not always a labelled section, it is crucial to good research and good research reporting. A poorly conceived study cannot be clearly stated in one, or even several, statements of purpose.

Thus, one criterion a reader uses to evaluate research is the clarity and precision of these statements, for the entire report, indeed the research itself, hinges on this statement.

Loban's study was massive, yet he could articulate his purposes in one statement and five interrelated questions. His use of questions to specify the purposes is not unusual, but the reader has to see that these questions are altered forms of statements of purpose.

Terry specifies the purpose of her study in the more typical manner, 'Specifically, the research was conducted for the following purposes'. She then lists her three concerns.

Kroll does not overtly state his purpose. Instead, he states his general hypothesis (cited above), then presents a clear statement of how he will test that hypothesis. 'To test this hypothesis at one grade level, the effect of communication modes (speaking and writing) on the communicative adequacy of fourth-grade children's informative discourse was investigated.' All of the essential elements of the study are specified: one grade (fourth grade), the two modes (oral and written), the type of discourse (informative), and the measure to be used (communicative adequacy). He has created code words for the reader who is now ready to learn more about them.

The statement of purpose, therefore, is quite like the thesis statement students are often asked to write. It, like the title, is a contract which provides the unity for the entire report.

There is a distinct advantage in labelling this statement. The reader can read it first to determine whether it is necessary to read the introduction. If the reader knows the terms and comprehends the logic, then the reader probably is prepared to read the rest of the report without reading the introduction.

Procedures

The Procedures (or methods) section is perhaps the most stylized of all. The reader expects it to include specific information and to be so clear and precise that the study could be replicated, but that does not mean that each step in the procedure is discussed. Some procedures are standard or the researcher may be using someone else's procedure. In these cases, a simple citation is sufficient. (This is another instance of the semantic abbreviation discussed earlier.)

The 'exposition by citation' is nettlesome to readers who don't know those references. However, this is one of the compromises one makes in writing and reading research. If each researcher using

Loban's 'communication unit' explained that measure and how it was used, we would lose the efficiency and parsimony we desire in research reporting. This is rather like my experience with German. The speakers would make references to what they considered common knowledge (for example, some literary or social reference), expecting me to fill in all the relevant detail. I wanted them to explain each reference more fully because I couldn't make sense of their reference. Talking with me must have been very difficult.

One way of determining how 'settled' a science is involves examining the repertoire of standard procedures. This is why the most often cited studies are those which define a clear, valid, and reliable method. Using common procedures is of decided importance. It allows the researcher to discuss the results in light of other studies and greatly extends the interpretations drawn from all of the studies.

The Procedures section is, however, more than just a clear exposition; it delimits the results, and, along with the theory, forms the lens through which the results will be seen and interpreted. Consequently, the Procedures section typically includes four types of information: the subjects used, the measures used, the methods used to collect the data, and the methods used to analyze the data. These prescribe the extent to which the results can be generalized.

Subjects used

The most obvious limitation is 'who was investigated'. The neutral term 'subjects' is used (or its abbreviation 'Ss') because it is a specific reference to only those studied, thus allowing the researcher to use the terms 'students', 'teacher', 'children', etc. for more general or extended statements. The choice of subjects is prescribed by the statement of purpose. Thus, the researcher must not only describe the Ss but also explain how and why those Ss were chosen. The description tells the reader to whom the results can be extended or generalized.

Terry used 422 students from four states with roughly the same number in each grade and roughly half from each sex. Thus, her findings could be generalized to all fourth, fifth, and sixth graders in the nation. Loban's Ss were from one city, Oakland, California, but represented a cross-section of the entire community. Therefore, assuming Oakland is not itself unique, his results could be generalized to the entire nation, at all grade levels. Kroll used only fourth graders in one school, selecting thirty-six students from the forty-four in the class. Thus, his findings cannot be as generalized, unless one assumes that all fourth graders are alike.

There is a paradox here. A fine-grained description of Ss must mean that they all shared restricted characteristics. Thus, the research gains power. Yet such a fine-grained selection necessarily reduces the generalizability of the results. Furthermore, any detail included in the description of the Ss is assumed, by the reader, to be of consequence. Otherwise the researcher would not have mentioned it. These issues are usually addressed when one explains why the Ss were chosen.

The overriding issue here is relevant to the purpose of the study; the secondary concern is what other research has shown or what common sense dictates. For example, the research on syntactic development has shown almost no difference between males and females; consequently, one would not have to select Ss on this basis, nor even describe the proportions of each. I know of no research indicating whether brown-eyed teachers are better or worse than green-eyed teachers, but I also know of no one who has even postulated that eye color makes a difference. However, if I mention gender and eye color when describing Ss, I imply that I consider this important, and the reader will expect me to report and to discuss some evidence concerning these characteristics.

Therefore, the reasons for selecting Ss become extremely important and warrant discussion. Terry chose her Ss on the basis of gender and grade. She established that there was reason to expect boys' preferences to be different from girls', and she supports her choice of grades by referring to an authority who states that 'It is along about the fifth grade ... that children decide poetry is not for them.' Her choice of grades four, five, and six, therefore, is appropriate because they encompass this apparently pivotal point.

Kroll chose the fourth grade because prior research had indicated that fourth graders performed better in written discourse than in oral, yet the theory, based on Piaget, would indicate the opposite. The choice, therefore, becomes obvious and rational.

Loban's reasons are equally rational. He wanted to ensure a representative sample. Therefore, he carefully selected kindergartners using gender, ethnic background, socioeconomic status, and intellectual ability. However, he notes that analyzing the data from all 211 subjects would be prohibitively expensive. Consequently, his report focusses on three groups of thirty-five Ss, one group of Ss selected because they were high in language ability, one because they were low in language ability, and one a randomly selected group.

Terry and Kroll do not state their reasons in the 'Subjects' section; rather, they establish those reasons in the introduction. Nevertheless, the reasoning is clear and well-motivated. The reader, however, must interact with the writing to understand it. This, once again, indicates a point worth repeating: reading research is not a passive activity. The reader is required to integrate, and interpret the information presented.

The method of selecting Ss is also important because it prescribes the way the data can be legitimately analyzed. There are four basic methods. A random sample is most highly valued. The researcher first determines the total group (called the 'population') to which the results will be inferred to apply. From this population, a small number (called the 'sample') of Ss is selected using any one of several devices which ensure that each member of the population has an equal chance of being a member of the sample. This method is seldom used because of these strict constraints and because it is prohibitively expensive.

Consequently, most researchers use what can be called a quasi-random sample. They make the assumption that the students (or teacher) in one place (a school system or college) are roughly the same as those in other places. Then they randomly select Ss from that group. In an experimental study, these Ss would be randomly assigned to each experimental group to decrease the probability that the two groups are systematically dissimilar. Kroll used this technique. He randomly assigned the fourth grades to each group.

The third method is called 'stratified' sampling. The population is divided into sub-groups using whatever criteria are theoretically relevant. Then Ss are selected so that each segment of the theoretical population is represented. National polls typically use this method, and so did both Loban and Terry. Loban segmented the population according to gender, ethnic background, socioeconomic status, and intellectual ability, and then selected Ss so that they represented a distribution of all four segments. Terry divided the nation into four geographic regions, and divided school systems into suburban, metropolitan, inner-city, and rural. From the questionnaires returned, she randomly selected fifteen schools from each state. This method allowed Loban and Terry to assume that their samples represented all students in the nation.

The fourth method is the most commonly used in education. It is best described as 'available sample', for the research uses whoever is available. Although this method technically restricts both the types of statistical analyses and the generalizability of the results, it is also the least time-consuming and the least expensive. When using this method, the researcher must explain, in some detail, the characteristics of those Ss so that the reader will know to whom the results might be applied. The results of the study using tenth graders in a rural Texas town might not be generalizable to inner-city Minneapolis tenth graders. This method is creditable, however, if the researcher carefully describes the sample and if that researcher does not generalize unreasonably. Thus, it is incumbent upon the reader to know how to read the 'method of selecting subjects' and to understand how and when to apply the results. Unfortunately, this is not always the case. I can think of several studies which used available samples which in my opinion were very atypical, yet many readers used the results to justify curriculum changes for students who didn't resemble the subjects in those studies.

Measures used

The second piece of necessary information is the measure(s) used. Hypothesis testing research depends upon using the most appropriate and the most precise units of measurement, a way of identifying and counting. If the measurements are not clear, precise, and relevant to the purpose of the research, neither the reader nor the writer can make insightful interpretations. Thus, unit of measurement is itself a bridge between the statement of purpose and results and discussion.

These measures may be developed by the researcher or be a standard, well-documented unit. However, in either case, the researcher should explain the choice. Well-documented measures require less rationalization; the reader can infer the reasons, given the literature cited and the purpose of the research. Thus, Terry, who counted the frequencies of her subjects' responses about their poetry preferences, made no additional mention of her way of counting.

Loban and Kroll, however, developed new techniques, and thus devote some time to their explanations. Loban's basic units were the number of words produced and a 'communication unit' which is roughly akin to either a simple or complex sentence. He does not discuss how he counted words, although other researchers looking at syntax have carefully explained what constitutes a word (for example, are 'contractions' to be counted as one or two words? are 'proper names' one or more words?), but he does explain and give examples of the communication unit. Thus, the reader understands why the length of a communication unit would be an appropriate and insightful way to look at children's linguistic growth. Kroll developed a technique for identifying the informative content Ss included in their explanations of a game. Consequently, he too devotes several paragraphs to explaining how he determined scores and why the scores are appropriate to the purpose of the study. Selecting an inappropriate measuring device results in what is called a 'fatal error'. No amount of revision can allow the researcher to recover, or to cover up. The research is useless.

Methods used to collect the data

The test for the appropriateness of a measure is simple, yet requires knowledge of both the existing scholarship and the topic and subjects being studied. It must have reliability, validity, and relevance, and the writer must establish all three. Even if the measures used meet these tests, the research can still fail if the methods for collecting the data are not also well-rationalized, valid, reliable, and relevant. The explanation of these methods should include information about the testing (how and why it was done that way), about the content of the tests, and, in experimental studies, about the intervention. These methods must be so clearly explained, either explicitly or by reference to prior research, that replication is possible. Here again, as in the case of subject selection, the methods prescribe the generalizability of the results; detail is of great import. Therefore, only important information is included.

In one well-known (but here unnamed) study, the color of the room in which the Ss were tested was controlled. Although no reason is given, the reader must assume that the researchers thought this an important variable. Consequently, the results cannot be generalized to students writing in rooms with different colors. This may seem absurd, but it indicates the importance of judiciousness in describing the methods.

Terry's methods were fairly standard, so little explanation was provided. She does, however, explain who selected the poems she used (she asked elementary teachers and authorities on children's literature) and how the poems were presented to the students, even noting that the poetry was read and recorded by a radio announcer who was experienced in reading poetry. Attention to such small details suggests integrity. This is no small point, for research is only as good as the integrity of the researcher, and the writer must assure the reader of that integrity.

Terry also explains that she field-tested two forms of the instrument she used. She wanted students to rate each poem on a five-point scale, from 'great' to 'hated'. In this pilot test, she found that the instrument which included illustrations (for example, Snoopy dancing for joy to accompany the 'It's great' response) 'elicited greater standard deviations per item'. Therefore, this instrument was used. In three sentences, Terry has shown the reader that this study was not casually done but, rather, involved a considerable amount of thought and pre-testing. Consequently, the reader has much more confidence in the study and in Terry's ability to discuss and interpret the result, for these are not mere numbers to her; she has that requisite 'feel' for the data.

Kroll's description of his methods is just as precise. He conceived a game which Ss learned to play and then taught to another person orally and in writing. The critical issue was the amount of information conveyed by the student. Although the design of Kroll's study is simple (learn, then perform in two modes), the game and the scoring are innovative and complex. Consequently, he devotes over three pages to these two points. As a result, the reader understands and appreciates both the method and the reasons for the method. Kroll includes small, but important details like: there was a low, translucent screen in the middle of the table separating the S and the listener. The screen allowed eye contact, but prevented the S from seeing the listener's game board, and also ensured verbal, but not non-verbal communication.

This attention to detail clearly shows the reader that Kroll was sensitive to those details which make an experiment valid. Kroll clearly had not just concocted a study. He had thought through the study, and had probably done some pilot testing. Such precision of thought and writing not only lends credibility to the research; it makes the researcher credible, a credibility which the reader transfers to other Kroll articles. Kroll has earned the reader's confidence.

Loban's methods were more standard. Other researchers had been using them, and thus the experienced reader would probably be familiar with them. Nevertheless, Loban specifically states that he is using standard methods, and he briefly summarizes them and provides references to the original sources. His new methods are described in detail, and he provides illustrative examples. Furthermore, he anticipates the reader's questions, describes the expected limitations of his method and explains how he surmounted them.

Loban is a well-respected researcher, a reputation earned through his prior writings. Despite this fact, he continues to provide precise details about his procedures. He even mentions one area which he did not analyze but should be looked into in future research. Thus, he is sharing his insights into the potential refinements of his methods. This certainly indicates that he has not just chosen measures; he has chosen carefully, and he has continued to analyze his choices. Consequently, a standard, stylized, descriptive Methods section becomes a device for improving future research.

Methods used to analyze the data
The last piece of information described in the Procedures section concerns how the data were analyzed. The types of analyses are prescribed by the other procedures and by the purpose of the research.

Since most statistical procedures are standard, only a simple reference is needed, or the writer may not mention this at all. Instead, the type of analysis can be inferred from the Results section.

Loban's purpose was to describe the language used by his subjects, and that is precisely what he did. He presents only descriptive numbers, primarily averages. Terry's purpose also was to describe, but she also tested some hypotheses; therefore, she presents the frequencies with which her Ss responded and makes some comparisons among groups. Since the testing of hypotheses requires a formal means of testing, she states that she used 'Chi-square', a test to determine whether two groups are statistically different. Kroll also tested hypotheses, but to know which statistical method he used, the reader must know a simple convention, that 't' means a t-test was used. Kroll did not explain the test because it is a standard device, discussed in basic statistics texts.

In many studies, the researchers state that a specified level of statistical significance was used, typically '.05' or '.01'. These, too, are just conventions. If the data analysis indicates that the difference (on some measure) between two groups is 'significant at .05', this simply means that accepting the normal curve distribution theory, the chance of being wrong is five out of 100. There is, however, no magic in '.05'; .06 is nearly as good. The level of chance one is willing to accept depends on how critical the decision is. Thus, the methods used to analyze the data need be explained only when an unusual test is used or when a test is being used for a particular reason. In normal use, the reader is expected to know both the test and the reasons why it is appropriate. However, this assertion by implication can lead to trouble, for if the test used is not appropriate and is not explained, a knowledgeable reader will question the results and any interpretations.

Results

This section may appear by itself or be combined with the Discussion section. The results, by themselves, tell little; they must be explained and interpreted in light of the theory which underlies the study. Consequently, one must know the purposes, design, and procedures to understand them.

A Results section is composed of the data generated (the numbers and the results of statistical tests) and some explanation. The data are usually presented in tables and figures. The need for, and the number of, tables and figures depends upon the amount and complexity of the data. For a simple study, such as one comparing tenth and eleventh graders' scores on a comprehension test, the necessary information may be presented in the text, without tables or figures. Tables and figures are presented to help readers visualize and interpret the findings.

Reading the numbers presented in the text can pose problems, especially when a great deal of data is presented. The reader cannot integrate or see the relationship among the numbers easily unless they are presented in a graphic representation. Using tables and figures circumvents this memory requirement and, more importantly, allows the readers to see numbers in relation to other numbers. This allows the readers to create their own impressions, their own interpretations. Furthermore, tables and figures provide immediately accessible reference points which the writer can use when discussing particular points concerning the results.

In most reports, some verbal description of the data is included, but the tables and figures can speak adequately for themselves. The clearest research reports will contain considerable explanation of the graphic displays. Experienced and efficient readers are familiar with the different types of tables and figures and what each means.

Tables
Tables are comprised of rows and columns of numbers. In some cases, these might be the actual scores from each student, but more often they display the 'means' (a measure of central tendency or averages) and standard deviations (a measure of dispersion from the mean). The table may include both descriptive data (means and standard deviations) and statistical (inferential) data. Loban's study was both complex and massive. Therefore, he includes nineteen descriptive tables, each presenting the means derived from the various measures he used. Terry's study also was large and complex; therefore, she includes fifteen tables, thirteen presenting the frequencies of responses and two presenting statistical analyses. Kroll's study was very elegant; thus, in his article, he has but one table, in which he presents the mean scores for each group on each task. Unlike Loban and Terry, who could not possibly (or comprehensibly) have presented all of their data in prose, Kroll could have included the means in his text. However, by creating a table (which is reproduced below), he allows the reader, at one glance to compare the performance of the subjects. His table 4.1 creates a dominant impression.

Tables may be as simple as Kroll's, with just two rows and two columns, or they may be very complex, with multiple rows and

Table 4.1:   *Mean spoken and written information scores for groups A and B*

	Session I		Session II	
	Spoken	Written	Spoken	Written
Group A	—	13.0556	18.7222	—
Group B	17.8333	—	—	18.7778

columns showing a great many relationships among many groups, sub-groups, and tasks (for example, the Ss may have performed several tasks, such as a re-test, two mid-term tests, a post-test, and a delayed post-test). The number of tables and the complexity of the tables depends on two factors: the complexity of the design of the research, and the length of the article. The latter is particularly important. In a monograph, such as Loban's or Terry's, the researcher has ample space to split the data into multiple tables, thus simplifying each. However, in a short article, fewer tables are allowed; thus, the data must be compressed.

One advantage of using tables is that data which are not discussed can also be included. These are not irrelevant data, but they may not be pertinent to the specific points the author is making. These data provide additional, more elaborate evidence for other researchers concerned with the same topics.

The table, then, is a type of shorthand which allows the author to present large amounts of data in a readable form and permits knowledgeable readers to draw their own conclusions and interpretations.

Figures

Figures represent of the general configuration of the data. This overall picture, however, actually creates a more powerful impression than either the text or the tables. In fact, a well-constructed figure will create what is called a 'dominant impression', an impression that each reader will long remember.

Figures are particularly useful in two instances: (i) when the study includes data from either several different groups of subjects, or more typically, when data are collected at several times; and (ii) when different but related data are collected from the same group.

Many studies focus on how different groups of students perform on some variable. For example, O'Donnell, Griffin, and Norris (1967) studied the syntactic complexity in oral and written discourse of students from kindergarten and grades one, two, three, five and seven. In their report, they include a figure which shows 'Words per T-Unit' (one measure of complexity). Figure 4.1 shows an increase across grades in both speech and writing, but the lines representing speech and writing cross at about grade four. The same information, the actual data, may be presented in a table, but the figure shows the extremely interesting and important cross-over effect in a much more memorable way.

Figure 4.1: Oral and written syntactic complexity across grades

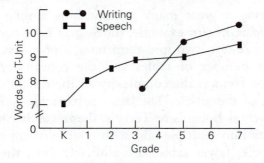

Many experimental studies use pre- and post-test measures. However, the use of only these two points does not tell us what happened between those points. Thus, the pre-test and post-test results of a study on the quality of tenth graders' writing when taught using two different methods might look like figure 4.2.

Figure 4.2: Pre- to post-test change in two groups

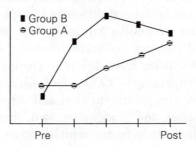

Figure 4.3: Change in two groups across five points

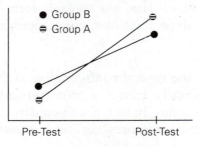

This figure shows that group A improved more than group B. Thus, method A would be considered better. However, if the quality of the students' writing had been measured at three additional times betwen pre- and post-tests, the results might look like figure 4.3.

Now it becomes apparent that the method used to teach group A created early growth in quality but did not sustain that growth. The students in group B improved at a slower rate for most of the year but rapidly improved near the end. If one uses this figure to guess about the students' subsequent improvement, it would seem that group B, given more time, might do better than group A. Therefore, method B would be better. Presenting these data in table form would not show the dissimilar trends as clearly as the figure.

The second instance when figures are useful is well exemplified in Loban's monograph. He includes fourteen figures, many presenting the same information he includes in tables. He was measuring students' writing by using several measures. Each figure indicates how the subjects performed when in each grade. Furthermore, his Ss represented three groups. Thus, each figure allows the reader to compare each group across grades or compare the three groups at each grade. When examined individually, the figures clearly show general growth for all groups but greater growth for the 'high language' group. However, the lasting impression from Loban's study does not come from any one figure; rather, it comes when one puts these figures together. All of the figures show the same configuration. The patterns of growth for these three groups are the same on almost every variable. Those patterns are what we might expect for any one variable or for general growth. Had Loban not included the figures, readers would be less likely to see that there is one overall consistent trend.

Thus, although figures are technically less precise than tables, they can be more important, for they allow the reader to see important relationships and thus to infer much more from the report. One note of caution must be added here. Whereas it is difficult to create false impressions with actual numbers (means and standard deviations), figures presented in graphic form can deceive. Consider figure 4.4 which presents growth in writing ability.

One's immediate impression is that the growth from pre-test to post-test shown in panel A is much more pronounced than that shown in panel B. However, actual growth is identical. By putting the two points (PRE and POST) close together, the growth appears to be at a faster rate and even greater. Figures, and all information presented in the research report, must be read critically.

Figure 4.4: Comparison of two plots of pre- to post-test change

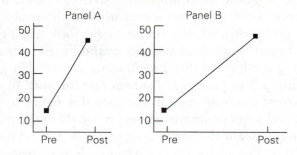

Discussion and Implications

Hypothesis testing research cannot, must not, exist in a vacuum. It has to be based on theory and must be motivated by a larger question. And it has to lead to evaluating the strength of a theory as well as more precise questions. The implications implied or specified by a researcher provide insight into how the research might influence practice and theory.

These parts of any research report can be the most important, for here the author combines theory, her/his overall purpose, the results and what she/he came to realize during and because of the research. The Discussion section is related only to the specific research project results; in the implications section, however, those results are put in a larger perspective, usually the context specified in the introduction. Thus, the implications seem to bring the project full circle, yet they don't return to the same beginning point. Instead, they create a new beginning.

The purpose of the Discussion section is to provide the researcher's interpretation of the results. Although the numbers themselves will carry much of the meaning, the actual significance, as distinct from the statistical significance, of the numbers is rarely self-evident. Therefore, the researcher tries to present the most convincing explanation possible giving his/her best analysis and explanation for the results obtained. Research very frequently produces surprises. I can't think of a piece of my research which didn't provide surprises; that's one reason why I continue to conduct research. Therefore, the Discussion section is the place where those surprises are explained and interpreted.

The most often stated complaint/criticism of hypothesis testing research in education is that it doesn't include implications for some 'real world context', such as teaching. The tendency is to want to know how the research relates to curriculum, pedagogy, or students' learning. However, such generic implications often cannot be drawn, for the researcher is well aware that the research and the findings are limited by the type of research being conducted, by the measures used, by the sample examined, by the theory, and by many other variables. Thus, the stated implications are typically conservative.

Nevertheless, knowledgeable readers (those who know how to read a research report) can and should create their own implications. However, any implications must be relevant to the purpose and the important findings of the research. Thus, for many studies, the most logical implications are not about teaching and learning. Rather, they concern research methodology.

Loban's research was descriptive and focussed primarily on syntactic development. Consequently, he did not make specific, pedagogical suggestions. In fact, he does not include a distinct section labelled 'Implications'. Instead, he comments on his conclusions, relating his research to other research and theory and to current practice. Yet the implications are there, both implied and stated. One of the conclusions supported by his data was that complexity of language (as determined by his measures) is 'related to social background'. Given this evidence and the assumption that although 'language is one effective means of maintaining social class stability (such stability) is not one of the aims of education in a democracy'. Loban can draw the reasonable implication that 'teachers need to understand how language and social caste are linked'.

Terry's research was also descriptive, but the nature and context of that research does permit her to draw implications. These implications are presented in a separate, labelled chapter in which she offers four 'suggestions for making poetry an inherent part of the elementary classroom curriculum'. But these are not just her own preferences; they are supported by the results of her research. For example, she suggests making 'books of poetry readily accessible to children' because her results showed that teachers relied mainly on anthologies, yet the poetry in anthologies is not necessarily the best poetry for stimulating interest in poetry.

Kroll, like Loban, only suggests implications and does this in his Discussion of the results. He is very cautious and controlled because he correctly sees his research as primarily a new step in research methodology, and thus he focusses his implications on reasonable and profitable future use of the method. It would take a number of related studies using this methodology with other populations differing in age, socioeconomic status, etc. to be able to draw wider implications. He makes no suggestions for application of his findings to teaching because his research, by design, could not provide them.

References (or Bibliography)

The References are probably the resource least used by novice readers of hypothesis testing research, yet the references provide a significant amount of information about the research and about the author. At a surface level, the references list works the author used or consulted in creating and designing the research. But much more can be apprehended by a critical and experienced reader, for those references provide a sense of the focus of the research, the foundation upon which the research was built. In most research reports, only the works actually cited in the text are included in the references. Thus, if one begins with the assumption that the researcher knows the relevant scholarship, then one would further assume that only the best and most recent scholarship will be cited. Therefore, the references, by themselves, become a way of seeing how the researcher created the theory, the design, and the methods used.

After one has read several research reports, four patterns in the references begin to emerge. First, certain works are cited in report after report. These are the standard works in a field. For example, a research report focussing on syntactic development in writing, would be expected to cite the research by Hunt, Loban, and O'Donnell. Each aspect of our discipline has such standards, and as an aspect becomes more defined and researched, the number of standards increases. Thus, by looking at only the references, a reader can ascertain the theoretical perspective, the focus, the methods used, and even the approximate date when the research was conducted.

The second pattern can be called 'entailed citation'. Since each piece of research is built on and extends prior research, the prior research is entailed in that piece of research. Therefore, citing one recent research study implies the research upon which it was built. Thus, in a study on sentence-combining, not all of the research on that topic will be cited. The author assumes that the reader either knows those studies or will read them. This type of entailment is often confusing to readers who aren't aware of this procedure. These readers often assume that either there is little scholarship in the field or that the author has not provided sufficient support for the research. By knowing that this procedure is used, the critical and knowledgeable reader can quickly ascertain whether the author has a good grasp of the relevant scholarship, for most of the references should be either recent or the standard citations mentioned above.

The third pattern is linked to the second. Because authors use the entailment procedure, they need to cite fewer references. Thus, the number of references does not determine quality. Furthermore, if a report focusses on a well established research topic (for example, sentence-combining or language development), there may be only a few references because the scholarship is both well known and interconnected. However, if the author is attempting to create a new line of research or a new method for research, the references will be more extensive because the author must rationalize the new way of thinking, typically by relating scholarship from several disciplines, disciplines which the readers may have little knowledge of.

The fourth pattern is called 'self citation'. Researchers who have been conducting research in an area for some time typically cite their own previous research. This is not for ego gratification; rather, that research is highly relevant because it is the foundation for the present research. Thus, with one quick glance, a reader can determine the extent of the author's involvement in an area of research.

By knowing these four patterns, one can learn a great deal about the research before reading it. Loban, Kroll, and Terry provide cases in point. The research Loban presents in his monograph was part of an emerging line of inquiry. Therefore, his thirty-nine references include research, some being 'standard' works, from several related areas. Since he could not possibly include many from each area, he is quite selective, citing recent publications which entail prior publications. Because he had been conducting research on language development for many years, Loban cites six of his own studies, each of which contributed to the current research.

Kroll, in contrast, was creating a new way of researching oral and written language. Therefore, he cites a wealth of scholarship (thirty-nine references) from several related areas, including standard works from four areas. Although some of his references entail prior publications not cited, Kroll provides references to support and elaborate his new methodology. Kroll includes no references to his own prior works because, at the time, he was beginning his research career and this was a new line of inquiry for him.

Terry, like Kroll, was beginning her research career when she conducted her study. Therefore, she does not include any 'self citations'. She does include some standard works among her twenty-one references, but because little scholarship existed on the topic, few of the citations entailed other publications.

Conclusion

Like any complex ability, the capacity to read and understand empirical research is mainly acquired by meaningful practice. Probably the best way to become a reader of research is to start investigating a genuine question related to your own professional concerns. If you really want to know what research has revealed and what questions still remain cloudy, you will be more likely to struggle with the inevitable difficulties which confront us all when we begin a new learning process.

The more you read, the more the grammar of the research report will become part of your own mental repertoire. You will select sections to read slowly and carefully. You will begin to distinguish between research that has been well done and clearly reported from that which was shoddy or obscure. Even the mysteries of numbers, statistics, and graphs will take on new meaning as their grammar becomes more familiar.

Along with your familiarity with the form will grow your own capacity to make appropriate connections between research findings and your own teaching. And, with persistence, you will be ready to join the growing numbers of teacher-researchers who are already helping us understand the incredibly complex interactions between learning and teaching. Although there will probably always be many more questions than there are answers in this domain, as the circle of researchers broadens, we will continue to expand the knowledge base on which effective teaching can be built.

References

KROLL, B.M. (1978) 'Cognitive egocentrism and the problem of audience awareness in written discourse', *Research in the Teaching of English*, 12, pp. 269–81.

LOBAN, W. (1976) *Language Development: Kindergarten through Grade Twelve*. NCTE Research Report No. 18, Urbana, IL, NCTE.

O'DONNELL, R.C., GRIFFIN, W.J. and NORRIS, R.C. (1967) *Syntax of Kindergarten and Elementary School Children: A Transformational Analysis*, NCTE Research Report, No. 8, Urbana, IL, NCTE.

TERRY, A. (1974) *Children's Poetry Preferences: A National Survey of Upper Elementary Grades*, NCTE Research Report No. 16, Urbana, IL, NCTE.

Chapter 5

Reading Hypothesis Generating Research

Ken Kantor

In her acceptance speech for the NCTE Promising Researcher Award, Sondra Perl (1979b) talked about research as a process of discovery, similar to that of composing. She told of how her background and thinking had led her to a 'felt sense' of what she wanted to do, and how the recursive movements of the research process led to further discoveries and shaping of her investigation. She related further how she tried out various alternatives, keeping her options open, thereby allowing the process to inform her and create the conditions for significant patterns to emerge.

The discovery process in writing and research to which Perl referred is highly intriguing, much like reading a picaresque novel, with its many adventures, unexpected turns in the road, and search for meaning. Getting there is, indeed, half or more of the fun. The appeal of the journey, of the open-ended narrative story line explains, I think, a good deal of the recent interest of teachers and researchers in our field in inductive methods of inquiry, in studies more concerned with generating than with testing hypotheses. The contrast seems much like Robert Hogan's (1970) analogies of hunting and fishing: sometimes we know precisely what we want, and go after it; other times we know (or sense what we want) but not precisely, and cast our nets in hopes of catching something worthwhile.

I must admit, though, that my initial attraction to inductive modes of research was also based on a negative motivation — a distrust of numbers. Like many others, I had associated hypothesis-testing with statistical analysis, and hypothesis-generating with qualitative inquiry. I was thus persuaded by polemical arguments and distinctions, implying preferences for one kind of research over another: qualitative vs. quantitative (Filstead, 1979), naturalistic vs. scientific

(Guba, 1980), aesthetic vs. scientific (Eisner, 1981), context-dependent vs. context-stripping approaches (Mishler, 1979). But as Reichardt and Cook (1979) point out, we ought not link a given paradigm with particular techniques. Qualitative studies may involve attention to context and generation of hypotheses; quantitative studies may require isolation and control of variables and testing of hypotheses. Increasing numbers of sound research investigations combine methods of qualitative and quantitative analysis so as to provide complementary data and findings.

The distinction between hypothesis-testing and hypothesis-generating does appear, however, to have some usefulness. While it is possible to do both in a given study, researchers tend to place emphasis on one or the other: theories are either stated *a priori* and tested out, or findings emerge as the study proceeds, as data are collected, analyzed and interpreted, leading to the discovery of 'grounded theory' (Glaser and Strauss, 1967).

The emphasis on the process of discovery does not mean, however, that the research lacks a systematic, empirical or rigorous approach. Research of any kind represents an inquiry into the nature of things, requiring close attention to detail, careful procedures, a concern with reliability and validity (see LeCompte and Goetz, 1982).

Characteristics of Hypothesis Generating Research

Nor is hypothesis generating research necessarily any easier to read critically even though a relative absence of statistical tables or presence of narrative passages may allow us more immediate access to it. Reading reports of inductive studies requires an awareness of its general characteristics (some of which are shared by deductive studies). I want to identify seven such characteristics, which may serve as guidelines for a careful and critical reading of these research reports:

1 Theoretical and Research Background
2 Initial Questions and Objectives — Designated Focus of Inquiry
3 Criteria for Selecting Participants and Settings
4 Design for Data Collection and Researcher Roles
5 Data Analysis — Process
6 Products of Data Analysis: Emergent Patterns and Hypotheses

7 Grounded Theory — Implications of Findings for Teaching and Research

I will now explain the importance of each of these characteristics in studies which generate hypotheses.

Theoretical and Research Background for Topic

The inability of current theories and knowledge to explain the occurrence of certain phenomena would provide the premise on which a hypothesis generating study is mounted. When we come upon a phenomenon which we believe is significant based on our expertise in the area, yet cannot explain our intuitions, we need to carefully observe repeated occurrences of the phenomenon. Through these repeated observations we create a hypothesis about what is occurring — predicting causally related events as a way of further testing the hypothesis. The need to find answers to real problems not accounted for within existing theories establishes the importance of studying the issue.

It is only when an individual is knowledgeable about existing theories that such an individual can determine either the inadequacy of current knowledge or where previous theories went wrong. Comprehensive knowledge of previous studies provides models for a researcher to adapt effective research strategies while avoiding ineffective ones. Citations of related work acknowledge the traditions underlying the study. This knowledge is essential in explaining how the findings emerging from the study differ from the state of knowledge — the theories and research reported prior to the study.

Initial Questions and Objectives — The Designated Focus of the Study

A researcher who intends to generate hypotheses, must focus on a specific phenomenon such as how people read fiction stories, or participate in class discussions. This specific focus results from the experience wherein events occurred which current theories did not predict (such as a 'non-reader' explaining the theme of a story or a student getting a turn-at-talk without being verbally recognized by the teacher).

The precise nature of the question to be researched evolves in the process of collecting and analyzing data. Thus the question which is posed initially is relatively vague. The questions are important in that they frame the procedures for collecting and analyzing the data. Thus, they should clearly follow from the theoretical and research background, and they should guide the design of the study.

Due to the lack of precision in the initial parts of hypothesis generating studies, extensive time during the study is devoted to refining the questions. Frequently interim and preliminary reports are published, preceding the final products. The continued reformulation of the research questions represents increasing understanding through the research process.

Criteria for Selecting Participants and Settings

Naturally occurring settings are the sites of hypothesis generating studies. Hypothesis generating studies intend to study phenomena which occur normally as individuals participate in life. The researcher studies what people do and how they accomplish their activities. The researcher selects settings for conducting the study in which the phenomenon is likely to recur.

All of the individuals in the setting would be considered participants. To get 'in-depth' information, researchers frequently find it beneficial to identify a subsample of that larger group of participants. This determination is based on the question being studied.

Researchers seek individuals within the setting who will (i) be verbal in articulating their implicit knowledge when queried by the research staff; (ii) be integral to the group; and (iii) be willing to share with the researcher. It is possible that numerous individuals would be included in such subsamples. The participants and settings are selected for their natural presence in the setting where the phenomenon occurs.

Design for Data Collection

Data are essential for hypothesis generating studies. They are the prime source of information from which the hypotheses result. The researcher is responsible for clearly describing the procedures implemented for collecting these data. Creativity is encouraged, indeed essential in the design of hypothesis generating studies. The researcher needs to design approaches which will simultaneously allow for the naturally occurring event to transpire while allowing the researcher to capture its essence. Videotapes, audiotapes, diary notes, and journal entries supplement products used and resulting from the activity. While recognizing that no medium, nor any individual will see 'all' or know 'all', these collections allow for further probing, and spark the memory. The design needs to account for accumulating as much information as is available, which the researcher will access as needed in the analysis process.

The data collection and data analysis processes overlap in these studies. As the researcher reflects on (or analyzes) the initial data collected, the desirability of changing focus, time, or strategies might become apparent. This revision of the collection process is possible in the design because the *data are accumulated over an extended time period*.

The researcher potentially serves numerous roles including observer, participant, and participant-observer. The role influences the quality and quantity of the data collected and must be clearly explained in the research report. Hypothesis generating studies tend to be open-ended in their data collection, some virtually causing researchers to drown in their collected data. This overkill is essential to create the thick descriptions for which these studies are known. The credibility of the findings frequently rests on a researcher's ability to convey sufficient detail for the armchair reader to at least visualize the experience. The concept of validity in data collection is accounted for when the data result from normal, naturally occurring situations.

Data Analysis Process

The data which are collected are considered 'raw'. There may be taped records of lessons, student writings, jottings in journals. By themselves, they do not provide answers to the initial questions. It is the responsibility of the researcher to find out what these documents and events mean by comparing them to other products, for example, by discussing how students developed stories from an idea to a full-blown story plot. The data analysis process should be described as explicitly as possible such that readers understand how the process was applied to the data that were collected.

Often found in hypothesis-generating studies are multiple sources of data. These sources provide for 'triangulation' (Denzin, 1978; Sevigny, 1981) or corroboration of evidence. A statement by a student or teacher in an interview may be confirmed or challenged by certain observed behaviors in the classroom or traits determined from the analysis of written products. This triangulation enables researchers to avoid getting locked into a single subjective position as they look for either supportive evidence or negative cases. The analytical process is considered reliable if others come to the same conclusions using the same procedures.

Products of Data Analysis: Emergent Patterns and Hypotheses

The analysis should result in the identification of categories for describing the data collected. During the entire process of conducting a hypothesis generating study, the researchers are concentrating on identifying the 'representative elements' which create the pattern for the setting being studied. Through systematically studying the data, hypotheses which are focussing on the identification of these patterns are tested and revised. These categories should be comprehensive in that they account for all of the data collected, and they provide the constructs for understanding all of the essential components in a phenomenon or process. These categories need to be discrete in that there can be no overlapping among the elements. The relative importance of the categories is reflected in the organization of the analyzed data. Frequently it is hierarchically organized such that there are two or three major or umbrella categories with numerous sub-categories related to each of the major ones.

These categories should be explicitly described such that others studying similar phenomena would, when independently studying the data, place the same labels on the phenomena as the original researcher. Inclusions of examples from the data help the readers to decide whether or not there is researcher bias in arriving at these significant patterns.

Hypotheses Generated, Grounded Theory and Implications

The patterns and categories identified and described by researchers thus lead to generation of hypotheses, and to the development of 'grounded theory' (Glaser and Strauss, 1967), a set of ideas or propositions which have grown out of the evidence provided by the data. This theory can then further suggest implications — not necessarily a set of 'proofs' or predictions — but understandings and insights which may guide teaching and further inquiry.

A word should be said here about the notion of generalizability. One of the purposes of an experimental study involving a representative sample and control of variables is to generalize from the findings to other populations and settings, to make predictions of similar results. In research involving a small number of case studies or a particular classroom context, however, the generalizability (in a conventional sense) of findings is more limited.

The original intent of the hypothesis generating studies is to generate hypotheses grounded in the accumulated data which contribute to a more accurate and comprehensive theory. The research report should provide these as evidence that it has accomplished its original purpose. These hypotheses are generated from the data which were collected and emerge from the process of analysis. They should:

(i)   be grounded in the data collected;
(ii) provide a new lens for studying the phenomenon;
(iii) lead to theory building grounded in 'real' data;
(iv) lead to research which tests the newly created hypotheses;
(v)   provide a new perspective for understanding the teaching-learning process; and
(vi) have the 'ring of truth' which the reader recognizes as consistent with their own experiences.

Studies Exemplifying these Characteristics

For purposes of illustrating these features of hypothesis-generating research, I have chosen ten reports of studies, all published in recent years in the journal *Research in the Teaching of English*. There have, of course, been a number of hypothesis generating studies published since that time. Because, however, the researchers conducting studies during this period were breaking new ground in research on language teaching and learning, they tended to provide a more extended discussion and defense of their methodologies in their published reports. Thus these articles offer clear illustrations of designs and procedures characteristic of this kind of inquiry. They are listed here in abbreviated bibliographic form (full citations can be found in the reference list).

Birnbaum (1982): A case study of urban and suburban fourth and seventh graders' abilities as readers and writers using a wide variety of observational methods. Among her most interesting hypotheses are: that good readers can be distinguished from less able readers by watching how they go about selecting a book to read, and that better writers are less committed to the texts they've already produced and, therefore more open to revision than their less able peers.

Brause and Mayher (1982): A preliminary report on a study of three classrooms in a bilingual urban elementary school, this study focussed on how students learn and participate in negotiating the rules which govern classroom interaction. One of the principal values of this paper is its careful attention to the process of hypothesis generation by recursive examination of the data.

Bridwell (1980): This study is in some ways the most 'experimental' of those discussed here in that Bridwell chose a relatively large sample (100 twelfth grade writers) and used a number of statistical techniques to analyze the patterns of their revision behavior. She categorizes revisions in terms of both time (first draft to last) and type (word, sentence, etc.).

Dillon and Searle (1981): A comparison of the school and home language of 'good' elementary students throughout the school day and in selected home situations. By looking at how language shapes their learning and academic success and at the relatively restricted kinds of language permitted in school, they raise important questions about how classrooms should be organized for productive learning.

Florio and Clark (1982): An in-depth ethnographic analysis of the community of a first grade classroom, this study describes the role relationships of all the participants and how they provide or restrict opportunities for meaningful writing. One of the strengths of this study is its insightful involvement of the teacher in the data collection and analysis process.

Galda (1982): Three fifth grade girls read and responded to two novels on a similar theme individually and as a group in this study. Using theories derived from the study of reader response and cognitive development, Galda hypothesizes that level of cognitive development determines the capacity of young readers to effectively transact with literary texts.

Hickman (1981): A naturalistic description of how children and teachers work together to respond to literature provides the basis for this study which spanned several elementary grade levels. Among her most interesting hypotheses are those concerning the role that teachers play in creating contexts for learning.

Lamme and Childers (1983): By taking pre-school children into a laboratory/play setting, the researchers were able to investigate how different settings and varied kinds of activities influenced their writing and reading behaviors. One of the most impressive strengths of this study, in addition to its careful description of what went on, is in the clearly stated list of hypotheses with which the study concludes.

Perl (1979a): In addition to being one of the first to look in-depth at how 'basic' writers compose, this study is notable for its careful description of methods of data generation, and particularly, data analysis. Her coding scheme for the composing process has proved valuable in subsequent research, and her findings that basic writers have stable, but harmful, composing processes has provided a helpful basis for pedagogical change.

Pettigrew, Shaw and Van Nostrand (1981): In order to determine the possibilities and constraints for writing instruction in schools, the researchers examined a number of classrooms to discover the roles played by such factors as administrative pressure, standardized tests, and textbooks.

My reasons for selecting these studies are as follows. First, *Research in the Teaching of English* is the major research journal in our field; manuscripts are subjected to a careful review procedure by qualified experts. Secondly, each article represents an intensive and/or extensive study of important questions in language education. Thirdly, this collection of reports reflects a range of significant topics in the field: oral and written language development, composing and reading processes, response to literature, and relationships among these areas.

A fourth trait of these studies is that they reveal the use of both quantitative and qualitative measurement, in varying degrees and appropriate to the purposes. Fifth, the articles are written so as to provide readers with a clear sense of procedures, findings, and implications. Finally, the most salient, the studies offer fine examples of inductive research, employing varied techniques but uniformly concerned with the discovery of significant patterns and grounded theory.

Following, then is a discussion of these ten studies in light of the characteristics of hypothesis-generating research I have identified.

Theoretical and Research Background

Several of the studies to be discussed here arise from the relatively recent body of literature on composing processes. Perl, for example, credits the small-scale case studies of investigators like Emig, Graves, Stallard, and Pianko, as informing her inquiry. At the same time she shows how she extends that earlier work by developing her own system for coding and analyzing composing behaviors. Similarly, the Pettigrew, Shaw, and Van Nostrand article recognizes studies of recursive composing processes, and further demonstrates how these processes are reflected in teaching and in the process of researching these questions. And Bridwell in her report acknowledges not only earlier empirical studies, but also theories of revision as proposed by scholars, educators, and professional writers.

A second group of these articles focusses on oral and written language development. The studies by Dillon and Searle and Brause and Mayher look to previous examinations of classroom language and teacher-student interactions for their inspiration. Sociolinguistic theories are drawn on, as well as views of classroom organization and transmission of knowledge. Florio and Clark also refer to sociolinguistic studies, and to the fields of ethnography and cognitive psychology, in establishing the basis for their investigation of the classroom community. And Lamme and Childers look to the research literature on composing processes of young children and behaviors accompanying composing for background appropriate to their study.

A third group of these reports deals with the areas of reading and literature. Drawing on theories of response to literature as set forth by Applebee and Rosenblatt, and case studies like those conducted by Petrosky, Galda uses these as a lens for exploring response in the context of group discussion. Hickman broadens the context further by examining response to literature in a classroom setting, using the techniques of ethnography to provide a methodological complement to studies of response. And Birnbaum consults a wide range of research on reading and writing relationships, including studies of composing processes, psycholinguistic views of reading, and correlational and longitudinal case studies.

Initial Questions and Objectives — Designated Focus of Inquiry

In their study of the functions of writing in a first grade classroom, Florio and Clark originally posed issues related to how speaking and writing were used by members of the classroom community: the role of writing in the children's lives, opportunities provided in school, the functions and forms of that writing, and the influences of teachers and others. This set of issues thus provided the framework for their investigation. Dillon and Searle state their purposes even more explicitly in terms of objectives, indicating their concern with how children learn language rules within a classroom, how language shapes their learning and academic success, and how their classoom language contrasts with that used at home. Birnbaum reveals in her initial questions her aim of discovering influences on reading and writing behaviors, patterns associated with levels of proficiency, and, like Dillon and Searle, relationships between academic and non-academic experiences.

An excellent example of research questions posed in the context of developmental theory can be found in Galda's study, in which she sought to determine how traits of concrete and formal operational thought affected children's responses to literature. Similarly, Lamme and Childers state their initial questions regarding composing processes of young children in relation to developmental aspects of talking, drawing and reading.

Additionally, some researchers are concerned with generating a systematic approach to studying given phenomena. Pettigrew, Shaw, and Van Nostrand, for example, identify their goal of constructing a valid and reliable description of writing instruction in a few representative settings, which could then be adapted to examination of other settings. In a related sense, Perl set out to develop a classification scheme for composing processes which could then be used for analysis of those processes with different individuals in various situations. Both articles include a detailed description of the coding systems that were eventually developed.

Criteria for Selecting Participants and Settings

In accordance with the objectives of a study that seeks to generate hypotheses should be the criteria for choosing the participants, or subjects, and the setting in which the research is conducted. These selections may, of course, either limit or expand the generalizability of the findings. Frequently the method of 'theoretical sampling' (Glaser and Strauss, 1967) is used, in which researchers focus their attention on the particular individuals and contexts that yield the greatest information related to questions and emerging hypotheses.

In identifying subjects, for example, Perl looked at writing samples that would qualify students as 'unskilled' writers. Contrastingly, Dillon and Searle solicited the opinions of teachers and principals as to which were 'good' students, while Galda and Birnbaum looked for students who were reading above grade level. Using a more traditional approach, Bridwell selected a representative sample of 100 twelfth grade students for her investigation of revising strategies. Rapport with participants is also an important consideration; Hickman and Brause and Mayher noted the willingness of teachers to participate in their studies, while Perl and Lamme and Childers cited the cooperativeness of the students with whom they worked.

School and classroom settings were also chosen with care in these studies. Birnbaum compared students in an urban and a suburban school, while Pettigrew, Shaw, and Van Nostrand looked at writing instruction in urban, suburban, and rural school environments; Galda conducted her study in a private school. Hickman describes the classroom she observed as having an open structure, both in terms of curriculum and architecture; Florio and Clark chose a classroom with moveable walls, learning centers, and alcoves, lending itself to team teaching and mixed age interactions.

Again, the selection of participants and settings is related to purposes. Examining the behaviors of a number of students of varied ages and ability levels allows researchers to generalize to a wider range of populations and contexts. On the other hand, observing the processes of students of a particular type in a more specialized (perhaps a laboratory) setting allows researchers to focus on specific features and accumulate more detailed, fine grained kinds of data. Conceivably the best of both is achieved in a 'pyramid' design like the one used by Graves (1975), in which increasing amounts and kinds of information are gathered on decreasing numbers of individuals, culminating in a single in-depth case study. (At a later point in this essay, I'll discuss at greater length the issue of generalizability in inductive studies.)

Design: Data Collection Procedures, Researcher Roles

One crucial matter has to do with the length of time spent in collecting data and the range of phenomena being examined. Dillon and Searle observed for one-half day per week for the first two months of the school year, looking at the full range of language contexts within the school day. Hickman observed for a four month period, also at the beginning of the school year, in three classes (grade K–1, 2–3, 4–5), in order to gain a developmental perspective. Perl and Lamme and Childers utilized laboratory settings, the former conducting ninety-minute sessions with each of five students, the latter conducting sixteen sessions of two kinds (personal communication and book writing) with one group of three children. These researchers therefore avoided the faults of what Rist (1980) calls 'blitzkrieg' studies, either of an ethnographic or experimental type, in which investigators spend limited amounts of time in settings gathering scattered pieces of data, and emerge with incomplete, inaccurate, or unfounded conclusions.

A second major concern has to do with stages of data collection; readers of inductive studies should look for delineation of these stages. Brause and Mayher, for example, describe the sequence of first making videotaped records of classroom events and secondly constructing written transcripts and logs. Galda's report reveals the three phases of interviewing children as to their reading interests, conducting discussions of two young adult novels with three case study children, and talking with each child individually about the stories. The process reported by Pettigrew, Shaw, and Van Nostrand has to do with the collaborative relationships between teachers and researchers, and the cycles of progressive coding, observations, and trinary group meetings.

In several cases the design calls for certain kinds of purposeful interventions, or structural situations within an otherwise naturalistic context. This approach is consistent with what Bronfenbrenner (1976) terms an 'experimental ecology' of education. Birnbaum, as an illustration, created specific tasks for her case study children, for reading in the genres of reality-based fiction, fantasy, and factual accounts; and for writing in expressive, transactional, and poetic modes. Similarly, Galda provided two particular texts, chosen for their appropriateness to the age, ability, and interest levels of the children, to stimulate response. And Bridwell devised a transactional writing assignment to stimulate the kinds of school-sponsored tasks to which subjects were accustomed.

At the same time as they may be structuring certain interventions, hypothesis generating researchers also attempt to be as non-intrusive as possible. Perl and Lamme and Childers, for example, point out ways in which they sought to avoid interfering with processes once they had begun. In naturalistic studies, a 'reactive field entry' style (Corsaro, 1981) is required, wherein the researcher is receptive to events as they occur, trying not to manipulate or alter the environment unnecessarily, at the same time recognizing the potential effects of their participant-observer role. And even Birnbaum and Bridwell, for example, devised their tasks to be as closely analogous as possible to the kinds of typical school tasks that their subjects would face in a natural situation.

This kind of sensitivity is especially important for working collaboratively with teachers, as Florio and Clark demonstrate in encouraging teachers to record their insights in written journals, and as Pettigrew, Shaw, and Van Nostrand show in working cooperatively with teachers to derive a model for writing instruction. Efforts like these also reinforce the phenomenological stance of viewing the perspectives of participants as an integral part of what is being studied.

In terms of design, perhaps the most intriguing study here is that of Lamme and Childers, who combine a laboratory setting with techniques of participant-observation. The inductive method is strengthened, I believe, by this experimental ecology, the merging of approaches which too often are considered as incompatible. Figure 5.1 reveals the kinds of data sources cited by the researchers in their reports.

Figure 5.1: Data sources cited in selected research reports

	Observational Notes and Transcripts	Audio-Tapes	Video-Tapes	Interviews/ Discussions	Written Products
Birnbaum	X	X	X	X	X
Brause & Mayher	X		X		
Bridwell					X
Dillon & Searle	X	X		X	
Florio & Clark	X		X	X	X
Galda		X		X	
Hickman	X	X		X	X
Lamme & Childers	X		X		
Perl		X		X	
Pettigrew, Shaw, & Van Nostrand	X		X	X	

Data Analysis Process

The use of multiple data sources is particularly important for phenomenological or ethnographic studies in which researchers seek out varied features of context and a diverse range of individual perspectives. The Birnbaum and Florio and Clark studies represent fine examples of such multidimensionality. At the same time, a more limited number of kinds of data sources need not restrict the power to generate valid hypotheses. Bridwell's study, for example, deals with written products at three stages of the composing process. Given her purpose of determining revision strategies, these texts provide compelling evidence of those processes at work. In addition, her research establishes a strong basis for a closer case-study investigation of revising behaviors in relation to larger contextual traits, previous instruction, and classroom, school and societal environments.

As with deductive research methods, we need to consider ways in which the data are treated, in this case, how the processes of triangulating sources of information shapes and defines the discovery of significant patterns. In hypothesis-generating research, there tends to be a greater overlap between data collection and data analysis, reflecting a more fluid and interactive process. To a great extent this parallels the 'retrospective structuring' which Perl refers to in writing, the recursive movements of looking back over what has been done in order to gain a sense of how to move forward. In particular, the methods of 'analytic induction', involving the scanning of information for categories and relationships among them, and development of working typologies and hypotheses, and 'constant comparison', involving discovery of relationships through examining and comparing recorded phenomena across categories (Glaser and Strauss, 1967) offer to researchers a systematic means of analyzing data.

Clear demonstration of these procedures can be found in several of the studies cited here. Birnbaum, for example, reveals the sequence of observation, discovery, and verification she used as she identified patterns in reading and composing episodes, and compared for individual variations in response to conditions and modes. Galda also discusses the way in which she examined her data until categories generated by responses to literature emerged. Interestingly, she found that the initial set of categories with which she was working were inappropriate to an analysis of group discussion; this process of trial and error thus brought about an important discovery.

In related ways, the method of progressive coding used by Pettigrew, Shaw and Van Nostrand provided for ongoing data analysis, in the researchers' terms, a means for generalizing, framing questions and hypotheses, and juxtaposing descriptions with observed behaviors. Using an ethnographic design, Florio and Clark describe how they posed their initial questions in the larger context of school life, then framed working hypotheses and tested them against subsequent events. Their aim was to seek out meaningful contrasts, particularly as related to those matters that made a difference to participants (teachers and students). Each of these investigations then, reveals in some manner, the processes of formulating, testing and generating hypotheses explicated by Brause in her study with Mayher, and in her article in this monograph.

In some cases the inductive process results in construction of a specific and detailed classification scheme, as with Bridwell's system for analyzing revisions at the surface, word, phrase, clause, sentence, and multi-sentence levels. Perl's procedure for coding operations of the composing process and Pettigrew, Shaw, and Van Nostrand's identification of 'activity constructs' in the teaching of writing, represent further illustrations which arise from the use of inductive methods.

Finally, in reading the results of research, we need to look for specific illustrations of observed phenomena, and in the case of ethnographic studies, some 'thick description' of events as they occur within contexts. An excellent instance of such reporting can be found in the article by Hickman, in which she includes a transcript from her research log, revealing the range and sequence of response events as children discuss the story *Where the Wild Things Are* with their teacher. Similarly, Dillon and Searle select one lesson from those they observed, as well as an excerpt from an at-home discussion, to exemplify significant patterns and contrasts. Galda and Lamme and Childers also do a commendable job in supporting their generalizations about case studies with specific statements made in discussions of samples of written products. Such descriptions and illustrations offer to the researcher (and reader) a means for data reduction without stripping the study of its contextual features.

Products of Data Analysis — Emergent Patterns and Categories

Most of the studies discussed in this essay are concerned in some way with patterns of language development. Galda, for example, shows how patterns of response to literature among her three case study subjects reflect levels of cognitive development, one child being highly subjective, a second 'reality bound', and the third able to see alternatives and assume a spectator stance in reading. Others reveal differences between skilled and unskilled readers and writers. Birnbaum determined that the more proficient readers monitored and reflected alternatives, expressed ideas more tentatively, and recognized other points of view, while the less proficient were more literal and 'textbound', and controlled by external forces, suggesting a less confident self-concept. In related ways, Perl's unskilled writers did demonstrate consistent composing processes, but their preoccupation with editing and correcting truncated those processes without markedly improving the form of their writing.

Additionally, a number of these researchers point out in their reports the elements of classroom contexts which emerged as significant. As an illustration, Dillon and Searle identify the basic sequence of teacher-student interaction as teacher initiating, pupil responding, and teacher evaluating. They found that teachers tended to control learning experiences, searching for correct answers and restricting children's use of language. These patterns were somewhat reversed in home settings, where children's language was more varied and extensive. Brause and Mayher's conclusions contribute to this view of classroom interaction and organization, as they point out linguistic and non-linguistic inputs, transitions, tracking, pacing, and teacher identification of acceptable behaviors.

Similarly, the activity constructs identified by Pettigrew, Shaw, and Van Nostrand clarify the picture of what actually occurs in classroom writing instruction, and also suggest some of the external constraints: administrative pressures, standardized testing, inadequate textbooks, and lack of teacher training resources. And highly revealing of both classroom and larger contexts for learning to write are the functions of writing discovered by Florio and Clark: to participate in a community, to know oneself and others, to occupy free time, and to demonstrate academic performance.

What arises then, in these inductive studies, is a sense of how language development occurs within various learning contexts. In the laboratory setting utilized by Lamme and Childers, children produced longer and more sophisticated products in the personal communication sessions than in the book writing sessions. The researchers also observed a good deal of play, rich language, reading and sharing in all the group writing sessions. In the more naturalistic settings of actual classrooms, Hickman noted the 'manipulable context', the degree to which teachers influenced the types and qualities of response events — listening, contact with books, oral language, sharing, dramatic activities, making things, and writing. Looking at classrooms of different grade levels enabled Hickman to identify developmental patterns of thinking and language.

An examination of the findings of research conducted within a range of contexts, from controlled laboratory settings to actual classroom situations, and employing a variety of methods, from experimental to case study or ethnographic techniques, can enable us as readers to formulate our own hypotheses concerning ways in which individuals learn language and how they can be helped in that developmental process.

Hypotheses Generated, Grounded Theory and Implications

What Galda or Florio and Clark discovered with specific children in a specific educational setting may or may not apply to other children and settings, even if they are similar in some respects. Researchers must be cautious (as I think those cited here have been) not to make excessive claims for their conclusions. At the same time, there is a kind of generalizability inherent in the findings of inductive research which has less to do with prediction than what I would call 'authenticity', the extent to which the discoveries presented are consistent with experience, knowledge, and common sense, the degree to which the researcher can depict the patterns observed in credible fashion, and make the reader see familiar settings in new ways.

This is not to say that the conclusions reached need always to be in agreement with what we had previously thought or believed. Indeed, one of the strengths of any good research study is that its findings question assumptions that have been commonly held. Dillon and Searle, for example, argue on the basis of their findings that the 'restricted code' which Bernstein and others deemed characteristic of home language may actually be more representative of school language. The approaches to teaching writing identified by Pettigrew, Shaw, and Van Nostrand may cause us to question some of our assumptions about skills, sequence, and planning, and Perl's revelation that unskilled writers do have stable and consistent composing processes challenges the conventional deficit theory and opens up new and promising directions for helping such students learn to write more successfully.

Implicit in many of these studies are criticisms of conventional teaching methods and the educational system, especially related to ways in which language development and effective teaching are thwarted by outmoded theories and institutional demands. The restriction of children's language revealed by Dillon and Searle, the tendency of school writing assignments to relieve students of important roles and responsibilities cited by Florio and Clark, or the kinds of administrative constraints enumerated by Pettigrew, Shaw, and Van Nostrand might lead us to be pessimistic about literacy instruction in schools. On the other hand, these researchers also make us aware of the potentialities that exist within schools for enhancing language learning. Florio and Clark found some writing to have value both as a school event and for personal growth; Pettigrew, Shaw, and Van Nostrand found in their procedures of progressive coding a worthwhile means of teacher training and staff development as well as research. And inherent in the teacher's ability to manipulate the context, as described by Hickman and Brause and Mayher, is the power to open possibilities for language learning, rather than simply to restrict those options.

One of the crucial contributions that hypothesis generating research can make is in the area of theory building. This involves making connections with other studies and other theories so that the results of the particular study can be interpreted broadly and can provide a framework from which other studies can be derived. Bridwell, for example, related her findings to other studies of the revision process and proposed a more comprehensive theory of revising which has been useful to subsequent researchers.

Ultimately, if educational research is to be of any value, it must make sense to practitioners. This entails a dual responsibility. Researchers need to report procedures and findings in such ways as to be accessible to research consumers, whether they be teachers, administrators, curriculum specialists, teacher educators, or other researchers. They might well follow the advice of Donald Murray (1983) to 'write research to be read'. Even given clearly written reports, however, the design and procedures may seem complex, the jargon difficult, the theoretical concepts remote from classroom realities. Our task as consumers, then, is to become more familiar with the research literature, to balance a critical attitude with an open-minded stance toward research findings (and not to expect that those findings will yield magical solutions to teaching problems), and if possible to conduct some research ourselves, following such guidance as is offered in this volume.

Teaching, like writing and the kind of research I've been describing, is also an inductive process, marked by hypothesis formulating and generating, and discovery of grounded theory. Prescriptions for teaching may be useful in some instances, but ultimately I think the knowledge and experience we gain as teachers and students of teaching and learning guide our instruction in the most meaningful ways. The contributions of inductive research findings, then, have less to do with providing ideas for immediate implementation than with their enhancing our processes of discovery, with enabling us as readers and consumers of research to make constructions of meaning, to generate insights for our own teaching.

References

BIRNBAUM, J.C. (1982) 'The reading and composing behavior of selected fourth- and seventh-grade students', *Research in the Teaching of English*, 16, 3.

BRAUSE, R.S. and MAYHER, J.S. (1982) 'Teachers, students and classroom organizations', *Research in the Teaching of English*, 16, 2.

BRIDWELL, L.S. (1980) 'Revising strategies in twelfth grade students' transactional writing', *Research in the Teaching of English*, 14, 3.

BRONFENBRENNER, U. (1976) 'The experimental ecology of education', *Teachers College Record*, 78, 2.

CORSARO, W.A. (1981) 'Entering the child's world: Research and strategies for field entry and data collection in a preschool setting' in GREEN, J. and WALLAT, C. (Eds) *Ethnography and Language in School Settings*, Norwood, NJ, Ablex.

DENZIN, N.K. (1978) *The Research Act: A Theoretical Introduction to Research Methods* (2nd edn), New York, McGraw-Hill.

DILLON, D. and SEARLE, D. (1981) 'The role of language in one first grade classroom', *Research in the Teaching of English*, 15, 4.

EISNER, E.W. (1981) 'On the differences between scientific and artistic approaches to qualitative research', *Educational Researcher*, 10, 4.

FILSTEAD, W.J. (1979) 'Qualitative methods: A needed perspective in evaluation research' in COOK, T.D. and REICHARDT, C.S. (Eds) *Qualitative and Quantitative Methods in Evaluation Research*, Beverly Hills, CA, Sage Publications.

FLORIO, S. and CLARK, C.M. (1982) 'The functions of writing in an elementary classroom', *Research in the Teaching of English*, 16, 2.

GALDA, L. (1982) 'Assuming the spectator stance: An examination of the responses of three young readers', *Research in the Teaching of English*, 16, 1.

GLASER, B.C. and STRAUSS, A.L. (1967) *The Discovery of Grounded Theory: Strategies for Qualitative Research*, Chicago, IL, Aldine.

GRAVES, D. (1975) 'An examination of the writing processes of seven-year-old children', *Research in the Teaching of English*, 9, 3.

GUBA, E. (1980) 'Naturalistic and conventional inquiry', paper presented at the annual meeting of the American Educational Research Association, Boston, April.

HICKMAN, J. (1981) 'A new perspective on response to literature: Research in an elementary school setting', *Research in the Teaching of English*, 15, 4.

HOGAN, R. (1970) 'On hunting and fishing and behaviorism' in MAXWELL, J. and TOVATT, A. (Eds) *On Writing Behavioral Objectives for English*, Urbana, IL, National Council of Teachers of English.

LAMME, L.L. and CHILDERS, N.M. (1983) 'The composing processes of three young children', *Research in the Teaching of English*, 17, 1.

LECOMPTE, M.D. and GOETZ, J.P. (1982) 'Problems of validity and reliability in ethnographic research', *Review of Educational Research*, 52, 1.

MISHLER, E.G. (1979) 'Meaning in context: Is there any other kind?', *Harvard Educational Review*, 49, 1.

MURRAY, D.M. (1983) 'Write research to be read' in MURRAY, D.M. (Ed.)

Learning by Teaching: Selected Articles on Writing and Teaching, Portsmouth, NH, Boynton/Cook.

PERL, S. (1979a) 'The composing processes of unskilled college writers', *Research in the Teaching of English*, 13, 4.

PERL, S. (1979b) 'Research as discovery', Promising Researcher Address, National Council of Teachers of English Annual Conference, San Francisco, CA.

PETTIGREW, J., SHAW, R.A. and VAN NOSTRAND, A.D. (1981) 'Collaborative analysis of writing instruction', *Research in the Teaching of English*, 15, 4.

REICHARDT, C.S. and COOK, T.D. (1979) 'Beyond qualitative versus quantitative methods' in COOK, T.D. and REICHARDT, C.S. (Eds) *Qualitative and Quantitative Methods in Evaluation Research*, Beverly Hills, CA, Sage Publications.

RIST, R.C. (1980) 'Blitzkrieg ethnography: On the transformation of a method into a movement', *Educational Researcher*, 9.

SEVIGNY, M.J. (1981) 'Triangulated inquiry — A methodology for the analysis of classroom interaction' in GREEN, J. and WALLAT, C. (Eds) *Ethnography and Language in School Settings*, Norwood, NJ, Ablex.

Part Three
Designing and Conducting Classroom Research

This section provides specific guidance in designing and implementing a classroom research project. The authors discuss in great detail such basic issues as: How do I know what to study? and How do I go about interpreting the information I collect? Exemplary studies are discussed in great detail to make the research process more approachable for neophyte teacher-researchers. Readers interested in designing their own hypothesis testing and/or hypothesis generating inquiries into their own teaching should consider the criteria discussed for such studies in chapters 4 and 5. Finally, there is a call for action, suggesting specific activities for initiating the process of becoming uncommonsense teacher-researchers.

Chapter 6

Finding and Framing Questions

John S. Mayher and Rita S. Brause

By posing questions we take a researcher's stance. Inquiring teachers, reflective practitioners, constantly subject to careful scrutiny all that we do as a way to improve our practice. Teacher researchers choose questions which are consistent with this concern. In this chapter we discuss both how we find our questions and how we phrase these questions so they are researchable.

Researchers strutinize assumptions, traditions and customs with the belief that those who blindly follow tradition are not professionals. Professional educators, and all learners, leave their assumptions at the door and are willing, indeed desirous of reflecting on experience as a way to improve future experiences.

When we perceive that our students could be learning more, we seek a new teaching strategy (grouping), new texts, or new materials (puppets). These might work for a short while, but unless we can determine why each is effective, we will soon return to look for a new recipe, a new idea, a fast fix. When students seem confused about their roles, we need to consider how our practice might be handicapping them, making them increasingly dependent on us rather than encouraging them to accept more responsibility for their own learning.

As teachers, we are often seeking something new in an attempt to stimulate more active involvement by our students in class activities. We, as teachers need to go beyond the isolated gimmicks, beyond the recipe which, according to the Chinese proverb will give us one meal, or one lesson, to learning how to fish, so that we will be able to eat for life, or have a theory about effective teaching-learning activities which will be useful for the whole year or longer. After becoming exhausted by the daily chase for a gimmick or a sure-fire recipe, we may become totally frustrated ... until we take a look at the broader issues which are causing our exasperation. When we take a more holistic and more comprehensive perspective, we are subjecting our isolated concerns to a more principled analysis. And at that point we value theory and reflective practice as guides to educational decisions.

The first step in planning a research study — in some respects both the most important and the most difficult — is identifying an area of inquiry. Although research studies can be designed for practically any issue, there are some concerns which are of greater importance than others. Educational researchers seek to identify an issue which, on reporting findings, will influence the ways in which we conduct our educational practice. The difficulty inherent in identifying a research topic involves determining an important issue and phrasing the question so that it addresses the heart of the problem we are seeking additional information about. Due to the importance of a highly focussed, single research question, we devote much time to the process both in our preparation to conduct research and in this book.

Educational researchers do not go shopping for a research question *per se*, and certainly teacher-researchers do not pick questions from a prepared list. Rather, we tend to research issues which are of particular concern for our own teaching. Thus, we have a vested interest in the findings — we hope that they will make us more effective teachers. It is with such personal investment in the findings that teachers elect to become researchers.

Teachers make an infinite number of decisions — but none of these are simple. All choices have many subtle ramifications — particularly influencing students' views of themselves as learners and their role in the learning process. Even something as seemingly simple as selecting a specific book, reveals sub-conscious beliefs, assumptions, and theories. In our professional stance as inquiring teachers, we subject these decisions to systematic scrutiny.

Finding Research Questions

Research questions are created by individuals focussing on specific issues of professional interest. This curiosity might evolve from reading a theory about how children's thinking develops — or from reflecting on what happened during a particular class activity, for example. These two complimentary sources — theory and practice — are the two major seeds for our questions. Research which tests hypotheses and research which generates hypotheses are reciprocal, interdependent research strategies. Both are essential for our construction of a more perfect theory to make practice more predictable and therefore more effective. Each research study, however, usually has one intent: either to test a theory or to generate a theory.

Research Which Tests Theories

In chapter 2 we looked at two theories which contribute to our understanding of the multitude of factors which influence our teaching: The Teaching Act Model, and The Neverending Cycle of Teacher Development. Other theories focussing on learning, reading, and writing, for instance, also inform our educational practice in important ways (see for example, Mayher, 1990; Smith, 1988, Vygotsky, 1978; Bruner and Haste, 1987). These theories provide us with carefully considered principles about the nature of the learning process, how reading proficiency develops, and how writing facilitates learning, for example. But these are not guarantees — they are only theories. We much accept the fact that no one can predict the future and no one can predict with absolute accuracy what will or will not work. Our lives are so complex that it is impossible to be 100 per cent sure of anything. But we do work from beliefs and theories, accepting the impossibility of guaranteeing outcomes, but carefully selecting those theories which are mostly substantiated by our experiences. We use these theories (mainly unconsciously) as we make educational decisions about how to organize a course of study, how to plan activities, and how to assess student progress.

We generally accept these theories if they intuitively seem to make sense, if we can account for our experiences using them — or if they are mandated by authorities. As educational researchers we can place aspects of a theory (called hypotheses) under a microscope. Such study provides information about the validity of an aspect of that theory in a specific context. Thus, we can say, after reading about the Teaching Act Model (Mayher and Vine, 1974), that it sounds like a valuable approach. Now I need to see if it really works, that is if following the theory helps me to get greater insight into the impact of decisions I am making as a teacher. And if my teaching strategies are influencing students' learning.

To test theory, we would need to focus on one aspect of the total theory, since most theories are too complex to test totally in one research study. These aspects are frequently termed factors or variables which potentially contribute to the predicted outcomes. Age, length of time, and previous experiences are typical factors which influence learning, for example. Researchers 'manipulate' these variables in their selection of participants and materials as ways to test the influence of those factors. They conduct experiments in which these potential variables are scrutinized to determine their individual or collective contribution to the predictability of the theory in specific contexts.

Hypothesis-testing research may support the hypothesized connection between age and student learning, for example, or it may not support the theory as currently presented. Upon the accumulation of findings from many research studies, a decision is made about the value of that theory as a predictor of outcomes. This accumulation of verifiable knowledge is at the heart of scientific practice. The theory is accepted, modified, or abandoned, depending on its accuracy in predicting the occurrence of a specific phenomenon.

Sample questions from the Teaching Act Model
The Teaching Act Model discussed in chapter 2 provides a good resource for listing a series of researchable questions for conducting a hypothesis testing study about the relationship between the contexts for our curricular decisions and planning, doing and evaluating instruction. Put in another way, we can study the connection between teaching and learning. Each question refers to one potential variable which is predicted to influence students' learning. As teacher-researchers we can test isolated parts of this theory as exemplified in the questions noted below, many of which originally appeared in Mayher and Brause (1985).

Contexts of curricular decisions

Teacher self-image

What are my areas of strength?
How can I use these to help students learn?
What are my perceptions about effective learning environments?
How much noise can I tolerate?
How flexible am I as a planner?

My pupils

What do I know about my students' interests and needs?
How do they feel about being in school?
How do they learn?
What are their perceptions of themselves as learners?
Have I identified their strengths accurately and comprehensively?

Subject

What is my conception of the subject(s) I teach?

How is that conception reflected in the tests, texts, and curriculum guides?

How do others in my profession construe the subject?

How does this subject connect with other subjects my students take?

Have there been changes in these constructs recently?

Teaching/Learning of the subject

What evidence do I have that students learn?

What are my conceptions of effective ways to learn?

Where do they come from?

Are they shared by my colleagues? Locally? Nationally?

Do they account for individual differences I see?

School community

What are the community's goals for instruction?

Are they consistent with my conceptions as a teacher and a subject specialist?

How supportive are my administrators of my approach?

Teacher's image of the situation

How congruent or consistent are these contexts with each other?

Does the setting fit my students?

With my conception of the subject?

With my conception of how it is best learned?

Have I set up my classroom physically to make effective use of the learning approach I am using?

Am I comfortable teaching in such a classroom?

Planning, doing and evaluating instruction

Goals for instruction

Are my goals for this class consistent with the students' proficiencies?

With the increasingly complex interpretation of learning this subject?

With the available materials?

With the way I will evaluate their learning?

With the way others will evaluate?

Plans

Do my plans for this lesson (week, unit, etc.) grow out of my long-range goals?

Do they contain an evaluation component?

Are they congruent with the learning approach I want my students to adopt?

Have I reflected sufficiently on alternative approaches rather than just doing today what I did yesterday? Last week? Last month? Last year?

Activities

What sources contribute to the class activities?

Are my students active participants in their learning?

Are the activities enjoyable for them and for me?

Are they varied enough?

Are they consistent with my constructs of the situation?

Does today's activity really contribute to my overall learning goals?

Evaluation of learning

Does every learning activity have a built in observation/evaluation component?

Who does the evaluation?

Do the students know how they are being evaluated?

Is the evaluation system consistent with the teaching/learning approach employed?

Is it consistent with the learning goals?

Does it give useful information for modifying plans and activities?

Feedback

How do the results of my observations and evaluations of student learning modify my constructs of the students' abilities and needs?

Of my approach to teaching?
Of my goals?

One thing the Teaching Act Model shows us clearly is the large number of variables which may influence teaching and therefore classroom learning. The structure given by the Teaching Act Model provides a valuable system for sorting out the central factors from the peripheral ones involved in teaching and learning. It provides us with an explicitly stated theory to test in our particular teaching setting. Research which tests a theory results either in a confirmation of the predictions identified in the theory or the specification of the need for modifying the theory to be more consistent with reality.

Research which generates theory
When our theories conflict with our experiences, we recognize the need to obtain a better theory — one which will more accurately predict what will happen in a given situation. What we need to do is identify how our students are learning — how the specific phenomenon we are striving for, gets accomplished. What effect on student spelling is realized by weekly spelling tests? ... by deducting points for spelling on essay tests? How do students learn to write dramatic stories? Why are some students better at understanding historical events than others? What experiences are most valuable for students to become persuasive in their discussions?

Research which studies naturally occurring phenomena, those not subjected to experimenter manipulation, are called hypothesis generating. Such studies result in the identification of hypotheses about a phenomenon which contribute to the subsequent development of a predictable theory. When we generate hypotheses we bring to a level of consciousness our understanding and predictions about the effects of our engagement in our everyday practices. By reflecting on a typical experience in Mrs Howe's class, we exemplify the identification of research questions which are intended to generate theory.

A classroom vignette
As Mrs. Howe enters her fifth grade classroom on Monday morning, the activities which will be central to instruction have already been planned. A visitor observing her class would see lessons devoted to writing, reading, American history, and then the class split for mathematics with half of them going to Mr. Williams across the hall and some of Mr. Williams' class coming to join hers. (On Tuesdays

and Thursdays the third lesson of the day is science, but otherwise the morning routines are fairly consistent.)

The subjects covered and the content of the lessons seem to have been primarily determined by the texts that the students are using with the exception of the writing portion of the morning. Each student learned to begin the school day with ten minutes for making journal entries. The rest of the hour is spent on an apparently bewildering variety of writing-related activities. Some students are writing; others are reading their stories to classmates; still others are working at the editing corner; a few are waiting to have conferences with Mrs. Howe, and a couple are looking out the window, pencil in hand. During this time the room has the productive noise level of a workplace.

Even a few minutes in Ms. Howe's classroom can illustrate how complex every classroom is, and how difficult it is to understand a classroom solely on the basis of what we can observe. These activities reflect assumptions about the nature of teaching and learning and what teachers' and students' perceived roles are in this process (Brause and Mayher, 1984). Our observations tell us the organization of Ms. Howe's classroom. We list nine of these and six from other classrooms in the first column in table 6.1. All of these practices are potentially researchable as to their impact on student learning. A parallel list presented in the second column in table 6.1 transforms the observations to inquiry.

When we reflect on routine approaches to organizing and enacting classroom instruction, we adopt an inquiring stance and question such issues as whether there are more effective ways for facilitating student learning. We can question whether 'the way it's 'spozed to be', from the perspective of students experienced in traditional classrooms, is effective in accomplishing our explicit long term educational goals. We must acknowledge a potential for dissonance between colleagues' and students' expectations of what schooling is supposed to be and our understanding of the types of experiences which are most beneficial in contributing to student growth. Once we accept a skeptical stance, it is easy to identify a large number of issues.

Sample questions

There are many potential sources for our questions including: Reflection on Professional Practice; Frustration; Boredom; Current Trends and Innovations; and Serendipity. Professional inquisitiveness encourages us to ponder about our professional practice. Some potential research areas are inherent in the following list of questions, provided to initiate your own question posing.

Table 6.1: Framing research questions from our practice

Observation	Question
There is one teacher and twenty-five students.	How effective for learning is the 1:25 ratio? Are smaller groups better?
All the students in the classroom are in the same grade.	What knowledge is common to students of the same age?
The class is meeting in a school building.	What resources for learning are found in the building?
The teacher plans the class activities.	How many students are actively involved in learning?
There are 'subjects' which serve as the focus for specific times: History, Math, and Science.	What activities during reading and writing are similar to those in American History?
Students use textbooks for reading, history and math.	What do the students learn from their textbooks?
They collectively and systematically progress through all these textbooks from front to back.	From their use of textbooks, what concepts do the students have about learning?
Writing is individualized.	How do I know each student is becoming more proficient at writing?
At math time, the composition of the class changes.	What grouping is most effective for math?
There is an aim placed on the board at the beginning of the lesson.	What evidence do I have that placing an aim on the board helps my students?
The students copy that aim into their notebooks.	How do students benefit from copying the aim?
The homework assignment is posted on the board for students to copy as soon as they enter the room.	What differences are apparent when the homework is assigned at the beginning instead of at the end?
The class copies and defines ten 'vocabulary words' prior to their silent reading of a story.	How do I know that my students really learned these words?
The whole class reads the same story, the one which follows the one read last week from the class textbook.	What are the advantages of all students reading the same work?
There is a teacher-led 'discussion' of the sequence of events in the story, and the definitions of assigned vocabulary words.	What do the students get from a teacher-led discussion?

—How do vocabulary and spelling tests affect students' uses of these words in their speaking and writing?

—How does the study of a list of vocabulary words influence student understanding of spoken and written texts?

—If students were instructed in the business letter form in fourth grade, is it necessary to repeat this in subsequent years? When is the optimum time for introducing this genre? Are there differences in the ways tenth graders use this genre from fourth graders?

—Does teaching the business letter form help students convey their ideas clearly?

—How might my instructional practice change if I knew more about x (say, the process of writing)?

—Why are students writing more (or less) than they wrote last year?

—Why are certain students nonparticipants in my class?

—Does it matter if I assign one book or let students choose books for the mythology unit?

—Is the most efficient way to organize a reading program for first graders to establish three groups organized around students' phonic test scores?

—Is the scope and sequence of objectives provided by the publisher of a basal reading program the right and only way to develop students' reading interests and abilities?

—Should instruction in writing stories be independent of the reading of published stories?

—When students get low grades are they motivated to study more diligently?

—When students are enjoying class can they also learn?

—What knowledge is revealed in student responses to teacher questions?

—Do teacher questions and their expectations about the content of student responses reinforce educational labelling as 'learning disabled' or 'gifted'?

—Do teachers expect different progress from students in different reading groups?

—How does increased wait-time effect the quality and quantity of teacher and student questions and responses?

—What aspects of student talk influence concept acquisition?

—What practices seem most productive for engaging students in learning?

Daily we enact our personal theories about the relationship between student learning and each student's involvement in classroom discussions and activities. When we call on non-volunteers who are able to answer, we reduce the strength of the belief that students who don't participate don't know the answer. Some participants contribute, but obtain low grades on tests. Some give brief responses. Some give extensive responses. There are significant differences in the ways students participate in class. But how does this influence their learning? Through systematic inquiry, we may get a better understanding of these professional issues.

Philosophical conflicts and instructional practices sometimes frustrate us professionally. As dedicated professionals we are concerned with providing the best setting for student learning. But inevitably colleagues may have different perspectives which influence the availability of resources, scheduling, grading practices and students' sense of responsibility in the classroom. To persuade others of the potential value of change in practice, research findings can be very useful. Teacher researchers conduct studies to document achievement, evaluate learning and determine the need for revising current practices. Is there something you'd like to do which is being thwarted by external forces, such as colleagues, the curriculum, administrators, external tests, parents, or students? Some of these issues are highlighted in the questions that follow. Again, we list these to spark your own questioning about practice in each reader's classroom.

— You may think writing develops increased grammatical sophistication, but your students are being tested on grammar and usage as isolated concerns. How does grammar instruction influence student writing?
— You may not want to 'bleed' every paper, but parents, students, and administrators expect it. How does a student who gets a bloodied, but corrected paper approach future writing tasks? What comments are valuable? At what times?
— Your students seem bored but cooperative. What activities during the day are best responded to?

Carefully collected data on these issues, strengthen our discussion of these practices as well as advocacy for change. As active professionals we gather ideas from many sources including colleagues in teacher centers, articles in professional journals, readings in courses, materials from publishers, comments from students, and presentations at workshops. These result in inquiries such as:

— How does verbal participation in collaborative small groups influence student understanding of concepts?
— How does writing daily in journals influence student writing? What does 'writing better' imply?
— What variations among student proficiencies are apparent in classes which are homogeneously grouped for reading, writing, and each subject?
— How closely matched are the questions in the teacher's manual to my students' questions about the text? What are they understanding with the text? How do the questions inspire them to continue reading?
— If students write about topics they have discussed in class, do they create better stories and essays? Rather than blindly stepping on the bandwagon, careful research will either support or refute the value of contemporary trends.

We may find a new way to travel when we mistake a turn at an intersection for the intended one. Similarly, we may find new ways of teaching from unexpected events including:

— Parodies about teaching in films and on television.
— Forgetting to plan or forgetting to bring needed materials.
— Temporarily moving to a new classroom which requires reorganizing the seating arrangements.
— Unintentionally skipping a unit in a text.
— Having twice the number of students as texts.
— Going 'off the topic'.
— Using materials allocated for other classes, grades, or topics.
— Asking or being asked a 'personal question'.
— Eavesdropping on student conversations.

Being open to new ideas and new perspectives, we nurture our professional development. The sources which contribute to teacher inquiry are as diverse as the individual experiences of each teacher. Inquiring teachers tend to question rather than accept. Now that we have initiated an inquiring stance, we need to frame our questions so that we will be able to design a research study to enact the project.

Framing Researchable Questions

Research questions provide the organizing structure for a research study. In framing a research question, we need to identify information which will provide a comprehensive understanding of the phenomenon under scrutiny. A primary consideration is to be highly focused. If a theory is being tested, then one aspect of the theory should be scrutinized in focussing a particular research project. If a theory is to be constructed, then the focus needs to be on documenting naturally occurring phenomena, such as how fifth graders go about getting a conversational turn at talk, or how a topic for discussion is negotiated and sustained.

There are several elements which are essential to include in the posing of a research question once the specific focus is clear. These include:

(i)   identifying the available population;
(ii)   selecting data which are accessible;
(iii) selecting data which are representative of a larger pool of information; and
(iv)   identifying the resources available.

The Population

It is impractical to consider studying all the people in the world. A realistic study focusses on one specific group or subset of the world population. This might be organized by gender, by age, by socio-economic background, by school placement in a private or public school, ethnic background, or language background, for example. The researcher does not arbitrarily make this choice. The selection depends on the theory and its relevant variables being tested as influenced by the researcher's particular interest in asking the question. So as a seventh grade English teacher I am more likely to want to know about how seventh graders are influenced by different phenomena, so I will choose to study a population that is more like the students I am concerned about teaching. Similarly, if my students are mainly from an urban area, I would be unlikely to choose a population in the suburbs. So I will identify the population which is consistent with my own personal concerns. If the theory I am testing refers to aspects of language development, for example, I will be sensitive in selecting participants with specific language backgrounds. Thus there needs to be great care taken in choosing the population to be studied.

Accessible Information

A major part of the study involves collecting information essential to answer the research question. Only information which is likely to be accessible will be reasonable for the researcher to plan to use. If an experimenter knows of a test which was used in another setting, but has no access to copies of it, identifying such a test as essential data for collection will make the study impossible to complete.

Representative Data

The researcher must consider the quantity of data which is realistic to accumulate when phrasing the research question. There is a finite amount of time and space for collecting information. The researcher must decide what size sample is adequate to answer the question posed. In part this adequacy is determined by the level of assurance that the researcher seeks in predicting what is likely to happen in certain situations with certain students. The more accurate the researcher seeks to be, the greater the quantity of data that is needed. With this mindset, however, it is essential to not lose sight of the fact that all educational issues involve people who are highly unpredictable in many respects, so the need for a high level of predictability might be illusory.

In addition to the quantity of data to be collected, the researcher needs to collect high quality data providing a fair representation of the students' proficiencies. Thus, the time allowed for writing must be reasonable to obtain a fair product from each student. If a researcher seeks to determine how often students participate, one five-minute, randomly chosen episode is unlikely to be adequate. Rather the researcher will need to collect data over a more extended time period — to ascertain what is typical during those time sequences. Then we choose from that larger data pool, samples which are typical. The real issue is not to devote time studying an idiosyncratic occurrence. We must focus on what actually occurs on a fairly regular basis.

Resources Available

Depending on a researcher's comfort with technology as well as with collaborating with colleagues, a teacher-researcher might choose to invite a colleague to participate in drafting interview questions, conducting interviews, videotaping sessions, or observing students and evaluating their work. A video camera might be useful in documenting activities for later review. Certainly having a videotechnician experienced in taping in classrooms would be ideal. But if such equipment or such personnel are not reasonable to expect, the researcher needs to design a study which is consistent with the available resources.

A major resource is time. How much time is needed to collect and analyze the data? Is the analysis so extensive that it will not be completed while the question still has relevance? If so, then why conduct the study? The researcher is responsible for clearly conceptualizing the enactment of the research study. Once a plan is drafted, a careful researcher 'pilots' the plan — to get the bugs out of it — to improve it on a small scale before conducting the major study. Critical reflection and revision at this time is very valuable in improving the quality of the research. Frequently there is a rush to do the study, eliminating the piloting, a major error in designing a study. Blunders are easily avoided, and improved data collection techniques can dramatically influence the conduct of the major study when we plan time for a pilot or feasibility study before the major study.

Sample Research Questions

We have identified numerous issues which may be the heart of research projects. Our next step is to formulate questions as they pertain to our own classrooms. Reflecting on our experiences allows us to pose questions which address issues of professional import which may either test or generate a theory.

1 How does the quantity and quality of three eighth-grade students' verbal contributions in small group discussions influence each student's understanding of specific viewpoints of the story?

2 What is the relationship between teaching sentence structure to fifth graders and the structure of sentences in their polished written compositions?

3 How does direct instruction focussing on ten specific science vocabulary terms influence students' uses of these ten words in their written science reports?

4 What are the differences in the organization of students' drafts and polished writing when they participate in peer conferences which focus on organization and when they write individually?

5 What differences are evident in student use of tape recorders when they have the opportunity to experiment with them in contrast to the students who listen to a lecture on how tape recorders function?

6 Do groups of fourth grade students who meet regularly in their reading groups use different strategies for discussion than groups which meet infrequently?

Researchable questions have specific characteristics:

* They have a clear focus based on either theory or practice.
* They carefully identify the meanings of terms.
* They clearly present their methods for studying the questions.

And now, we encourage you to frame a research question which focusses on an issue of major import to you in your professional capacity. We know that the ways we frame questions determines how we conduct research which is the topic we discuss in the next chapter on data collection and analysis.

References

BRAUSE, R.S. and MAYHER, J.S. (1984) 'Asking the right questions', *Language Arts*, 61, 5.

BRUNER, J. and HASTE, H. (Eds) (1987) *Making Sense*, New York, Methuen.

MAYHER, J.S. (1990) *Uncommon Sense: Theoretical Practice in Language Education*, Portsmouth, NH, Boynton/Cook.

MAYHER, J.S. and BRAUSE, R.S. (1985) 'A structure for inquiry and change', *Language Arts*, 62, 3.

MAYHER, J.S. and VINE, H.A. Jr. (1974) 'The Teaching Act Model', *New York University Education Quarterly*, 6, 1.

SMITH, F. (1988) *Insult to Intelligence*, Portsmouth, NH, Heinemann.

VYGOTSKY, L.S. (1978) *Mind in Society*, Cambridge, MA, Harvard University Press.

Chapter 7

Collecting and Analyzing Classroom Data in Theory and in Practice

Rita S. Brause and John S. Mayher

Researchers systematically collect and analyze information which will provide insights into specific problems or issues, typically called research questions. Intentionally studying a particularly issue, researchers approach the task in a highly organized and systematic fashion. A technical term referring to the information collected for a particular study is 'data'. The word 'data' is synonymous with information and is typically used in its plural form. Thus, we find reports stating 'data were collected over an entire semester'. The term 'data' can refer to an infinite list of materials. Everything around us is potentially 'data'. Depending on the research question being posed, some data are more valuable than others. It is the researcher's responsibility to systematically select the most appropriate information to answer a specific research question.

The researcher designs the total study deciding what data need to be collected, how best to collect those data, and how to analyze the data, all consistent with the question or problem which initially sparked the research project. This chapter will focus on these issues, exemplifying the process of data collection and analysis with two classroom studies.

What Data Inform Classroom Studies?

Classrooms are settings in which people engage in a wide range of activities. The data inherent in such a setting are infinite including:

—the participants' ages and family backgrounds;
—the precise words spoken by the teacher and the students;

—the materials posted on bulletin boards;
—the texts used;
—the notes taken by students;
—the students' journal entries;
—students' notes passed surreptitiously;
—teacher plans;
—laboratory projects;
—role playing activities;
—announcements broadcast over the public address system;
—clothes the students are wearing;
—condition of the flooring;
—order in which materials are stored in closets;
—organization of desks and other furniture.

You could add much more to this list taking either a holistic perspective on the classroom – or a more atomistic focus on a specific event. Studies focusing on one specific activity are conducted more often than those which take a holistic focus. While it is interesting, and indeed important, to study such concerns as how the classroom environment influences learning, these more holistic studies tend to require more extended time periods. A single lengthy study is frequently replaced by a small group of more highly focussed studies. The assumption underlying such aggregations is that it is possible to get a sense of the totality of the classroom by weaving findings focusing on distinct elements. While there may be a large leap of faith to accept the pooling of isolated pieces, there is probably no design which would be considered perfect or uncontroversial. There are limitations to all designs and compromises which researchers constantly make. Acknowledging these limitations researchers tentatively accept findings, keeping open minds about the possible contradictions reported in new studies.

A researcher focussing on instruction in vocabulary development might choose to collect only a transcript of the classroom lessons. While information about the bulletin boards may be interesting, the researcher decides this does not directly refer to the focus of the study. The researcher defers attention to these issues, heeding instead, those which are judged more likely to answer the specific question posed. This is a judgement call by the researcher. The more accurate the decisions, the better the study is likely to be. Those who are more knowledgeable about the activities, the participants, and the materials, are likely to have the advantage in knowing the range of possible sources and the best ways to get access to them. Insightful teachers, then are better able to speculate about the data which are likely to be helpful than those with little familiarity or expertise in the lives of classrooms.

Data collected to answer one research question will not necessarily represent the best data to answer a different question. It is wisest to collect new data for each research project. But in this less than ideal world, where we try to hurry everything, it is not unusual to use one set of data to understand multiple issues.

A careful researcher takes many preliminary steps in preparing the design for collecting data. A basic issue is whether to collect data by carefully controlling the setting, or as it naturally occurs without manipulating the setting. The researcher needs to decide if it is more important to discover what really happens in real situations (to generate hypotheses) — or to find out what happens in a situation created by the experimenter drawing on a theory (to test hypotheses). At certain times each is preferable. But rarely are both appropriate to inform the researcher's questions. It is the researcher's judgement about the validity of current theories which influences this decision.

Another major issue involves deciding what data will be the most appropriate for the specific question being posed. There are several procedures which researchers engage in while preparing a project. These include observation, 'piloting' and 'feasibility' studies. As a result of these activities, researchers revise their designs, creating the best plan for collecting data that they can conceive. Thus, the design is the creation of the researcher over an extended time period. The quality of the design is a clear indication of the quality of the researcher's thinking about the issues. In the process of creating the design, the researcher is influenced by knowledge of research and theories as well as reflections on personal experiences in classrooms, for example.

Careful observations provide the researcher with a rich sense of the multitude of activities occurring in a lesson. Serious contemplation on these events allows the researcher to design or identify activities which address the specific research issue.

Piloting involves trying out some of the potential procedures to determine the mesh between the researcher's expectations and reality. Piloting usually results in revising plans to enhance the outcomes. This is usually conducted on a small scale, creating a microcosm of the major study. If a test is to be given, each item needs to be looked at carefully, to ascertain that there is a clear mesh between the respondent's and the researcher's interpretations of the questions and the choices. This relationship is essential since the researcher makes inferences about the participant's knowledge from the participant's responses. If these inferences are inappropriate, then the study is of little value in answering the research question. Piloting also allows the researcher to identify redundant questions, and many other important issues (see chapter 4 for an extensive discussion of this concern).

While the researcher may envision grandiose plans of videotaping all day long for example, the feasibility that these plans may be realized in the specific setting needs to be determined. The researcher needs to actually implement the plans on a trial basis, using this feasibility experience not only to determine if it is possible to accomplish what is designed, but also to consider if there are more expeditious or more effective ways of collecting the needed data. Throughout the entire design process, it is essential that the researcher think about the consequences of the decisions as these relate to the quality of the data collected. After these preliminary steps the researcher plans the major study, revising activities after reflecting on experiences in the feasibility and pilot studies.

The more comprehensive the procedures for data collection, the more accurate the findings are likely to be. From another perspective, researchers are frequently reminded by many critics, 'garbage in, garbage out'. Serious researchers take care to develop designs for data collection which will be the most informative for the particular problem being addressed in the study.

How Much Data is Needed?

Once the procedures are decided, the next issue to determine is the quantity of data needed. How do I know when I have enough data? On the one hand, the best advice to give is that the more data the researcher collects, the more accurate the findings are likely to be. But there may never be an end to data collection with this perspective in mind. Especially problematic in this light is the possibility that the researcher may drown in the data. The researcher must make a compromise — collecting adequate data to understand the complexities of the issue being studied, while being pragmatic about the shortness of life and the need to allocate time appropriately. Such a realization results in the decision to do the best one can in a specific time period using heightened awareness to focus on one issue.

Researchers thus, take a 'representative sample' from the larger potential pool believing that by wisely, but selectively sampling, we will obtain results which are representative of the larger whole. A problem with sampling is determining what 'the whole' really consists of. When studying educational issues, this may be realized in deciding to focus on fourth graders. The difficulty with this decision is the realization that some fourth graders are 9 years old and others are 10 or 11; for some English is their only language while others are multi-lingual; some have travelled to several continents while others have never left the immediate neighborhood. The issue of representation is not easily resolved, but all researchers acknowledge this concern and make a judgment call for the specific question they are studying. There is no easy answer and all answers have limitations. But it is the acknowledgement of limitations that is essential in honestly interpreting data collected, recognizing the unique qualities of each individual and the possibility that any of these might influence actions and outcomes.

There are no easy recipes for designing good research projects. The knowledge and sensitivities of the researcher are the critical ingredients. With experience, researchers become more expert, highlighting the importance of 'getting one's feet wet' as soon as possible so that with time, expertise will grow.

When do I Analyze Data?

Analysis may take many forms. It might occur while the data are being collected and/or it might occur only after all the data have been collected. If there is overlap between the data collection and analytical procedures, future collections might be influenced by the early analysis. In some designs the researcher seeks to modify procedures once the study has started. In this context, early analysis enables the researcher to make changes based on reviews of the early data. This less formal structure is typical of hypothesis generating studies. In hypothesis testing studies, however, there are two clearly contained periods. One is solely devoted to collecting data, and a second exclusively focusses on analyzing it. This formal structure is consistent with the presumptions on which the hypothesis testing study is based, specifically, that explicit hypotheses are being subjected to careful scrutiny in specific contexts. The time for data analysis, then, depends on the intent of the study, be it to test hypotheses or to generate them.

Rita S. Brause and John S. Mayher

How do I Analyze Data?

There are two major issues in analyzing the data. First the researcher interprets the data collected exclusively within the confines in which the study was conducted. Thus the initial analysis deals specifically with the setting in which the data were collected. After this stage, the researcher abstracts from the specific setting, connecting findings to published studies and theories, generalizing and theorizing about the phenomenon under study. There are two major procedures for analysis of the data: quantitative and qualitative. Some studies use just one of these. Many combine them both. Thus we can find hypothesis testing studies which analyze data numerically and qualitatively. Similarly, we can find hypothesis generating studies which analyze data numerically and qualitatively. The researcher decides how to analyze the data based on the specific question which is guiding the research.

Quantitative Analysis

Quantitative analysis involves converting information to numbers — the number of times a person spoke in a group, the number of correct responses to specific questions, or the number of words in a composition. While counting might seem quite simple, this is far from the truth. The researcher makes inferences from the data, determining what constitutes an utterance, what answers are correct, and what counts as a word. For example let's consider three students' written sentences presented in (i)–(iii):

(i)   I am going to the lunch room.
(ii) I'm going to the lunchroom.
(iii) I'm lunching.

The researcher needs to consider if lunch room (in (i)) and lunchroom (in (ii)) count as two different words or one, and if *I am* in (i) is quantitatively different from *I'm* in (ii) and (iii). While these differences may seem trivial, they will influence the total numbers arrived at in a quantitative analysis. This decision is the researcher's and must be noted when reporting the procedures for analyzing data as well as during the interpretation process.

Quantitative analysis is atomistic in that it counts units (words, for example) without any concern for the content of those words. The objectivity of that analysis is very compelling, despite the difficulty in determining what the numbers really mean. Are longer sentences necessarily better? Are infrequently heard words (lunching in (iii)) preferred over more commonly used ones (lunch)? Numbers do not mean anything by themselves. It is the researcher who makes important inferences and decides what they mean. The consumer of the research considers these issues when placing a high or low value on the research findings. In this volume we have been distinguishing between hypothesis testing and hypothesis generating research. Research which tests hypotheses is frequently *quantitative* in design, but it need not be exclusively quantitative. Thus, the analytical procedures (be they quantitative or qualitative) do not distinguish the purposes or intents of educational research as discussed in chapter 3.

Qualitative Analysis

In a *qualitative* design the researcher believes that the exclusive consideration of numbers of words in (i)–(iii) misses potentially important differences in linguistic sophistication and style. Qualitative analysis involves inferring meaning from more holistic chunks of information such as the meanings of whole sentences or whole discourse. In the samples noted above, the relative uniqueness of (iii) would be contrasted to (i) and (ii) which might be considered more conventional. On the other hand, the formality of (i) might be contrasted with the informality of (ii) and (iii). Thus, the content of the utterances would be given priority over the numerical counts in a qualitative analysis (see chapter 9, for more information on qualitative analysis). Hypothesis generating research typically uses qualitative procedures for data analysis, but frequently incorporates quantitative procedures as well.

Findings as Abstractions from the Specific Data

Once the findings of the specific data collection are clear, whether from a qualitative or a quantitative perspective, the researcher considers the impact of the findings from a broader perspective. For hypothesis testing studies, the researcher connects the findings to the specific theory being tested. If the findings are consistent with what the theory predicted, the research study serves to strengthen the theory. When findings are inconsistent with the theory there is reason to believe the theory may need some revision.

In hypothesis generating studies, the abstracting process results in the specification of tentative hypotheses and theory building which need testing in future research studies. The researcher formulates these hypotheses based on the specific findings generated through the initial research study. There may be some suggestion about people in general, or all fourth graders, based on data from a small sample. The intent, ultimately, however is to create a theory which will be consistent with reality. Thus, although hypothesis testing and hypothesis generating have different short term goals, ultimately they are intimately connected. The theory derived from a hypothesis generating study is eventually tested in a hypothesis testing study. The theory found wanting in a hypothesis testing study becomes grist for the mill in a hypothesis generating study. (We consider this interdependence in chapter 3.) Let's now consider two different studies as these exemplify the data collection and data analysis concerns we have been addressing.

Sample Studies

To illustrate the collection and analytical processes discussed in this chapter we will draw on two different studies. One was a teacher-researcher study (Levine, 1982) from which we highlighted and more intensively examined one aspect of that study in Mayher and Brause, November/December 1983. Levine designed the original study as a classroom teacher to understand the relative impact of different activities on sixth — eighth graders' vocabulary development. It uses both qualitative and quantitative data techniques.

The second study we will consider is a segment of an ethnographic study conducted by researchers visiting a second grade classroom (Brause and Mayher, 1983). It was part of a much larger study which focussed primarily on the nature of classroom interaction during whole class lessons. Within the large data collection, we selected one lesson which focussed on an aspect of vocabulary development which will serve as another example of qualitative and quantitative data collection and analysis.

A Teacher-Researcher Vocabulary Study

Denise Levine, a teacher in an urban alternative program, was concerned with the effects of the instruction she planned to help students increase their vocabularies. She stressed that her interest was not so much that students accurately match synonyms on vocabulary tests, but rather that students understand concepts integral to the technical vocabulary identified in their science curriculum.

Levine wanted to find ways to help each student in her class learn the 'curriculum' as represented by their understanding of key vocabulary terms. She had read Britton (1982) and was convinced of the combined need to use language-to-learn concepts and to personalize and contextualize learning. She took these several issues into account when evaluating the impact of the activities she designed to help them understand the characteristics of liquid solutions.

For each unit, Levine identified 'key terms'. She recognized the need to limit the number of terms she studied choosing those which appeared most frequently in readings, presentations and written activities. In preparation for students' future encounters with technical terms, Levine assigned dictionary work. Students were assigned to copy the subject-specific definition, the pronunciation, derivation, root and syllable configurations. In practice, students chose the scientific definition for solution, 'a mixture that is clear, transparent' rather than 'the answer to a problem'. After consulting the dictionary, they were responsible for using each word in a sentence.

Once the unit was underway the terms appeared in many different contexts including:

— Class lessons
— Worksheets with blank spaces to fill in new vocabulary
— 'Clarity Statements' students wrote at the conclusion of an activity, summarizing what each had learned.
— Quizzes with multiple choice, matching, short answers, and essay questions.

Levine had identified many potential data sources.

The data collection covered a wide array of materials. Levine gathered her lesson plans, and sampled half the class' completed worksheets, tests and writing folders which contained their clarity statements. While she had planned the unit in a way comparable to the others in the curriculum, she had never systematically studied what students had done as learners. Mainly due to time constraints she taught and tested without subjecting the students' work to any systematic study to determine if there were some activities which were more productive in promoting students' understandings than others. Once she had collected all these materials, she decided to analyze the papers as a way to get a handle on what and how students seemed to be developing their concepts about solutions.

Table 7.1: *Relative frequency of appearance of defined words*

Concepts	Contexts			
Vocabulary	Instructional Activities		Evaluation	
	Lessons	Demonstrations	Laboratories	Student Writing
Solution	X	XXX	XXX	XXX
Solute			X	X
Solvent		X		X
Soluble				
Mixture			XXX	XXX
Dilute	X		X	XXX
Concentrate	X		X	X
Saturate (Super-)	X		X	XX
Particles		X		X
Homogeneous	X		X	X
Transparent		X		X
Opaque				

XXX indicates great frequency of use
XX indicates moderate use
X indicates minimal use

To address her concern, she analyzed some data qualitatively and some quantitatively. From a quantitative perspective she counted the numbers of times students heard or used specific terms. These numerical findings are presented in table 7.1.

From an analysis of table 7.1 Levine could see that there was a close match between the words that students used in connection with laboratory projects and the words they used in their writing. The terms which appeared most often in demonstrations and laboratories were also used most frequently in the evaluation. Dilute and (super)-saturated were used frequently, although they had minimal use in the class activities. In discussing this table with Levine we speculated that this increased use in their evaluation might be attributed to their personal experiences particularly out of school.

Two terms (opaque and soluble) which students only looked up but never used in class, never appeared in student writing. In contrast, those which were used frequently in laboratories, demonstrations, and lessons were also the terms which appeared in student writing. Their appearance in hands-on instructional contexts probably promoted their use in student writing. These findings suggest the intimate relationship between the learners' experiences and their understanding. When students used these terms in hands-on contexts, with increasing frequency, they were likely to be used meaningfully in writing as well.

Levine noticed that although the words appeared in some student work, they were not all used in the same way. There were differences in students' understanding which were not reflected in the frequency counts. For example, students were confused about the extremes of dilute and concentrate, yet this confusion was lost in the display of frequency of use. Levine realized that by tallying the frequency with which some words appeared, she had no indication about the appropriateness of these uses. Frequency counts only provided superficial evidence of learning, at best. The number of uses did not necessarily reflect any depth of understanding.

Additional analysis was needed to inform this concern. Levine decided on doing a qualitative analysis of students' understanding of these ideas through sampling students' writing. By studying the students' writing in response to specific teacher-assigned activities, we can see development in student understanding. This analysis is a qualitative one. We are assessing students' understanding of the characteristics of solutions as evidenced by their use of technical terms in different writing activities.

In our analysis of these data, we looked at student responses to sentence completions, essay questions, and clarity statements written individually, to summarize each lesson. By contrasting students' responses across the two-month duration of the unit, we established a three-point scale for evaluating students' writing distinguishing among inappropriate statements, acceptable statements and integrative statements. Integrative statements provide a synthesis as in (iv).

> (iv)   Concentrated is something that is real strong like orange juice, frozen orange juice. (Veronica, 11/12/82)

Acceptable statements used the term appropriately, albeit in an isolated context as in (v).

> (v)   We made it more concentrated.

Many of the answers which were in the acceptable category seemed to be regurgitations of definitions. These didn't give us any indication of what the students understood or what they were confused about although they did use the term appropriately. Inappropriate statements included the technical term with no clear indication of understanding its meaning as in (vi).

> (vi)   The food coloring started to dilute.

Using this three point system, we can usefully contrast Charles' early explanation of a concentrate with his later one in (vii) and (viii).

(vii)   Something made weak. (10/13/82)
(viii) Means strong. Ex. We put more rum in the rum cake to make it stronger [more concentrated]. (11/15/82)

Charles' initial explanation indicated his awareness of the relationship between types of solutions and degree of intensity. But he has confused concentrate and dilute, thus (vii) is considered inappropriate while (viii) is considered acceptable. Although his later explanation is closer to the mark, from the example he provides we can't be sure that he understands the difference between adding more quantity of rum flavor or increasing the strength of the rum flavor by concentrating the liquid state. Certainly by increasing the quantity of rum, the rum flavor will be stronger, but that does not necessarily equate with being more concentrated. As Charles increases his understanding of this distinction, he will gain greater understanding of the term. This will be noticeable in the increased clarity of his statements.

When students are asked to use the term 'concentrated' and the use is inappropriate as in (ix) or unclear as in (x), this is an indication of the need for additional experiences before we can be sure the student understands the concept in an integrated fashion. Since Maritza's response (ix) was presented early in the unit, it is not very troubling albeit not related to science *per se*. Lorraine's (x), which appeared towards the end of the time allocated for this unit suggests a more personal understanding of the term and concepts.

(ix)   Concentrated means a prison camp where political enemies, prisoners of war, or members of minority groups are held by government order. (Maritza, 10/13/82)
(x)   When something is on the bottom it is concentrated. (Lorraine, 11/12/82)

Even at the end of the unit there were differences in the students' definitions for the term concentrate, reflecting a wide range of understandings among members of the class. Representative samples are listed in (xi), (xii) and (xiii).

(xi)   When it has a lot of acid in it. (Rhonda, 11/12/82)
(xii)   Concentrated means the opposite of diluted; it is strong. (Marcelino, 11/15/82)

(xiii)   Concentrated is something that is real strong like orange juice, frozen orange juice. (Veronica, 11/12/82)

Rhonda in (xi) used technical terms which have been defined in this unit. She displays some familiarity with the concept concentrated in that it may be acidic. Her brief statement is not expansive enough to provide assurance that she understands what concentrated means. She may be sprinkling her response with terms, hoping the mere use of the words will impress her audience. Her response is rated inappropriate. We can contrast (xi) with (xii) and (xiii). Marcelino (xii), while using the term concentrated presents a very clear definition. He provides both a contrast and a synonym. His response is rated acceptable. Veronica (xiii) not only gives a synonym, but an example as well. It is possible that while she was writing she realized that orange juice is not as strong as frozen orange juice, and that the frozen form was the concentrated form. Her connection of the term concentrated with her daily experiences of mixing frozen orange juice from its concentrated form provides her with a clear, more integrated sense of what the term means. Her response is rated as integrated.

Qualitative analysis offers us insight into the different students' understandings from similar in-class experiences. Further examples are provided in (xiv), (xv), and (xvi) which are students' responses to Levine's query: Is orange juice a solution?

(xiv)   Some of the vitamins go to the bottom and top. (Charles, 10/13/82)

(xv)   I think that anything that is a solid will not make a solution. (Charles, 10/19/82)

(xvi)   A solution is a liquid that you mix with water or something else and it is clearer. (Manuel, 10/19/82)

Although we can tell Charles is aware of a concern for mixing elements in (xiv), we note a change in his focus between instances (xiv) and (xv). In (xiv) he is using the term 'vitamin' as a way of suggesting dispersion of a concentrate in a solution. He has not answered the teacher's question as to whether orange juice is a solution. He is focussing on vitamins, an issue possibly discussed at home or in other classes, suggesting he should drink orange juice daily 'for the vitamins'. While he is trying to connect his prior experiences with the new concept, he has confused some of the information. In (xv) we note a tentative nature in his response, particularly in his use of the term 'I think'. He is still unclear on the concept of a solution.

Manuel's explanation in (xvi) about transparency, liquids, and solutions uses terms stressed in the unit. If he had given an example of each of these items, his understanding would be more apparent. The eventual clarity of some students' understanding is apparent in their use of terms describing activities they engaged in during the unit. Robert's statements in (xvii) and (xviii) are interesting contrasts which appeared within the same written assignment.

(xvii)　Yesterday in the science lab we diluted food coloring. We added seventeen cups of water to one drop of food coloring. We could still see some of the red food coloring but it was being dilute. (Robert, 11/9/82)

(xviii)　Diluted Concentrated Tea
Lipton Cup-a-Soup
Soup Coffee
Instant Tea

In (xvii) he seems to be regurgitating terms without making sense of them. The comparative list he appended in (xviii) more clearly identified his understanding . . . and his problem. Although this list confuses concentrated and diluted solutions (diluted concentrated tea), Robert has connected the discussion to his experiences with food. He probably understands that diluted mixtures are weaker than concentrated ones . . . and that tea, for example may appear in either diluted or concentrated forms. But it's not clear if he understands that it is either concentrated or diluted.

The major issue for Levine is to determine which activities promoted development of the students' understandings of the characteristics of solutions. We consider three students' responses in (xix), (xx) and (xxi) as a basis for assessing this issue.

(xix)　In science we made an experiment of water and food coloring. We put a drop of food coloring and then added water to that one little drop of food coloring. When we added the water, the food coloring started to dilute. The more water we put the lighter the color got. I learned that water can dilute food coloring. (Veronica, 11/15/82)

(xx)　This experiment is about lollipops. You fill up two cups of H_2O and get two lollipops to see which one dissolves first. So we said that just let one lollipop sit in the cup of H_2O and stir the lollipop and see which one dissolves first. So at the end, the lollipop we stirred dissolved faster than the

lollipop in H_2O- I learned that stirring the lollipop in H_2O
is faster than sitting in H_2O. (Robert, 11/15/82)
(xxi) The stirred one melted the fastest. (Victor, 10/14/82)

Victor in (xxi) has equated melting with diluting, a process he is
familiar with in eating ice cream and using ice to cool beverages. He
has conveyed his observation accurately but has not used appropriate
language for the experience. We can agree, however, that he understood the basic idea of the lollipop experiment. Similarly, Veronica in
(xix) displays her understanding commenting that 'the more water we
put, the lighter the color got'. This observation is critical in understanding the nature of diluted solutions. These two responses contrast
with Robert's in (xx). Although Robert uses scientific terms ('H_2O'
and 'dissolve'), his understanding of why one lollipop dissolved more
rapidly is no more apparent than Victor's (xxi). Thus, the use of
technical terms does not provide clear evidence of his understanding.
Another student's response to a science experiment in which he related
personal experiences with filtration are found in example (xxii) from
Britton (1982), an original source for Levine's inquiry.

(xxii) How I Filtered my Water Specimens When we were down
at Mr. Harris's farm I brought some water from the brook
back with me. I took some from a shallow place by the
oak tree, and some from a deep place by the walnut tree. I
got the specimens by placing a jar in the brook and let the
water run into it. Then I brought them back to school to
filter ... The experiment that I did shows that where the
water was deeper and was not running fast there was a lot
more silt suspended as little particles in the water. You
could see this by looking at the filter paper, where the
water was shallow and fast there was less dirt suspended in
it. (p. 87)

The student in (xxii) integrated the technical terms in his explanation
of filtration. Clearly a dictionary definition would not provide this,
whereas his personal experiences did. Similarly Levine saw how students' personal activities influenced their acquisition of the science
concepts more than copying notes or copying dictionary definitions.
    In contrast to (xix)–(xxi), (xxii) provides a synthesis of what
happened with an explanation of why things happened. Although
(xix), (xx), and (xxi) provide observations, the students have not

attempted to connect all of the isolated events. All happenings are viewed as equally important. One student's lab report noted that all of the students sat on the window ledge. The relationship between this information and the experiment was not explained. Although observation is an important component of science, explaining observations is even more so. Levine's students do not explain how the laboratory experiments they conducted helped them understand the nature of different types of solutions or how solutions are formed. The answers they have provided do not suggest that the students have integrated their study with their daily lives outside of the classroom. In contrast to the example in (xxii) where the student has personalized and explained the activity, Levine's students are having little personal involvement with their learnings. This may be understood from the difference in the initial teaching structures. Levine provided direct instruction in technical terms and the laboratory was an isolated classroom. Britton's student started with an experience at a farm and worked through the understanding of filtration through experiments which were personally designed.

From looking qualitatively at the learning that the students revealed as they wrote, Levine was able to question the effect of isolating words through dictionary activity. She also now questions how many students understood the major, overriding concepts about the nature of solutions. Although she believes that students focussed on learning the terms that she identified initially, she is not sure that actual dictionary search was helpful, particularly at that time. She also is unsure if vocabulary usage alone can be equated with understanding of the concept. She believes that the diverse activities during concrete tasks were probably more influential in learning. As part of her observation she noticed that students understood the terms more fully with time, as when they made analogies between the scientific phenomena and their personal, out-of-school experiences. She plans to take a closer look at a few students' work as they naturally integrate technical terms without her specific direction.

Focussing on the frequency of use of specific vocabulary items, does not seem to be a productive approach to determining student understanding of concepts. The laboratory activities and individual clarity statements encouraged connections to their own lives and seem more effective in helping students understand concepts and use the technical vocabulary. By doing a qualitative analysis of student responses and then abstracting from these specific instances, several issues have become clearer.

1   Focussing on the acquisition of concepts rather than on the acquisition of isolated vocabulary emphasizes the more important concern. Once students understand a concept, their use of appropriate terms follows.

2   The teacher must plan concrete ways for connecting concepts to students' individual lives.

3   Students' unique connections to new experiences personalize and enhance the learning process.

4   When students connect new experiences with familiar ones, they acquire a better understanding of the new experiences than if these are isolated.

5   Concrete activities accompanied by student and teacher talk provide a ripe setting for exploratory use of new, technical terms.

6   The more frequent the exposure to new terms within a concrete experience, the more likely that these terms will appear in student writing.

These generalizations are consistent with the theories of cognitive development and language development presented by Britton (1982), Mayher (1990) and Vygotsky (1962). They emphasize that technical terms are learned incidentally and as a byproduct of direct experience with a phenomenon, particularly in collaboration with peers. Levine's analysis allowed her to recognize the limitations of direct instruction and isolated classroom instruction, particularly causing her to consider alternative strategies for developing students' concepts and their technical vocabulary as well.

A Classroom Lesson: A Transcript on Synonyms

An excerpt from a transcript of a second grade classroom provides the database for another sample of data collection and analysis. This excerpt is typical of the total lesson and several other lessons on this topic in one classroom, which is similar to many other classrooms across the grades and across the nation.

To gather the data needed for this project, researchers videotaped in classrooms over an extended time period, enabling participants to get accustomed to the equipment's presence and thereby dismissing it as a concern as they went about their lessons. There were many aspects of the data collection which are irrelevant for our current purposes, so we will not muddy the waters with these here. (For additional information see Brause, Mayher and Bruno, 1985.) For our purposes, we need to know that a classroom lesson was in progress which was captured on videotape. According to the teacher, the purpose of the lesson was to increase the students' vocabulary. She wanted the students to know the words *synonym, antonym, and homonym*. She specifically wanted them to know these terms because 'they are in the curriculum for second grade'. In addition, she said the students needed to use a greater variety of words instead of constantly repeating the same words. So she saw the lesson as one which would encourage their expanding vocabularies. We taped the lesson, transcribed it, and then analyzed it to see if the goals which she had identified were realized.

To create the transcript, we videotaped in the classroom and then subjected that tape to systematic transcription. This is a tedious process of recording the constant flow of words on paper. It was essential that each word be recorded correctly. Recognizing the rapidity with which we talk, the different dialects represented among the participants, the frequency of multiple simultaneous speakers in a classroom, and the limitations of recording in classrooms, we were amazed at the possibility of getting a verbatim transcript despite the difficulties inherent in the process.

It is awe-inspiring to consider the capacity of each teacher's and student's mind to cope with the quantity of data presented in one lesson. The transcription process involved individuals listening simultaneously, verifying what each other heard. In transcribing one three-minute sequence, one hour was taken by four researchers working in concert. This is a time-consuming, exhausting process. However, it is essential if one wants to study what goes on in classrooms. We now go to the videotape....

We find ourselves at the beginning of a forty-five-minute word-study lesson. Synonyms and antonyms are reviewed prior to studying homonyms, the major focus of the lesson. To save space, one three-minute episode is presented in figure 7.1 as a sample of the verbal transcript of the teacher-student interactions.

From the teacher's questions we identify two issues related to synonyms which she considers important:

(i)   defining the word synonym;
(ii) stating synonyms for specific words.

Acknowledging that this is a review (line 1: who *remembers* what a synonym is?), we notice that approximately half the time is devoted

Figure 7.1:   *Transcript of a three-minute excerpt of a word-study lesson*

Line Number		
1	T:	Who remembers what a synonym is?
		(Ss raising hands)
	T:	Pharaoh.
		Pharaoh: Same words.
5	T:	Uh, close. Who can say it better?
	S:	Oh.
	S:	Me.
	S:	Me.
	T:	Me, me, I don't know. . . . Karen.
10		Karen: The same meanings.
	T:	O.K., but the same meaning what?
		You didn't say the whole sentence.
		(Acknowledging another student whose
		hand was raised) Yes.
15	S:	The same meaning that means the same.
	T:	The same meaning that means the same of what?
	S:	Of the word.
	T:	Right. Two words that have the same or similar
		meaning. Now we're learning similarity also in
20		math, so we know very clearly what both terms
		mean. Um, if I say glad, what's a synonym?
		S(Calling out): Happy.
	T:	Happy. If I say sad, what's a synonym?
		Ss: Mad.
25	T:	No.
		Ss: I mean happy.
	S:	Happy.
	S:	Synonym?
	S:	Grouch.
30	T:	If I say sad, what's a synonym?
	S:	Selfish.
	S:	Unhappy.
	S:	Unhappy.
	T:	Who said that? . . . Right . . . unhappy. Unhappy is a
35		synonym of sad, not mad. You could be sad and
		you don't have to be mad. Mad is a synonym of
		what?'
	S:	Happy.
	S:	Angry.
40	T:	That's right. Mad is a synonym of angry.
		(Walking towards blackboard) Alright, so we know
		synonyms. Let's review with another example.
		Alright, let's write this. 'Words . . . that have . . .
		That have what, children?
45	S:	Same meaning.
	T:	Same or similar meanings . . . such as . . .
	S:	Such as what?
	T:	Give me an example.
	S:	Ill, sick.
50	T:	Ill and sick, very good. This is an example, alright . . .
		ill . . . and the ones that we just gave . . . unhappy and
		sad, glad and happy . . . and whatever else. Okay.

T = Teacher
S = Student
Ss = Multiple students responding simultaneously
(from Brause, Mayher and Bruno, 1985)

Table 7.2: *Frequency of appearance of the word* synonym

Classroom Participant	Frequency of Occurrence
Total Use	9
Teacher	8
Student	1

Table 7.3: *Number of turns to match synonyms*

glad — (1) *happy*
sad — (7) mad, happy, happy, grouch, selfish, unhappy, *unhappy*
mad — (2) happy, *angry*
ill — (1) *sick*

to getting a definition — which none of the children seems able to provide. Only the teacher has the acceptable definition (lines 19–20; lines 44 and 46) despite the fact that students are reviewing synonyms, and that they have just heard the acceptable definition from the teacher only a minute before (lines 19–20). We can assume that the students do not know an acceptable definition for synonyms — and by analogy probably do not know an acceptable definition for antonyms, both of which were studied on previous days. Later in this transcript we note the same confusion in defining antonyms.

From a quantitative stance, we can determine that not one student gave an acceptable definition for synonym. We could count the number of times the word *synonym* is used; the number of times students used the word in comparison to the number of times the teacher used the word; the number of synonyms they presented correctly; the number of students who answered correctly; or the number of turns at talk needed to define the term correctly. Some of these data would be impossible to ascertain. For example, we could not reliably state how many different students responded since there is no indication of students' names to distinguish one 'S' from another in the transcript. Nor can we determine how many students called out answers in lines noted 'Ss'. Thus, there is a limit to the amount of data we can obtain from this transcript. But using the data available, we could make a table for each of these analyses.

Table 7.2 displays the numbers of times the word synonym appeared in this transcript, with an indication distinguishing the teacher's use from the students'. We note that only one student used the word, in contrast to the teacher who used the word eight times.

In table 7.3 we can compare the number of responses which were needed before the teacher identified an acceptable response. Four words were provided as samples. Of these four, there were two words (the first and last considered in the class) which needed only one respondent. When the teacher offered 'sad' she was given words which rhymed, words which were antonyms, and words which might result from being sad (selfish and grouch). Even the response which was accepted initially went unnoticed until it was repeated. The students' confusion about what words would be acceptable as synonyms suggests that they do not understand what synonyms are.

A qualitative analysis of the same data would yield different information. We see an emphasis on general turn-taking procedures such as volunteering for a turn-at-talk. Although the teacher implicitly imposes the need for hand raising in line 9, the rule is not followed later. The fact that the teacher uses instructional time to impose this rule, however, serves to focus student attention on the way to get a turn, not on the content of their responses. Since no activity is provided to help formulate the content of their responses, their total focus remains on the format or procedure. The class functions as an oral workbook. Students seem confused about what a synonym is. They can neither define it nor match one. But students do not tell the teacher overtly that they do not understand. The teacher states in two different places that the students *do* know what synonyms are (lines 18–21; and lines 41–2). She also implies satisfaction with their knowledge by moving on to the next topic (line 52: Okay.)

Lines 28 and 47 mark the only student-posed questions in this episode. The first question is in response to the series of attempts to match a pair with the teacher's *glad*. The student seems to be seeking clarification as to what a synonym is, especially after the many unacceptable responses. Yet the question goes unanswered. The second question is directly related to the student's assumption that the teacher expected him to do something. This caused him to call out his question. In both instances, students felt they were supposed to be doing something but were not confident that they understood what the teacher wanted them to do. In this classroom, they realized that they needed to match mindsets with the teacher and these two questions highlight student attempts to accomplish this feat. But neither received assistance either from the teacher or from peers.

Following the teacher's pacing provided a harmonious atmosphere for the conduct of the lesson. The students and the teacher were exceptionally polite to each other. The teacher did not coerce students to participate. Nor did she ostracize those who did not provide acceptable answers. In a similar sense, the students never pressured the teacher to provide a clearer presentation of the concept under consideration. It seems almost as if they had a very 'civil' agreement that permitted all to function without a sense of threat or fear of being questioned. One effect was a 'safe' environment for all, hence the workbook comparison. Neither student nor teacher knowledge or confusion would become the highlight of the lesson.

Pharaoh was called on by the teacher to answer the question posed in line 1. Even though the teacher says 'Close', an analysis of the following fifteen lines doesn't really clarify where he was close or where he wasn't. The teacher never returns to him to find out if he understands what an acceptable definition for synonym is.

Only correct responses are sought. 'That's right' and 'Very good' were uttered five times by the teacher. Correct answers were acknowledged and repeated. When an incorrect response was uttered (lines 24, 31 and 38), it was not acknowledged. There is never any discussion as to why these answers were not accepted. The students are not provided instruction or feedback to help them understand why some answers are better than others. Their specific learning about synonyms is unclear from all the dialog which transpires. Their confusion however, *is* clear.

As we've seen, most of the classroom talk seemed to operate as an oral workbook with the teacher playing the workbook role and the children dutifully filling in the oral blanks, as in:

line 16: The same meaning that means the same of what?
line 21: If I say glad, what's a synonym?
line 43–44: Words that have ... that have what?
line 46: Same or similar meanings ... such as?

Another focus on the form of the response is conveyed in the teacher's statement in line 12, 'You didn't say the whole sentence'. It seems more important to respond in complete sentences than to indicate an understanding of the concept of synonym. Although the teacher calls for complete sentences, the form of her subsequent questions invites a conversational one- or two-word response. The students appropriately provided short answers.

The students are confusing synonyms and antonyms, even though this is designated a *review* of synonyms. This confusion suggests there is some lack of clarity on the students' parts. However, they do not seem to discuss this issue. Although the teacher makes a statement connecting the word-study lesson with their 'learning similarity also in math, so we know very clearly what both terms mean' (lines 20–1), there is no evidence that her assumption is accurate. *Her* understanding of both terms (same and similar) may be clear. The students' answers suggest that there is still a problem in their understanding of the concept. Even if all of the answers from the few participants were correct, we could not assume that the whole class understood the concept. We as teachers often make such an assumption, even though we as students have participated in lessons where we were relieved that we hadn't been called on. This recognition of different understandings by each participant is an important component in analyzing student learning. Admittedly, there is insufficient data presented here to conclude anything definitive about the learning in this lesson. However, the slice provides us with a valuable sample for the procedures in analyzing classroom transcripts from a qualitative and quantitative perspective.

Analysis from a Hypothesis Generating Perspective

We can abstract from these mini-studies, suggesting wider tentative understandings about teaching and learning from these findings. These are phrased as hypotheses which have been generated from the studies.

(i) Students do not learn meaningful concepts from isolated definitions. Defining a term is not synonymous with understanding what that term means. Analogously, well-intentioned teachers tell students, but students do not learn from being told. Nor do they learn concepts from memorizing facts presented to them. Many theorists have written on this topic, including Bruner (1978), Mayher (1990), Smith (1988). Students' understanding develops from concrete to abstract. Students need to personally experience a phenomenon in order to develop or construct the concept in their own minds. They need to explore new activities using prior experiences as a base, consciously building bridges and connections.

(ii) Students' explanations of their understandings need to be probed — to clarify their confusions and connect isolated elements. Teacher evaluations (almost, O.K., and ignoring incorrect statements) do not help students understand in what ways they are close, what is right or what is wrong. Lengthier discussions in which students engaged in dialogs exploring options, speculating about alternatives, and/or explaining their reasoning would help students to clarify their understandings.

Within this context, students need to be encouraged to take risks — to take a chance, as a basis for moving their thinking onward. When there is a penalty for being in error, students are reluctant to place themselves in such a position. Students who depend on the teacher's positive evaluation (good!) never learn to develop their own criteria for correctness or acceptability. Nor do they learn to think independently. They regurgitate what the teacher seeks them to say. These students read the teacher's mind. While this strategy may be successful in certain classes, it does not contribute to an individual's cognitive development.

(iii) In teacher-centered classroom discussions there is a greater emphasis on getting through the lesson than for any individual student learning of concepts. Students are asked to repeat information previously given, not to have any personal involvement with the topic. In fact the topic itself is totally teacher driven, not connected to each student's personal experiences outside of school. Vygotsky (1962) and Britton (1982) have shown we learn by comparing similarities and differences between our previous experiences and our new ones. When a topic is not specifically connected to us, we need to establish a relationship between the new information and our knowledge. Without this bridge, there is no connection, resulting in the accumulation of seemingly unrelated bits of data. By helping Pharaoh connect the study of synonyms to his choice of words in stories, he might find a real world purpose for his studies. There was no indication that the teacher had any such plans.

There was no evidence that the students understood how the concept of synonymy was related to anything beyond the lesson. The issue of using this knowledge for some real purpose was not discussed. Why is this concept being taught? There does not seem to be any evidence to suggest the students need to use this information in their school projects. The teacher tells us it is 'part of the curriculum', but from her presentation the curriculum is comprised of hundreds of such isolated facts, rather than an integrated holistic perspective on society.

(iv) The curriculum which we implement should help enhance

our students' use of language, as well as their concepts. We see no such focus in this lesson. Dixon (1975) advocates that through using language, students increase their understanding of life, an important objective of education. Such a focus would diminish the value of labels and enhance the value of communication within a language arts curriculum.

(v) Knowledge is acquired slowly, systematically and contextually. It is difficult to assume that all students in one class have the same understanding or that they acquire information identically. Pharaoh might have been assisted in his concept acquisition by participating in a small group project based on his interests, attending to the influence of word choice on getting his message across, as shown by Wells (1981), and Levine in some of her laboratory experiences.

(vi) Although the students clearly know how to play the school games required, it seems unlikely that they are learning the concepts of synonymy, etc. well enough to connect them to their own lives. They will be unaffected as synonym users, and we would seriously question the value of a curriculum which demands that students become synonym labellers. Accumulating educational trivia cannot be the goal of instruction.

The two studies we have considered have provided us with very important insights into what happens as students engage in classroom activities. Through careful qualitative and quantitative data analysis, we are able to understand how we might improve classrooms to make them places where students grow.

References

BARNES, D. (1976) *From Communication to Curriculum*, Harmondsworth, Penguin.

BRAUSE, R.S. and MAYHER, J.S. (1983) 'Learning through teaching: Classroom teacher as researcher', *Language Arts*, September, 60, 6.

BRAUSE, R.S., MAYHER, J.S. and BRUNO, J. (1985) *An Investigation into Bilingual Students' Classroom Communicative Competence. Final Report to the National Institute of Education*, Rosslyn, VA, Clearinghouse on Bilingual Education.

BRITTON, J.N. (1982) *Prospect and Retrospect*, (edited by Gordon Pradl) Montclair, NJ, Boynton/Cook.

BRUNER, J.S. (1978) 'The role of dialogue in language acquisition' in SINCLAIR,

A., Jarvella, R.J. and Levelt, W.J.M. *The Child's Conception of Language*, New York, Springer-Verlag.

Dixon, J. (1975) *Growth Through English*, Oxford, Oxford University Press.

Levine, D. (1982) 'Subject specific vocabulary in school', paper prepared for Fordham University.

Mayher, J.S. (1990) *Uncommon Sense: Theoretical Practice in Language Education*, Portsmouth, NH, Boynton/Cook.

Mayher, J.S. and Brause, R.S. (1983) 'Learning through teaching: Teaching and learning vocabulary', *Language Arts*, 60, 8.

Smith, F. (1988) *Insult to Intelligence*, Portsmouth, NH, Heinemann.

Vygotsky, L.S. (1962) *Thought and Language*, Cambridge, MA, MIT Press.

Wells, G. (1981) *Learning Through Interaction*, New York, Cambridge University Press.

Chapter 8

Testing Hypotheses in Your Classroom

James L. Collins

It is early in the semester and I am discussing techniques of conferring with individual writers with fifteen teachers enrolled in my graduate course, *Teaching Basic Writing*. I'm advocating the use of writing conferences to help unskilled writers revise for fuller meaning. By encouraging writers to develop the latent and ill-formed content of their writing through asking questions designed to make the writer's meaning more explicit, teachers can get writers to say more about what's already been said, turn one paragraph into three, one page into four. This advice prompts a question from one of the teachers: Doesn't this lead to many more errors to correct?

Thus began one of the more interesting research projects I've been involved with. In this chapter I tell the story of that research to illustrate how teachers can test hypotheses in their own classrooms, schools and districts. My emphasis is on using quantitative methods to perform these tests. I will discuss key guidelines for selecting and using statistical tools. My purpose is not so much to help teachers understand statistics as it is to help teachers to use quantitative research to better understand their own teaching situations.

The phrase 'quantitative research' can be somewhat problematic, and the problem is not with the word 'research'. Teachers are already researchers. We observe children and make decisions based on our observations. When we teach research skills, we have our students use the library and survey the literature, and we are aware of the discovering, organizing, and communicating powers built into writing a research report. Conducting research probes, inquiries, and studies is really only a refinement of what teachers already do, however informally, as part of the business of teaching.

Mention quantitative methods, however, and we often feel inadequate about our numerical abilities and therefore reluctant to try such methods. In part, this is a natural tendency. We often avoid quantitative methods because we invest them with too much value. We forget that numbers are only as meaningful as the measures used to determine them. In the question raised by my students, for example, a key issue is what counts as an error; clearly, this must be decided before we start counting errors.

A frequent mistake made by beginning researchers, and many experienced ones, is placing methodology in a position of greater importance than knowing. This can keep us from clarifying what we want to know. An undue concern for methods can also weaken the research once it is underway. When studies are weak, for example, they are usually inadequate on the conceptual end rather than on the empirical end. The data are there and have been dutifully gathered and analyzed. The problem is that the study makes only a minimal contribution to theorizing, conceptualizing, or to just plain knowing. The questions beginning researchers often start with suggest that more attention is being paid to doing the research than to placing research in the service of knowing: How many subjects do I need? Should I use a control group?

This risk of 'the doing' having dominance over 'the knowing' seems especially high in quantitative studies, perhaps because numbers can lend prestige to an otherwise uninspired research project, perhaps because most of us are unfamiliar with statistics, and sometimes because the numbers themselves usurp our attention when we get involved in manipulating them. At any rate, there is sometimes a tendency to equate research and statistics, to confuse a question with a quantitative method used to answer it, so that the question is made to fit the method rather than the other way around.

I recommend a simple solution to these problematic aspects of quantitative research. Keep firmly in mind the idea that research methods are only tools. Methodology is the mechanical or instrumental aspect of research. Or perhaps an electronic metaphor is more appropriate these days; quantitative methods count and arrange numerical data as computers do, but computers don't determine what the numbers mean. The computer specialist's phrase: 'Garbage in, garbage out' is particularly important to remember in evaluating quantitative research. We ought not to worry about statistics, at least not to the extent that such worry causes us to avoid doing or reading research or to allow quantitative methods to dominate the research we do.

Statistical methods are tools used to record and analyze data. But these tools are useless (or worse, confounding) if we haven't clarified what we want to know: by observing classroom realities; by reading what other researchers have had to say; and by deciding what to count and how to quantify observations. Quantification is merely one step among many in the research process. Granted, there can be times when a research question is simply handed to us, and the spotlight seems to be immediately on quantitative methodology: if a principal wants English teachers to justify continued reduced class sizes in developmental sections, for example, or if a supervisor will only agree to inservice training for elementary teachers if the training includes a quantitative design for measuring its effectiveness.

These cases often seem to demand numerical treatment. The principal's request might be fulfilled by a study to determine relations between class size and language performance. The supervisor's demand might be met by a study using published instruments to measure teacher behaviors before and after in-service training. Even in these cases, however, we should not rush unprepared into the statistical treatment of data. In either of these cases, it would be crucial to determine exactly what the variables or factors to be measured would be: What exactly is being claimed as the effect of reduced class size? Or which aspects of teacher performance are supposed to be influenced by the in-service program? A descriptive phase of the research should precede hypothesis testing, since it is necessary to create any hypothesis before we test it.

Creating Hypotheses

Before we can test, we must describe. The descriptive phase of hypothesis testing research includes deliberations based in observations of reality and in the study of prior research. We don't count or test or measure until we determine what we want to know. In hypothesis testing research, this guideline can be simply stated: Come up with a reasonable hypothesis before you bother testing it. Any hypothesis is really a guess or a prediction, and the best guesses or predictions are those in tune with available evidence. If the house is cold, for example, we hypothesize that the thermostat should be turned up, and if turning it up isn't followed by the familiar noise of the furnace, we further hypothesize that the pilot flame has gone out, and so on. We eliminate other guesses, such as the gas company has shut us off (since we know we have paid the bill) or that the furnace has blown up (since there's no fire) because they are contrary to the evidence. The only difference between a scientific or researchable hypothesis and our every day guesses and predictions is that hypotheses are derived from uncommonsense theories (see chapter 1).

And so it is with educational research. We spend some time choosing our best guess. Hypotheses are made, not born. In the research project I referred to in my opening paragraph, our hypotheses were the result of reading (for example: Beach[1], on analyzing writing conferences; Cooper[2], and Collins, 1981, on teacher-student conferencing strategies; Shaughnessy, 1977, and Perl, 1980, on basic writers). They were the result of careful observation, since we were a group of experienced teachers who looked at actual drafts of student writing and studied transcripts and tapes of actual writing conferences. And our hypotheses were also the result of class discussion and debate during which we turned initially strong but amorphous beliefs into researchable hypotheses: writing is a highly complex and recursive activity; students are generally anxious about writing and extremely sensitive to criticism; parents, principals, and politicians want us to get errors out of the writing. We argued two main opinions: conferring with writers to help them develop content is more useful than only correcting errors, and encouraging writers to elaborate content might increase the number of errors in their writing.

Our discussions led to clarification of our research question. We decided that the question (Won't content-oriented conferencing lead to many more errors to correct?) refers to comparisons between revisions of essays rather than to comparisons of first drafts. We supported this interpretation of our question by examining 'naturally occurrring' patterns of error between initial and revised drafts; that is, we wondered what happens to errors as students revise their writing without the teacher (or peer) intervention provided by conferencing. Our sense was that students, left to their own designs, would tend to merely copy their writing, reproducing first draft errors in second drafts. We used some descriptive statistics to examine this hypothesis.

My point here is that statistical procedures can be part of the describing phase of research which precedes the testing phase. These procedures allow us to discover latent patterns in numerical data. I will illustrate some key descriptive statistical tools with an example from our study.

One such tool is figuring percentages. In a class of twenty-six students, we discovered that initial drafts contained a total of 231 errors, and that 24 per cent of these were eliminated or corrected in revised drafts. By itself, this statistic seems to indicate a reduction in errors between drafts. However, another tool, the figuring of mean numbers of errors in both drafts, gives us a quite different picture. The writers produced an average of 8.88 errors in first drafts but 9.15 errors in second drafts. Thus, using mean numbers, we can see that errors are not reduced; the number stays approximately the same across drafts. Apparently, for writers in this class in response to one task, the tendency is to correct or eliminate some errors but introduce an almost equal number. Another tool of descriptive statistics, figuring the spread or dispersion of scores, adds a little more information to the picture by showing us that on both first and second drafts the range of errors for individual writers is from two to twenty.

By now we begin to suspect a strong relationship between errors in first drafts and errors in second drafts. This is a refinement of our earlier hypothesis that students tend to copy rather than correct while revising, and it can be examined using a technique called correlational analysis. This technique involves measuring variables and determining if they are related by co-occurrence. Height and weight are frequently used examples of such variables; these go together or are associated with each other, yet we make no claim that height causes weight, since it is possible to be short and heavy. Perhaps another familiar example is the use of product-moment correlation to determine reliability between ratings of essays for competency testing or other writing assessments. Here we want to know the extent to which one reader's score agrees with a second reader's.

Correlational analysis can be used to measure the strength of the relationship between first and second draft errors in our example of twenty-six writers. This is done by graphically plotting data on a scatter diagram. Using graph paper (it makes the job easier), we draw a vertical axis and a horizontal one, and along both we number points, using even numbers ranging from two to twenty-two (no need to include odds). Then we put a dot where each writer's first draft score intersects with the writer's second draft score. The final diagram is presented in figure 8.1.

This scatter diagram shows the relationship between the numbers of errors on first and second drafts for twenty-six writers, in one classroom, writing in response to one task. We can be confident we have discovered a rather strong relationship because the plotted scores cluster within a narrow elliptical outline, illustrated in figure 8.2 with a broken line.

We can next use a statistical formula to see how closely our relationship aproximates a perfect one. Such a formula gives us a decimal fraction, and the closer it comes to 1.00, the stronger the relationship. Using the formula for Pearson product-moment corre-

Figure 8.1: *Scatter diagram of number of errors on two drafts for twenty-six writers*

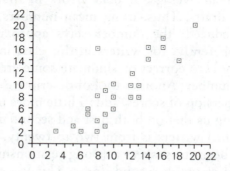

Figure 8.2: *Outlining clustered error scores*

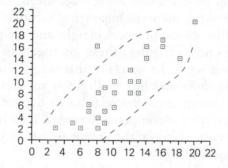

lation, we figured our correlation in the above example at .90, thus supporting the observation that we had discovered a strong relationship between first and second draft errors.

With this first mention of a statistical formula, I want to take time out for a couple of words about such formulas. The words are Don't Panic. Formulas are not inherently difficult; indeed they are meant to be standardized short cuts. The real problem with statistical formulas resides not in using them. Rather, it's remembering how and when to use each fomula which creates difficulties. Research is not a high school physics test; we're not cheating if we look up formulas and guidelines for using them. In the example just reviewed, we used a calculator to work through a twelve-step process for figuring the correlation, and one step included an additional nine-step process for figuring standard deviations. More importantly, we used a statistics textbook (Shavelson, 1981) to guide us in our calculations. Once we knew which formula to use (the brain part of the process) we followed the 'recipe' in the text (the no-brain part of the process). Skills involved in using statistical formulas are learned the same way other skills, like cooking or writing, are acquired, by doing, and by getting help when it is needed.

Correlational analysis, thus, gives us insight into strengths of relations between variables. At this point, we have tentative hypotheses in mind: students, left to their own designs, will only copy their writing and therefore reproduce errors; students will find and correct errors; students will revise and introduce new errors in the process, but we are not yet testing any hypothesis. Correlational analysis, by itself, cannot get to underlying causes. What it can do is show us that a cause is worth probing for, that a hypothesis has some merit.

Like the hypothesis-generating research discussed in other chapters of this book, descriptive statistics can help us to understand our teaching situations. In the hypothesis testing process, these methods help us choose our best bets. In our example, we identified two such bets. We agreed we were betting that conferences in which teachers direct students to work on elaborating the content of their writing would cause them to produce longer essays than students in a control group, and longer essays would cause students to produce greater numbers of errors than students in the control group. We realized that in the second of these two hypotheses we would have to measure the rate of error production and not just the frequency. Ten errors in a 100 word essay, for example, are not logically equal to ten errors in a 200 word essay.

Even after hypothesizing that content oriented writing conferences would increase the rate of error in student writing, we were prepared to accept a decrease as well, since some members of our research team were betting on one. Some of us felt that revising for content requires close reading, and close reading leads to a reduction in the rate of error. Others believed that revising for content requires the writer to take additional risks, and a higher level of risk-taking leads to a higher rate of error. This disagreement is attributable, I suspect, to the quality of our group; we were sixteen good and experienced teachers working together in a graduate course, and any hypothesis we totally agreed on would probably not be worth testing because it would be an obvious fact. We weren't worried about our opposing bets concerning our second hypothesis because we were getting ready to test a *null* hypothesis, a prediction that no change would result, that no statistically significant difference would be found in our comparison data. I will come back to this idea later; for now, I only want to make the point that the exact wording of a research hypothesis is temporary. The hypothesis should predict change in an expected or 'hoped for' direction, owing to the influence of a variable introduced to create change. Still, we are never so committed to our hypothesis that we blind ourselves to other possibilities, namely, no change, or change in the opposite direction.

Before leaving this section on creating hypotheses, I want to highlight the importance of the review of related research. The guideline here is to lean heavily and critically on prior scholarship. The best way to build a conceptual base for hypothesis testing, or any research, is to study what has gone before. Too often the review of the literature aspect of research is seen as a mere academic exercise, something to be avoided or tucked away in a particularly boring section of the research report or dissertation. This is nonsense. The review of related scholarship is an integral part of research. It informs our definition of the question or hypothesis, the means we use to carry out the investigation, and the ways we interpret our findings. Skipping this step would probably lead to a casual inquiry, one which asks 'So what?' questions such as these, taken from a recent survey of parents in a suburban, upstate New York school district:

8 How would you compare your feeling about the composition program in (our) schools with programs you have heard of elsewhere?
— better
— about the same
— inadequate

9 Would you help us improve our composition program by writing a brief analysis of our composition program based on the response you gave above in #8?

_____

_____

10 How would you rank (our) composition program in terms of the program you experienced as a child?
— better
— about the same
— inadequate
— different

The purpose of such questions seems more political than educational; the school system seems to be fishing for a 'We're OK' evaluation of its writing program. This observation is supported by the fact that question 9 is the real heart of the matter and could have been the subject of many questions rather than just one asking for a three-line, difficult to tabulate, response. The observation is also supported by language in the cover letter accompanying the survey where existing 'high academic standards', 'talented children', and 'exemplary system' are mentioned. Ironically, the cover letter also promises that a review of research will be conducted as part of the study of the writing program. What should have come before the project will come after, probably insuring that we will stay with what (we think) we know already.

In our conferencing and errors study, we avoided the mistake of not reading prior scholarship. Our bibliography on writing conferences, for example, included forty-nine items. And we were critical readers. We noticed that an earlier, informal, study of the effects of content-oriented conferencing on error production claimed that writers produce 25 per cent fewer errors in second drafts compared to first drafts, but that the information provided in the report did not support this generalization. No control group was used in the study, prior instruction had emphasized error correction, and we were not able to tell how errors were counted, that is whether the researcher had included only errors occurring in first drafts as they recur or not in second drafts, or whether new errors in second drafts were counted as well; we also had trouble deciding exactly what types of errors were included and whether frequency of error or rate of error was measured. We profited from our deliberations concerning this study, not by rejecting it outright, but rather by determining to avoid the same problems in our own study.

Testing Hypotheses

So far we have seen that the process of testing hypotheses begins with a research question from which we create one or more research hypotheses. In our conferencing and errors example we derived two hypotheses from the initial question:

Research Question: Will conferences encouraging writers to say more about the content of their writing cause them to produce more errors?

Research Hypothesis (H1): Content oriented conferencing will cause essays to be longer than essays produced without such conferencing.

Research Hypothesis (H2): Content oriented conferencing will cause essays to show a higher rate of error than essays revised without such conferencing.

The actual testing of hypotheses involves several more steps: identifying variables and measures to include in the study; selecting a research design; sampling; statistical testing; and determining what our findings mean. I shall say more about each of these steps, but first I want to discuss the matter of achieving validity in hypothesis-testing studies.

Hypothesis testing means examining causal inferences. Hypotheses predict that something causes something else — a discussion approach to *Hamlet* will produce better writing about the play than a lecture method; the study of words in meaningful contexts will produce higher scores on vocabulary tests than the study of word lists; word processing accelerates the development of writing abilities; and so on. Testing hypotheses, therefore, means determining the tenability of causal inferences. For a causal inference to be tenable, three conditions must be met. The first is a statistically significant difference between experimental and control groups in the study. Statistical significance reduces the probability that observed differences are due to chance or sampling error. The second condition is a proper time sequence; the cause has to come before its effect. This seems perfectly obvious, but the condition is not always easily met. Should a study showing a strong relation between writing ability and writing apprehension, for example, lead to the hypothesis that either one causes the other? No, since we can't tell which comes first, or indeed, whether both writing ability and writing apprehension are caused by some other factor. The third condition is that no other plausible explanation can account for the observed effect. This condition is achieved or approximated by control over variables and by random selection. Notice that only one of these necessary conditions has something to do with statistics. The others result from decisions we make while designing the study and interpreting our findings.

These conditions, when properly met, establish validity of two general types, external and internal. The external validity of a research study is the extent to which the findings of the study can be generalized to people or situations other than those directly observed in the study. Internal validity is the extent to which the outcomes of the study result from variables measured in the study, rather than from other variables (Shavelson, 1981). In each of the steps which follow, it is a concern for external and internal validity which more than anything else determines the decisions we make.

Identifying Variables and Measures

Here we are after precise, working definitions. We begin this step by considering the independent variable, the one we've selected to observe its relation to another variable, the dependent one. Independence in this sense does not mean 'independent of the researcher'. Instead, it has nearly the opposite meaning; the independent variable is the one we create or introduce to examine its effect on the dependent variable. The independent variable provides the hypothesized cause, and the dependent one manifests observed effects (and hence depends on the independent variable).

In our study we had two independent variables: content-oriented conferencing and the combined influences of teachers and classroom situations. The first variable had two interrelated aspects: what teachers say to students and how they say it. Conferring with writers about the content of the writing means, first, having some specific things to say, and it means, also, saying them in certain ways. We spent some time deciding what to say and how to say it, and we practiced these techniques on each other. We limited our comments to questioning writers (the 'how to say') about items already mentioned in the writing (the 'what to say'). If a person's hair, for example, was mentioned by a writer, we might ask for useful information about the hair: How long? What color? How styled?

Our second independent variable was included because we wanted to see if the effects of content-oriented conferencing varied with teachers and classrooms. Not including this variable would have meant lumping together the influence of conferencing and the influence of teachers working in classrooms. This would have kept us from generalizing beyond teachers in the study, since our independent variable would have consisted of 'conferencing as conducted by these particular teachers in their classrooms'. (Identifying two independent variables affects other steps in the hypothesis testing process, as I will show later.)

The objective in this step is to narrow the independent variable, to precisely or operationally define it, so that it becomes a specific behavior to be applied uniformly to experimental groups in the study. Notice there is a trade-off in this process of narrowly defining variables. The closer the independent variable comes to precisely specified behavior, the less it resembles what teachers actually do in real classrooms.

I should mention that we did not actually observe the teachers. We assumed that in delivering the conferencing, they would be as specific, questioning, and content-centered as we wanted them to be. In some ways this is a potential weakness in the study, since without actually observing the teachers in conference we couldn't be completely sure they were behaving within our specified limits. This is an example of how logistical and other practical problems influence research designs.

We identified two measures for our dependent variables: *mean length of revised essays* and *mean rates of error*. Dependent variables are those influenced (or not) by independent ones; they are what we observe and measure in terms of response to independent variables.

Hypothesis testing, once all else is under control, comes down to examining this connection between variables. This means precisely defining and measuring the dependent variable, for both experimental and control groups, to set up the opportunity of noticing its possible causal connection to the independent variable. We defined our dependent variables by deciding what counts as a word and as an error. We decided, for example, that proper names and contractions would be counted as one word, and we used National Assessment of Educational Progress (1980) 'Mechanics' scoring guidelines to decide, for example, when a sentence fragment is an error. We measured both length and errors by simply counting.

As I mentioned earlier, we expressed our measure of errors not as a frequency but as a proportion. We converted frequency of error to rate of error by dividing total errors in each essay by the total words in the essay and multiplying by 100; this adjusted our data to rate of errors per 100 words so that texts of differing lengths could be compared for differences in errors. Counting words proved to be relatively straightforward, but counting errors was more difficult. Deciding when to score a sentence for awkwardness, for example, can get complicated.

This difficulty can be overcome by using independent raters, people other than the researchers, to perform reliability checks. Reliability is the extent to which a design actually measures what it proposes to measure. We could have determined reliability by statistically checking agreement (correlation again) between the two sets of ratings provided by independent raters trained in the use of the measures. In our study, we used an even simpler method than correlation for establishing reliability. We eliminated from further consideration in the study those errors which were not scored exactly alike by the independent raters. Thus, we only counted those errors which independent raters agreed were errors.

In addition to the variables specified by the hypothesis, other variables deserve our attention. We must control variables which might introduce the 'other plausible explanation' I mentioned earlier. These, appropriately enough, are called control variables. The idea here is to neutralize any variables which might influence the causal connection we are probing for. We try to isolate the independent and dependent variables from all else which is actively varying. Such isolation, of course, is an ideal which the researcher can only hope to approximate. Still, we do the best we can. In our study, for example, we administered the same writing task, worded in exactly the same way, to both experimental and control groups:

Describe the physical appearance of someone you know well to someone your age who has never seen the person.

We also defined what teachers would do in the control sections. The control teachers, we decided, would give writers a chance to revise but not direct their attention to content. Teachers would circulate among writers and be available to answer questions, as in experimental sections, but would not initiate conferences and question writers about the content of their writing. Further controls were these: we gave both experimental and control groups the same amounts of time to write and revise; we controlled for the effects of prior instruction, as best we could, by using the same teachers in experimental and control classes, and we controlled for variations in writing ability by including only writers identified as relatively unskilled.

Notice, again, that in exerting these controls we trade what really goes on in classrooms for conditions which begin to resemble those of laboratories. Surely this must influence the way we interpret our findings. By controlling the teacher variable, for example, we sacrifice some independence between our experimental and control groups. To not control this variable, though, might mean we are actually measuring teaching styles or differences in curriculum. So we made our trades, and we kept them in mind when we decided what our findings meant. Thus, when we interpret our results, we do so in light of both existing research and theory and the strengths and limits of the methods we used.

Selecting a Research Design

When the hypothesis is one predicting an effect from a cause, we choose an experimental design. The basic idea in an experimental design is that we compare two equivalent and independent groups before and after, or at least after we have administered a treatment to one of the groups. Following Campbell and Stanley (1963), I shall present several of the more frequently used experimental designs. In this discussion, the letter X indicates an experimental treatment, and the letter O indicates an observation (i.e., a test of some sort). Campbell and Stanley divide experimental designs into three categories: pre-experimental, true experimental and quasi-experimental; they also include a correlational category, as we have done.

An example of the pre-experimental category is the *one-group pretest-posttest design*. In this case, we would introduce an experimental treatment between making pre-test and post-test observations of one group only. The conventional way of representing such a design is:

$$\text{Example 1: O1} \longrightarrow \text{X} \longrightarrow \text{O2}$$

This design could be used, for example, to explore relations between instruction and achievement, as when we give students a standardized reading test (O1) then a particular program of instruction in reading (X), followed by another version of the reading test (O2). This process might indicate an improvement in reading abilities, but we cannot claim the program of instruction caused the improvement.

To make such a claim (or to reject it), we have to use a true experimental or a quasi-experimental design; that is, we have to include a control group in the design so we can compare students receiving the treatment with peers who did not receive it. One such design of the true experimental variety is the *pre-test-post-test control group design* and is represented as:

$$\text{Example 2: R} \begin{cases} \text{O1} \longrightarrow \text{X} \longrightarrow \text{O2} \\ \\ \text{O3} \longrightarrow \text{-} \longrightarrow \text{O4} \end{cases}$$

In this example, R represents the process of randomly selecting members of control and experimental groups. The experimental group is observed, treated and observed again. The control group is also observed twice, but in their case the experimental treatment is withheld.

Ideally, we should have used a true experimental design in the conferencing and errors study, but since we had to use intact classes, and since a pretest-posttest design was unnecessary, we selected a modified *post-test-only control group design*. This design is represented as:

$$\text{Example 3: R} \left[\begin{array}{l} X \longrightarrow O1 \\ \\ \text{-- -} \longrightarrow O2 \end{array} \right.$$

Our implementation of this design used experimental and control groups, but it did not include randomly assigning individual subjects to these groups. In our case, we made classes our unit of analysis and randomly assigned pre-existing classes to experimental and control groups. Quasi-randomization was as close as educational realities would let us come to true randomization, since we decided that providing and withholding certain types of writing conferences to individual students in the same classrooms would be confusing and unnecessarily burdensome. (It would also be less likely to represent a teacher's educational practice, and therefore, less likely to give us the kind of generalized result we were looking for.)

Sampling

This step involves selecting subjects and assigning them to groups in the research study. Here the rule is to make sure that the sample chosen for participation in the study is randomly selected from any larger population to which we want to generalize our findings. If the purpose of the study, for example, is to learn something about tenth graders in one suburban high school, then the sample can be limited to, or drawn from, that population. Limiting the sample, however, limits the generalizability of findings, since we cannot infer that tenth graders are necessarily alike across schools and districts. To achieve randomness for larger populations, we first decide the degree to which the population is a homogeneous mass or a collection of heterogeneous units. Generally, samples must be larger and more widely distributed for heterogeneous units than for relatively homogeneous ones, though an even more general rule is always that larger samples are better than smaller ones, within the constraints of manageability.

Heterogeneous populations require proportional representation of sub-groups in the sample. This is called stratified sampling, since we want to make sure that various strata, such as urban-suburban schools, grade levels, achievement levels, present in the population are present proportionately in the sample as well. For both types of populations, homogeneous and heterogeneous, we go from the total population to create a sample using a process of random selection, and this is usually achieved through a table of random numbers. Such a table is appended to almost any statistics textbook, and the book also contains directions for using the table. The basic idea here is that all members of populations must have an equal chance of being selected as members of the sample to be studied.

Now for the practical side of these remarks concerning sampling techniques. In school settings, students are organized into classes, meaning that it is usually not possible to select populations and samples consisting strictly of individuals. Subjects in the study, most likely, will be decided in part by whatever administrative decision has assigned students to particular classrooms. This is not a problem, as long as we keep some guidelines in mind. Comparing pre-existing classes or groups of students can be done if we are confident that the groups are similar and if we randomly assign groups of subjects to experimental and control groups in the study. This means some observing or pre-testing for pre-treatment equivalence between experimental and control groups (or using a test for statistical significance which appropriately compensates for initial differences). And it means tossing a coin, or some such random method, to assign classes of students to groups in the study.

In the conferencing and errors study, we used the following method of choosing a sample of subjects for the study. From the more than sixty English classes taught by teachers in my course, we selected twenty classes containing unskilled writers. We limited the research to less competent writers because ours was a course in teaching basic writing, and we determined which classes contained unskilled writers by teacher perceptions and, where available, by scores on competency tests or placement tests of writing ability. From these twenty classes we selected six comprising three matched pairs. Each pair of classes was taught by the same teacher and represented one of three grade levels, grade ten through twelve. Next we randomly assigned three classes, one from each pair, to the experimental group and the three others to the control group. All students in these classes received either experimental or control treatments, and twenty-four from each class were randomly selected for data analysis; we made this final selection to establish samples of equal size.

Statistical Testing

This step in the hypothesis-testing process consists of several procedures: rewording hypotheses as null hypotheses, choosing an appropriate statistical test and setting the probability level, gathering and analyzing data, and deciding whether to phrase the question as a null hypothesis.

Rewording hypotheses as null hypotheses means transforming hypotheses that are not yet ready to be tested into ones that are. We do this by becoming explicit about the changes we expect. Our research hypotheses, for example, don't say how much longer essays will be or how much higher the rate of error will be. Research hypotheses are made specific enough to be tested by restating them as null hypotheses, predicting in our example, as in most cases, that no differences due to factors other than chance will be found:

> *Null Hypothesis (H0)*: Content-oriented conferencing will cause essays to be no different in mean length than essays produced without such conferencing.

> *Null Hypothesis (H0)*: Content-oriented conferencing will cause essays to be no different in mean rate of errors than essays produced without such conferencing.

Once we have a null hypothesis we select statistical techniques and a probability level and apply these to the data gathered from our experiment, to decide whether or not to reject the null hypothesis. The appropriate statistical test is determined by the research design. Two of the more common tests are the t test and the F test or ANOVA (for Analysis of Variance). A t test is an appropriate one to use to compare two sets of sample data, as for example in comparing the effectiveness of two methods of instruction or in determining if two versions of a test are comparable. The methods of instruction, or the versions of the test, are the independent variable, and we try them out on two different samples of students to compare the methods or tests. A one-way ANOVA can be used in research studies including one independent variable and more than two samples of data, as when we compare the effectiveness of three methods of teaching reading; the three methods comprise one independent variable and we randomly assign students to each method. A two-way ANOVA is used when we have more than one independent variable; this permits the simultaneous examination of the effects of two independent variables on a dependent variable. Two-way ANOVA, thus, was the appropriate statistical technique for analysis of data in our conferencing and errors study, since we included two independent variables. For more information on using these, and other, statistical tests, consult any standard statistics textbook.

Setting the probability level refers to deciding how much risk we are willing to take of being wrong when we decide whether or not to reject the null hypothesis. Researchers usually set this risk level at $P = .05$ or $P = .01$. In our study we set the probability level at $P = .05$, meaning that if we decided to reject the null hypotheses, the probability was $P = .05$ that we were making the wrong decision. Notice that the probability level is always set prior to running the experiment; setting it after the data are collected can lead to the accusation that a level was chosen to accommodate the data.

Once we have our hypotheses, variables and measures, research design, samples, and statistical tests, we set the process in motion. We run the experiment collecting our data for analysis. If our planning has been thorough enough, there will be no surprises at this stage. Two caveats, though, are worth mentioning.

The first concerns research ethics. Here the guideline is to obtain permission from anyone who is likely to become upset or angry about our research. These people can include parents and administrators, and of course, they also include the subjects or participants in the research. This guideline is a flexible one. In my own research, I make a distinction between ordinary research, that which closely resembles what normally happens is schools, and an extraordinary variety, that which would interrupt normal school processes. I stay away from this second type entirely, and I seek permission for the first.

We should tell participants in a study when we are probing for information we don't ordinarily have access to, and we should give them a chance to accept or reject the opportunity to participate. This guideline is stricter for university-sponsored or funded research. You should always check for 'Human Subjects at Risk' or informed consent requirements.

This brings me to the second note of caution I referred to, which concerns telling subjects in an experiment that they are participating in an experiment. The guideline is: Don't tell them that. This second caveat does not contradict the first. We can tell people about our research without using the language of experimentation. And we should, because people tend to perform better when they know they're part of an experiment. This tendency is called the Hawthorne Effect, named after the location of the factory where research on the effects of lighting on production was conducted. Researchers 'discovered' that the lower the lighting, the greater productivity became. What really happened was the experimental group wanted to show the researchers what they could do, even under adverse conditions.

Finally, after all of the data are collected (in our study, after tasks were administered and all of the words and errors were counted), we are ready to statistically test our hypothesis. I shall illustrate the mechanics of significance testing with data from our study. The process begins by constructing a matrix of cells with samples in the study assigned to separate cells, as in the matrix below. Here N refers to the number of subjects in each sample, and the matrix is referred to as a 2 X 3 ('two by three') ANOVA, because there are two rows (horizontal) and three columns (vertical) in the six cells of data (see table 8.1). This

Table 8.1: *Matrix pattern for presenting sample studied*

	Experimentals	Controls
Teacher 1	N = 24	N = 24
Teacher 2	N = 24	N = 24
Teacher 3	N = 24	N = 24

matrix pattern allows us next to examine sample means or averages for each of our two hypotheses. For the hypothesis concerning length of essay, expressed as total words we establish table 8.2. And for the hypothesis concerning rate of error, expressed as errors per 100 words we present table 8.3. Clearly, the sample means are different, but we want to know if the differences are statistically significant. Statistical testing determines the probability that a null hypothesis is false based on the likelihood that an obtained difference between means is due to chance. We decide not to reject the null hypothesis if there is a high probability that the difference between means for experimental and control groups could have resulted from chance. We decide to reject

Table 8.2: Comparing length of essay

	Experimentals	Controls
Teacher 1	86.5	68.3
Teacher 2	116.7	90.9
Teacher 3	123.4	115.8

Table 8.3: Comparing error rates

	Experimentals	Controls
Teacher 1	9.4	11.5
Teacher 2	8.9	12.9
Teacher 3	11.0	8.9

the null hypothesis if there is a low probability that the difference between sample means is due to chance. Notice that the statistical testing only determines the probability that the findings occurred by chance; whether the difference in mean scores is the result of the experimental treatment or other factors is something we decide as we interpret the statistical findings.

Using the two-way ANOVA technique allows us to perform three tests on each of our null hypotheses: test the difference between experimental and control groups (represented by the two columns of data); test the difference among influences of the three teachers and their classroom situations (represented by the three rows of data); and test for an interaction effect, so named because it examines the way in which teaching method (content oriented conferencing or its absence) interacts with teachers and classroom contexts. The two-way ANOVA technique uses quite complex calculations to determine whether each of these tests is statistically significant. The conventional way of presenting the results of a two-way ANOVA is presented in table 8.4 showing our results for length of essay.

These findings indicate that we should reject the null hypothesis claiming no difference in length of essays between experimental and

Table 8.4: Two-Way ANOVA for Length of Essays

	Sum of squares	Degrees of freedom	Mean square	F	
Between rows	43113.167	2	21556.583	11.741	P < .001
Between columns	10404.001	1	10404.001	5.667	P = .018
Interaction	1988.166	2	994.083	.541	P = .982
Within cells	253368.416	138	1836.003		
Total	308873.749				

Table 8.5: Two-Way ANOVA for Rate of Error

	Sum of squares	Degrees of freedom	Mean square	F	
Between rows	22.676	2	22.676	..245	P < 1.000
Between columns	66.423	1	66.423	1.437	P = .231
Interaction	232.479	2	116.239	2.516	P = .083
Within cells	6376.822	138	46.209		
Total	6698.399				

control groups, since .018 is below the .05 probability level we set. Notice also that length of essays varies between rows in a highly significant way ($P < .001$), indicating that length of essay is being influenced by some other factor, such as grade level or prior instruction. The test for an interaction between experimental treatment and teacher/classroom influences was not significant, indicating that one kind of variation in length, with conferencing, does not depend on the other, with teacher or classroom.

The results of another two-way ANOVA presented in table 8.5 show that our second null hypothesis cannot be rejected. This time probability levels are all above .05, and we do not reject the null hypothesis. Differences among sample means are not statistically significant in this case.

Interpreting Findings

Once the hypothesis has been tested for statistical significance, it is time to interpret the results. Here, as throughout the study, we proceed with caution. In the example I've used, we interpret our findings by saying that teacher-student conferences emphasizing revision for content led to longer essays but did not increase the rate of error. The question which prompted the research: — Doesn't conferencing for increasingly explicit content lead to more errors to correct? — is answered. Such conferencing leads to longer essays but not an increased rate of error. Still, the question generalizes more than does our study, and additional research would have to be done to really answer it. Do writers find and correct some errors and introduce others? Is rate of error really independent of anything teachers say to writers? Would our results be similar if we used truly independent groups of writers, say from different districts or different states? Or were we really measuring very similar writers in our study, since they came from the same teachers' classrooms?

Such questions and others lead us always to carefully qualify research findings. And they lead, where the spirit is willing, to additional research.

Conclusion

In closing this chapter, I want to return to my starting point. I have focussed on some key concepts and techniques in my portrait of statistical hypothesis testing, and it is time to step back and look at the whole picture again. Statistical methods are tools. They are not the research. Research really means thinking as hard as you can about the subject at hand. We should consider statistical procedures as aids to our thinking, and we should let the thinking itself, the purpose of the research, decide whether, when, and how to use numbers. Rather than deciding, or not, to do a statistical probe, inquiry, or dissertation, we decide what we want to know. The purpose of the research then guides decisions about which tools to use.

When the purpose of the research is to describe, statistical procedures can fit in as a way of summarizing and tabulating data. We might, for example, want to know what English faculty at two local community colleges would like entering students to have read, because, let's say, two-thirds of our graduating seniors attend these schools, according to our guidance office records. We design a rather straightforward questionnaire, listing titles, providing spaces for other choices, and asking respondents to indicate ten choices. This is an example of nominal or classification data; the titles of books become the categories of information. In this case we could survey the entire population of professors and summarize their collective recommendations for each title to reflect their preferences revealed by each questionnaire. Clearly, such a project involves a kind of hypothesis testing, since we are examining the assumption that our curriculum and instruction prepare our graduates for college.

Similar applications of descriptive statistics would also be valuable. We might, for example, examine the way literacy is portrayed in selected adolescent novels by counting references to reading and writing in five or ten of them and then classifying the references into types such as 'low level' for street signs, brief personal notes, shopping lists, etc., and 'advanced' for books, newspapers, documents, etc. Here the hypothesis is that we are, or are not, giving students hidden messages about literacy in the reading we have them do.

When the purpose of research extends beyond description to inference-making, other statistical procedures might be selected. In the 'recommended texts' example, the purpose of the research might move beyond an easily accessible population such as English faculty at two local community colleges, beyond types of recommendations to strengths of recommendations, and beyond uniformity in responses to diversity such as public versus private schools, English versus other disciplines, or contemporary fiction versus other types of texts.

In all this we can see that the purpose of the research is what determines its scope and content. Similarly, the purpose of our research is the best guideline in deciding when to use numbers and how to manipulate them. One final note: Although I have discussed quantitative research, what I actually did to write this chapter was do a case study of my research group. Appropriately, the next chapter will focus on case studies.

Notes

1 BEACH, R. (1980) 'Development of a category system for the analysis of teacher/student conferences', paper presented at the meeting of the Conference on College Composition and Communication, Washington, D.C., March.
2 COOPER, C.R. (1975) 'Responding to student writing' in FINN, P.J. and PETTY, W.T. (Eds) *The Writing Processes of Students,* Report of the First Annual Conference on Language Arts, State University of New York at Buffalo.

References

CAMPBELL, D.T. and STANLEY, J.C. (1963) 'Experimental and quasi-experimental designs for research on teaching' in GAGE, N.L. (Ed.). *Handbook of Research on Teaching*, Chicago, IL, Rand McNally.
COLLINS, J.L. (1981) 'Speaking, writing, and teaching for meaning' in KROLL,

James L. Collins

B. and Vann, R. (Eds) *Exploring Speaking-writing Relationships: Connections and Contrasts*, Urbana, IL, National Council of Teachers of English.

National Assessment of Educational Progress (1980) *Writing Achievement, 1969–70* (Vol. 1), report no. 10-W-01. Denver, CO, Education Commission of the States.

Perl, S. (1980) 'A look at basic writers in the process of composing' in Kasden, L.N. and Hoeber, D.R. (Eds) *Basic Writing*. Urbana, IL, National Council of Teachers of English.

Shaughnessy, M.P. (1977) *Errors and Expectations*, New York, Oxford University Press.

Shavelson, R.J. (1981) *Statistical Reasoning for the Behavioral Sciences*. Boston, MA, Allyn and Bacon.

Chapter 9

Hypothesis Generating Studies in Your Classroom

Rita S. Brause

Hypothesis generating research explores phenomena which are unexplained by contemporary theories, such as the many ways students get turns-at-talk in classrooms. The intent of hypothesis generating studies is to increase knowledge and thereby improve professional practice. The purpose of this chapter is to provide guidance in the conduct of such inquiries as part of our teaching. As an introduction we will briefly consider two instances in which hypotheses are generated naturally as everyday events.

Hypothesis Generating Experiences in Life

In *Alice in Wonderland*, Alice came upon people and events that confused her. As Alice explored and became frustrated, she wondered about how to get food, how to get help, and how to make friends. Her wondering led her to create alternative, working hypotheses and speculative predictions which guided her subsequent actions. As she traveled in the Wondrous World down under, she was subjected to seemingly arbitrary rules. This experience caused her to revise her assumptions. She slowly inferred some of the rules for participating in Wonderland. When the Mad Hatter spoke to her at tea in an unusual way, she wondered and made hypotheses about how to get along better with him. There were inconsistencies between people's actions and her predictions about their actions. When she recognized that her predictions were not realized, she generated additional hypotheses and questions, speculated about future actions, and tested her hunches. The approach she used, albeit unconscious, is consistent with researchers who conduct hypothesis generating studies.

Let's consider an episode from my teaching as another instance of hypothesis generating. During a discussion about the characteristics of language used in different situations we recognized the need for real 'data' such as the transcripts of actual talk. Five students opened their books to transcripts — five books and twenty students in one class! If only I had xeroxed one transcript for all of us to look at! Now what do I do? We needed data to ground our discussion. I spontaneously suggested we move into five groups with each group sharing one book. The students negotiated access to the text. Collaboration was inevitable as a few individuals tentatively made comments and asides. With my encouragement, all freely shared their impressions within the small group. I 'hopped' from group to group to monitor and guide progress. I wanted to encourage more speculative participation to occur than it did in the large group format. All of the students were under more pressure to participate than when they were in one group with the teacher leading the discussion. The students were productively engaged and task-oriented. After twenty-five minutes we came back together to share and extend perceptions in the large group setting.

When the class was over I felt pleased with what happened — but not quite sure why. I made a mental note to consider why I was so elated. Reflecting, I focussed on how the small groups worked — and how the groups seemed to be more involving than the large class arrangement. The spontaneous decision to form small groups served as an opportunity for me to see my class in a new light. I saw the students actively involved both trying to make sense of data and connecting the transcribed utterances with the theories presented in their readings. I subconsciously made a hypothesis from that experience: If I systematically organized class time to allow for working in groups, students would learn more because they would be actively involved in creating and refining their ideas. As teachers we implicitly generate hypotheses and test out these hypotheses albeit without consciously labelling it as hypothesis generation.

Designs of Hypothesis Generating Studies

Hypothesis generating research contributes to the building of new theories, particularly through intensive study of how people normally act. Inherent in this process is the collection of vast quantities of data from naturally occurring situations. Hypothesis testing researchers who study classroom interactions, for example, seek to obtain the perspectives of students as well as the teacher in building theories about the rules which function in classroom interaction. Hypothesis generating studies are conducted as either ethnographies or case studies with larger studies frequently combining both approaches to data collection.

Ethnographic Studies

An ethnography is a written description of a group's implicit or tacit rules and traditions which are followed by members of that specific community and bond the members of that group together. Educational ethnographers tend to focus on one aspect of settings, for example, the rules for getting along in a classroom (Brause and Mayher, 1982 and 1983; Brause, Mayher and Bruno, 1985) or how language is used at home and at school (Wells, 1986). The researcher studies the actions which occur naturally in a given setting. From observations of the group, the researcher generates a set of hypothetical rules which the participants follow. The researcher does not 'manipulate' actions.

To gather *extensive* data, researchers study whole settings such as the whole classroom. Studies taking this holistic stance, seeking the implicit rules which the community of participants negotiates as they engage in these settings are labelled *ethnographic*. One outcome of an ethnography is a 'thick description' which presents an interpretation of the experiences from the participants' perspectives. This description contributes to the development of a theory about how people accomplish specific activities as members of a community. Ethnographies describe in such rich detail that strangers are able to use the rules to function like a native in that society. The intent in conducting an ethnographic, hypothesis generating study is to contribute to building a theory which transcends unique individual students' experiences predicting how individuals negotiate their membership in a community. *Critical ethnographies*, a recent direction in educational research combine a search for what happens with a clearly identified philosophical perspective which results in a critique of practice (see Brause forthcoming).

Case Studies

Another approach used to generate hypotheses for theory building is the *case study* in which investigators study one individual or a small number of individuals as each accomplishes specific activities. The metaphorical use of 'case' is helpful in explaining the concept of case studies. We talk about 'casing a joint' when we study a place very carefully with a specific focus in mind: Is this a good school to teach in? Are there good people here? When someone 'has a case on another' we know that first person focusses amorous attentions exclusively on the second party. 'Having a solid case' refers to legal battles where extensive evidence has been accumulated. These uses of the term *case* convey the intensity and depth of inquiry which are involved in case study research.

To gather *intensive* data, researchers may study selected individuals as each reads and/or writes over a period of time. Studies taking this intensive perspective identify the rules which each individual implicitly enacts when engaged in activities.

In the process of doing case studies, researchers accumulate rich databases which we then subject to systematic analysis. The intensive analysis of these data derived from a few people provides the basis for generating hypotheses and new theories about how people engage in different processes. The resulting hypotheses transcend individuals by focussing on more generic strategies.

When Alice was studying her total environment, she was an *ethnographer*, however unwitting. As we focus on her strategies for surviving, we can label the discussion a *case study* since we are focussing on her as a 'case in point'. These are two distinct options in conducting hypothesis generating studies. Kantor (in chapter 5) discussed the characteristics of ten hypothesis generating studies which appeared in *Research in the Teaching of English*, a journal sponsored by the National Council of Teachers of English. Five are more consistent with case study design and five are more typical of ethnographic design (see table 9.1).

Table 9.1:   *Examples of hypothesis generating research design*

AUTHORS	HYPOTHESIS GENERATING DESIGN	
	Case Study	*Ethnography*
Birnbaum	+	
Brause and Mayher		+
Bridwell	+	
Dillon and Searle		+
Florio and Clark		+
Galda	+	
Hickman		+
Lamme and Childers	+	
Perl	+	
Pettigrew, Shaw & Van Nostrand		+

The limited space available for articles in journals precludes the possibility of presenting the comprehensive data collected and analyzed in a hypothesis generating study. These are more frequently published as books than journal articles (see, for example, Mehan, 1979; Taylor, 1983; Heath, 1985; Wells, 1986; McLaren, 1989; Cochran-Smith, 1984; Freedman, 1990; and Brause, forthcoming). These articles and books provide good examples of the processes involved in hypothesis generating research which are presented in the following section.

Processes for Conducting Hypothesis Generating Studies

Seven elements of hypothesis generating research serve to organize the discussion of how to implement a hypothesis generating study: Acquiring a Theoretical and Research Background; Establishing Initial Questions and Objectives; Selecting Participants and Settings; Collecting Data; Analysing Data; Findings from Data Analysis; and Grounding Theory from Findings. We will consider each of these in turn.

Acquiring a Theoretical and Research Background

Hypothesis generating research is mounted when existing knowledge is inadequate to explain specific phenomena. For example, our current understanding of how people learn is far from sufficient, yet we, as educators, are charged with guiding student learning. Our professional responsibility therefore, mandates numerous simultaneous strategies which include: understanding of published theories and research; reflection on the adequacy of this knowledge base, particularly as it helps us plan educational programs and assess student growth; examination of what students actually do when they learn; and speculation about the effects of alternative experiences on student learning. We need to distinguish between the known and what needs to be known. What is known should be constantly subjected to careful scrutiny (especially through hypothesis testing studies). What is needed to be known is an appropriate focus for hypothesis generating studies. Only through considering the inadequacies of our predictions, are we able to distinguish between the known and the unknown. Of necessity we incorporate hypothesis generating strategies in our thinking.

Rita S. Brause

Establishing Initial Questions and Objectives — Designated Focus of Inquiry

In hypothesis generating research we start out with a specific question (for example, Why did the small groups go so well?). As we continue gathering and analyzing data, we revise the question, reflecting and focusing on specific aspects within the experience (for example, How did the quality of the responses within the small group discussions differ from whole class discussions?). We try to avoid prejudicing our answers by being open to all events which occur naturally. Researchers conducting a hypothesis generating study make decisions tentatively, keeping open the desirability of expanding and/or modifying choices as the study progresses. Questions which are both of professional and personal interest are potentially the most important, exciting and productive ones.

Selecting Participants and Settings

By conducting research of regular classroom activities, hypothesis generating studies avoid the use of contrived settings which is a common phenomenon in hypothesis testing studies. Teacher-researchers have valuable knowledge about their students and therefore are able to select students who are likely to provide the richest data. Teachers devote extended periods of time to classroom activities. Those same, naturally occurring settings are ideal for conducting hypothesis generating research. Hypothesis generating studies tend to be long-term, longitudinal projects in which extensive data are collected on a limited number of participants in contrast to hypothesis testing studies which tend to collect data from a large number of participants in very brief time periods.

Collecting Data

When considering the issue of data collection, the researcher identifies potential data sources and collection procedures. The determination of the most informative data sources occupies considerable time in hypothesis generating studies. The exploratory quality of hypothesis generating studies is evidenced by the tentative identification of a vast array of potential sources. These data are intensively read, reviewed, and interpreted. Researchers need repeated access to these data, so permanency is an essential consideration.

Sources

Observations of ongoing classroom activities make us aware of the complexity and diversity of activities incorporated in daily experiences. Observations are as comprehensive yet unobtrusive as possible.

Fieldnotes recorded during and/or immediately following an observation help us to remember and organize details. Fieldnotes may be recorded concurrent with other devices such as videotaping. Fieldnotes include such information as what happened when the teacher went off-camera, what students were writing in their notebooks, or why the class was particularly excited. Initially the notes may be totally unfocussed, because the most important issues may not be known. Writing promotes reflection, and on re-reading, facilitates the highlighting of recurring themes and patterns.

Interviews are usually conducted in a location removed from the activity. Participants may be asked to remember and discuss what they did, why certain things happened, or what they might do at a particular time. The format for inquiry may be focussed or open-ended. The quality of the interview is influenced by the preparation and insightfulness of the interviewer. Mishler (1987) provides sensitive guidance in this activity, as does Briggs (1987) who suggests interviews should be conducted as shared conversations rather than one-sided interrogations. The interviewer intends, in these discussions, to obtain participants' perspectives and to explore tentative inferences about the participant roles. It is helpful to record these sessions on audio- or videotape for subsequent reference.

Verbal transcripts of teacher-student interactions are derived from video- or audiotaped sessions in conjunction with fieldnotes. The most accurate transcripts result when individuals who are present at the taping, record verbatim utterances through repeated playing of tapes. The process of creating transcripts is labor-intensive and extremely time consuming — but essential in many studies, as noted in Brause and Mayher (1982).

Participants' products, material resources and documents may also provide valuable information. Writing samples accumulated during an academic year, the multiple drafts utilized in arriving at a 'publishable' document, lists of activities pursued, pages referred to in books, teacher plans, and student notes are all potentially rich sources. A careful researcher squirrels away all of these documents, along with his/her fieldnotes for use at a later time.

Procedures

The role(s) of the reaearcher during the collection process vary depending on the focus of the study. The researcher may observe, or be a participant in the activity. Regardless of the role(s), the researcher seeks to obtain the participants' perspectives — and to understand the implicit rules governing the participants' actions. A common strategy used in hypothesis generating studies is labelled as *particpant-observer* (P-O), and includes both the stance of participant and that of observer, In P-O the researcher is a participant at some times while at other times the researcher exclusively observes. Just as one cannot be in two places at one time, one cannot act in two capacities simultaneously.

Analysing Data

One of the clear problems for the researcher is that every observation is influenced by the observer's point of view. This includes, not only what one can actually see, but also all the prejudices, preconceptions, and biases that any observer inevitably and naturally brings to the task. Just as every text is construed differently by each reader, so the classroom text is susceptible to multiple interpretations. While these biases can never be completely eliminated, they can be reduced by having more than one observer participate in the data collection, by seeking numerous instances of a phenomenon (avoiding idiosyncrasies), by comparing analyses with research-team members, by comparing inferences with participants, and by being consciously accountable for personal biases.

Ethnographers state that meanings 'emerge' from the data. Donmoyer (1985) challenges this view, and suggests that the meanings are imposed by the researcher. Contemporary theories of interpretation and learning emphasize the interaction between text and reader (Rosenblatt, 1978; Vygotsky, 1978; Mayher, 1990). The researcher is charged with confirming the interpretations both by interviewing participants and by accounting for all the data as the participants do when they engage in the activity being studied. I will discuss procedures for analysis, providing an example of how to implement these (Brause and Mayher, 1982). The process begins while the data are still being gathered.

Data collection and data analysis, considered as two independent components of the hypothesis testing research process, are intimately connected in hypothesis generating research. Concurrent with the accumulation of data, researchers review their collected data to obtain a more cohesive perspective which accounts for seemingly isolated events.

There are two reciprocal aspects to the data analysis process: data reduction or the discovery process and data verification or the validation process as presented in figure 9.1. The data reduction process involves the identification of significant patterns and the formulation of tentative hypotheses. The verification process focusses on the strategies for testing the accuracy and comprehensiveness of the inferences made in building the tentative hypotheses. The processes of data collection and data analysis are interdependent, with much overlapping between the two.

Figure 9.1: *Components of the analysis process*

Data Reduction ⟷	Data Verification
The Discovery Process	*The Validation Process*
Identification of the range of activities which occur	Triangulation Repetition Prediction-Testing
Tentative hypotheses about rules which guide participant activities	

Data reduction or the discovery process

After we have collected hundreds of documents, we need to make sense of these. There are many ways to accomplish this. Typical strategies are discussed here to provide general guidance for beginning researchers. The first step is to group documents which provide similar information. In this process we might identify several groups such as: evidence of personalizing information, and evidence of collaboration to synthesize information. Within these groups, we identify the clearest examples, thereby focussing our attention on a smaller subset of our accumulated data. We tentatively identify a smaller subset from the mass of data which is one 'representative sample of a frequently occurring activity'.

We have reduced our data in two ways in this process, grouping and then highlighting the clear examples. We subject this sample to intensive analysis and offer a tentative interpretation of that data. Then we return to look at additional slices from the same subset to determine the accuracy both of the representative nature of our slices and our interpretations. The process is cyclical and recursive. We tentatively choose units which represent important activities to the participants, grouping these to accurately reflect the participants' perspectives. We

Figure 9.2: *Processes involved in generating hypotheses*

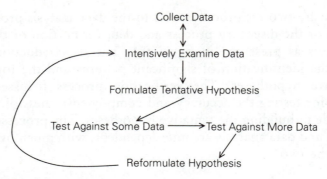

(After Brause and Mayher, 1982)

clearly describe these groups so that others will understand precisely how we segmented the total data (see figure 9.2).

Figure 9.2 presents visually the cyclical processes in analyzing the data. It is especially important to note how each process leads to and from others. Through repeated reviews, comparisons and contrasts are made. These contribute to the researcher's designation of significant, representative events which are called the units of analysis. For example, a unit of analysis might be a lesson or a conversation between two students.

Unique patterns are created in the researcher's mind as a combined result of the collected data and experiences. Initially these are considered conjectures or tentative hypotheses which are 'emerging' from the data. This is called the 'discovery process'. This discovery process focusses on the *tentative* identification of data which are the most significant. We infer significance from the context noting the frequency of the occurrences and the relative importance of the event to the participants.

By studying patterns, we reduce the possibility of considering an idiosyncratic event to be significant. Only those events which recur are isolated as patterns. These patterns 'emerge' as we review the data, striking our memories as repetitions. We compare and contrast these events. We note the similarities in the ways these events occur. They may be similar in an infinite number of ways, such as the language participants use or the time of day when they occur. These 'patterns' are embedded in the activities which the participants engage in.

As the analysis progresses many patterns become apparent. It is important to identify events which the participants consider different (such as contrasting conversations between age peers and those between adults and children). An example of a discrete difference is the mathematical process of addition (in contrast to subtraction). Researchers seek to create discrete categories or patterns to distinguish among processes/events in which participants engage. One clear test which distinguishes patterns finds different rules followed at discrete times. The researcher groups data which are similar, calling these groups 'patterns' and defines these groups by identifying their discrete characteristics. The clear identification of these characteristics or defining criteria are essential because they guide the researcher to be consistent in the grouping of the data. It is common practice for the researcher to group some data, then extrapolate a tentative description of commonalities for the grouped data. This description is the first approximation of a definition.

Since data analysis frequently highlights important issues, it results in the identification of additional information to be collected. The consideration of potential patterns and categories helps in focussing the continued data collection. When a researcher gets a hunch about the potential significance of specific actions in one event, additional observations of similar events are planned. If the hunch allowed the researcher to accurately predict an occurrence, the researcher states a *tentative hypothesis* describing what happens. This process is a very complex one. To further elaborate, I've identified the major steps in data analysis using examples from a study of the rules which govern participation in classroom lessons conducted with John Mayher (Brause and Mayher, 1982).

Review all the data collected to date to select example of events or behaviors which seem to represent the total activity being studied. In this case, a representative set of episodes is characterized by the teacher calling on students to respond to her questions.

Tentatively isolate one segment or episode from what was 'typical' (or patterned) in the larger sample. In this case, the teacher explicitly told the students they needed to raise their hands to be called on for a turn-at-talk.

Repeatedly review this one, isolated segment in order to formulate a tentative hypothesis about its characteristics. In this case, we hypothesized that students could get a turn at talk only by raising hands.

Test these hypotheses to see if they account for the behaviors revealed in the segment under consideration. In this case, we looked to see if all cases of student turns at talk could be accounted for with this rule.

Accumulate additional examples and test these hypotheses against other similar episodes to see if they continue to account for the behavior under consideration. In this case, we found that although the hypothesis did generally characterize the situation, there were cases where some shouted out answers were responded to by the teacher. (These were exceptions to the first rule — and showed us the rule needed revision.)

Reformulate a modified, more precise hypothesis which will account for or explain all of the data examined so far. In this case, we hypothesized (1) that students needed to not only raise hands, but make eye contact with the teacher when the teacher requested responses to her questions, or (2) if a child shouted out an acceptable answer after several incorrect or unacceptable answers, those answers would be responded to.

Reexamine other segments of the data to continue to expand and modify the tentatively reformulated hypotheses. This process is recursive in that it continues until all of the data are accounted for. In this case, the modified hypotheses continued to hold up and provide a useful key to understanding the nature of the rules governing classroom participation.

Determine the relative importance of aspects of the event hierarchically. In this case, student turn allocations were only one of numerous responsibilities for students engaged in classroom activities.

Discuss tentative hypotheses with participants for verification. In this case we collaborated viewing the tapes with and without sound. The participants predicted the rules for turn allocation and who might get a turn at talk. The children were particularly perceptive about how to get a turn at talk. When we showed them the videotapes they were easily able to identify times when they could get responded to by calling out — and their reactions confirmed our own observations. The teacher, on the other hand, had no idea that she was consistent in this process. Before viewing the videotape she thought she was only calling on students who raised their hands. This verification included 'triangulation.'

Label phenomenon using participants' terms. In this case, the students called one portion of class 'talking about' time which included opportunities for them to get a turn-at-talk.

The verification and validation process

The accuracy and comprehensiveness of the tentative hypotheses need to be verified. *Triangulation* is a technical term used by ethnographers to describe a process for verifying and clarifying interpretations. Triangulation involves the use of three data sources. Frequently we use interviews with different participants, repeated observations, lesson plans, blackboard notations and test questions. The intent in using three different sources is to obtain multiple perspectives on the same events. The repetition of occurrences across events and/or participants' explanations are used to support tentative or working hypotheses. The validity of the data analysis is strengthened by these convergent interpretations from diverse sources (Glaser and Strauss, 1967; and Strauss, 1987).

Another aspect of verification is the predictability of events from the tentative hypotheses. By using the hypotheses to predict the occurrence of phenomena within the data collected, the researcher provides additional verification for the tentative hypothesis. The validation aspect of data analysis includes testing tentative hypotheses and inferences by triangulations, repetitions, and predictions. Goetz and LeCompte (1984) provide helpful advice in addressing these issues.

Findings from Data Analysis

As a result of the intensive data analysis, patterns and hypotheses are created. The patterns are descriptions of the processes studied. The hypotheses reflect major findings. They represent the first step in the process of moving from the particular context in which the data were gathered to more general statements and theory building. In the example cited earlier, we were studying one second grade classroom, but our hypotheses were expressed in more general terms. That is, we hypothesized that responsibilities differ during two different times in class, namely talking-about time and writing time.

Each of these hypothesized generalizations, derived from systematically accumulated data, contributes to the formulation of a theory about classroom participation. The theory is built by coupling empirical findings from numerous hypothesis generating studies with testing of those hypotheses in new contexts. Thus, the data provided by each specific study is useful in building a more complete and coherent theory of the phenomenon under examination. Ethnographies and case studies are time-consuming activities. Patterns which emerge may be different from those discovered in previous studies. The researcher's insight, as reflected in our careful documentation of our procedures determines the value of the study for each reader.

Grounding Theory from Findings

Grounded theory refers to the sources of the theory. In hypothesis generating studies the theories are grounded or based on the data collected in 'naturally occurring situations'. Theories are built from these hypotheses. The intent of identifying theoretical constructs is to get closer to knowing the 'truth'. Hypotheses or tentative generalizations need specific testing. The initial sources from which they were derived were intentionally limited to provide for intensive analysis. Inductive and deductive approaches to research are not antithetical to each other, but complementary and each plays a vital role in supporting the other. Hypotheses which stand up to careful testing become components of theories. Theories may be abstract or grounded. The implications of findings can be useful in several ways. Our daily classroom decisions are grounded in theories, intuitions, assumptions, beliefs and reflections on experiences. Through the systematic collection of data, teacher-researchers contribute to a more comprehensive theory of the learning process. The knowledge provides a firmer foundation for formulating classroom activities, for responding to student contributions, and for evaluating student progress.

Teacher-Researchers

As teachers we observe students learning in numerous settings including the library, the corridors, the cafeteria and our own and our colleagues' classrooms. We also review student work in the process of completion from random notes and jottings to polished personal statements for college applications. As we observe, we internalize hunches about the diverse influences on specific student learning, and students' unique strategies and attitudes about knowledge. We may be surprised that when we intend to challenge students to participate, one student withdraws from the competition, while another craves the same competitive forum and seems to flower in that context. As we engage in the activities in our classrooms, numerous unpredictable events occur. When we systematically reflect on these events, we take a researching stance. When we experience something which surprises us, we might be motivated to study — or research the phenomenon systematically. When we conduct hypothesis generating research we add to our knowledge base.

We get hunches about strategies for teaching. These hunches evolve from our experiences. For example, we speculate that when we encourage students to share their work with their neighbors they will take greater care about presenting their ideas coherently. We 'generate' hypotheses intended to account for why things happened. We speculate about predictability given certain circumstances such as talking with peers. Our conscious exploration of an issue may lead us to generate a hypothesis which reflects our current hunches of why certain things happen as they do.

A wise stance for educators to adopt is a reflective stance. Teachers routinely, if subconsciously, do informal research to make educational decisions. Therefore, we control what happens in our classrooms. We can and must critically evaluate the effects of specific materials and practices on our students' learning. By taking a reflective stance, teachers consciously become researchers and participate in the building of theories related to classroom learning (Mayher and Brause, 1986; Schön, 1987).

Many teachers find that when systematically inquiring into how best to promote students' learning, every aspect of work becomes more rewarding and more effective (Mayher and Brause, 1985). Even more important than the professional self-satisfaction and energizing qualities that can come from becoming a teacher-researcher, is the fact that in many ways, practising classroom teachers are in a uniquely powerful position to do important educational research. Teachers who reflect on classroom activities enact responsibilities of professional educators. Teachers who have participated in research studies attest to their enhanced understanding of the teaching-learning process and their increased commitment to helping students learn (Mayher and Brause, 1984).

Sample Hypothesis Generating Studies

There are an increasing number of studies utilizing hypothesis generating approaches in education. Several of these have been published in *Research in the Teaching of English*. More typically, hypothesis generating studies become full length works owing to the need for thick descriptions and the presentation of careful documentation. Journal articles are more accessible, causing us to select such studies, to provide representative examples which might be useful for classroom teachers. (To understand the abstract issues presented here, and throughout the book, we strongly urge readers to read the original research reports in tandem with our explanations and discussions.) In addition to discussing these studies, suggestions for future classroom research are noted at the end of the three sub-sections: writing studies, reading and interpreting texts, and vocabulary development studies. These activities (writing, reading and speaking) occur in all classrooms across all grade levels as ways to facilitate student learning. They help us understand how our students are learning as well as how we may be more instrumental in facilitating that development.

Writing Studies

In 1975 Donald Graves carefully detailed his data collection techniques in studying the writing processes of Michael, a 7-year-old. He observed two different conditions — assigned and unassigned writing. In addition to recording all that Michael wrote (including his illustrations which preceded his production of text), Graves noted Michael's use of supplementary materials, his reading of the text, his voiced writing and reading episodes, and other activities such as sharpening pencils (see table 9.2). This was supplemented by 'interventions' using probing questions by the observer to provide insight into previous and prospective activities of the participant.

Graves recorded his data in the left column of his transcription which included all of the words that Michael wrote. He then put numbers under each of them as well as under significant pauses. The middle column recorded the time and the kind of activity that Michael was engaged in. The right hand column was used for researcher's comments, keyed to particular numbers of words or pauses. This data presentation format allowed the analysis to be integrated with the recording of Michael's performance.

A teacher-researcher intending to do an intensive analysis of a student's writing processes might be well advised to adapt a format similar to the one used by Graves as shown here. One of the advantages of this format is that it allows researchers to share the process of hypothesis generation that characterized the initial research.

Table 9.2:   Example of a writing episode

Michael's Writing	Time Activity	Researcher's Comments
A whale is eating the	10:12	9-Gets up to get dictionary.
1 2 3 4 5	R	Has the page with pictures of animals.
men. A dinosaur is		
6 7 8⑨⑩ ⑪ 12		
trying to eat the whale.	IU	10-Teacher announcement
13 14 15 16 17 ⑱		11-Copies from dictionary and returns book
A dinosaur is frowning		to side of room
⑲⑳ ㉑ 22 23 ㉔		
a tree at the lion . and		18-Stops, rubs eyes
㉕26 27 28 29 30 31 32	RR	19-Rereads from 13 to 19
the cavmen too. the men	OV	20-Voices as he writes
33 34 35 ㊱ 37 38	OV	21-Still voicing
are killed. The dinosaur	IS	24-Gets up to sharpen pencil and returns
39 40 41 42 43		
killed the whale. The	RR	25-Rereads from 20 to 25.
44 45 46 47 49	RR	36-Rereads to 36. Lost starting point.
㊽		
cavmen live is the roks.		48-Puts away paper, takes out again
50 51 52 53 54 55 ㊾	RR	56-Rereads out loud from 49 to 56.

KEY: 1-2-3-4 Numerals indicate writing sequence. 4- Item explained in comment column on the right.//// -erasure or proofreading. T- Teacher involvement; IS- Interruption Solicited; IU- Interruption Unsolicited; RR- Reread; PR- Proofread; DR- Works on Drawing; R- Resource use. Accompanying language: OV- Overt; WH- Whispering; F- Forms Letters and Words; M- Murmuring; S- No overt Language Visible.
(Graves, 1975, p. 232)

One of the most distinctive features of Graves' case study was that, although he focussed on Michael, he did so in the context of gathering some data on, not only the other children in Michael's class, but in three other second grade classes as well. Through this 'pyramid' design (see figure 9.3), Graves was able to build a firmer base for his generalizations and hypotheses than he would have been able to on the basis of looking at only one child. He started by examining the writing folders of ninety-four children and gradually narrowed his focus of attention to Michael. This pyramid design enabled him to capture some of the virtues of both ethnographic and case study approaches.

Graves presented hypotheses concerning such issues as: learning environments, sex differences in writing and developmental factors in the writing process. He presented seven specific hypotheses derived mainly from his case study focussing on four categories: assigned and unassigned writing; concepts of the good writer; developmental factors, and general factors. Thus, this case study, in context, serves as a model for data collection and data analysis with important implications for teaching not only Michael, but children in general.

Glenda Bissex (1980) studied her son as he developed in writing

Figure 9.3:   *Study phases and procedures*

PHASE IV — CASE STUDY
Michael
N-1

PHASE III — INTERVIEWS
Interviews on children's views of their own
writing and concept of the 'good writer'
N-17

PHASE II — THE WRITING EPISODE
The observation of fifty-three writing episodes
N-14

PHASE I — THE WRITING FOLDER
1. Thematic choices of children
2. Writing Frequency
3. Types of writing (assigned-unassigned)
N-94

Formal Classrooms		Informal Classrooms	
Room A	Room B	Room C	Room D
N-24	N-25	N-24	N-21

(Graves, 1975, p. 229)

and reading from ages 5 to 10. This case study, unlike Graves', did not have the context of other children, but did include lots of information on Paul's life and activities at home. She collected data on his beginning efforts as a writer and a reader prior to his entrance into school. One of the striking discoveries she made was that he began writing before he began reading and learned to read, in part, in order to read his own writing. His imaginative uses of writing are fascinatingly described, and although he is obviously an unusual child in some respects, his urge toward meaningful communication in writing seems quite generalizable.

His enthusiasm and imagination in writing at home provided a sharp contrast to the school activities he was assigned once he got there. In addition to contrasting home and school writing and reading, Bissex provides greater generalizability for her hypotheses by carefully comparing Paul's development with a wide range of studies of other children, both in school and out. Her insightful analysis of Paul's evolving understanding of the purposes of writing and the range of responsibilities of the writer was derived from her collection of all of his writing, interviews she had with him, and observations while he was writing and reading.

Since Bissex's research was published in book form, it provides an excellent example of the breadth and depth which is possible to achieve in a case study. One of the limitations of journal reports of hypothesis generating research is the page restrictions of a typical research article. These make it difficult to adequately present enough data for the reader to make an independent judgment about the insightfulness of the researcher's interpretations. As noted earlier, interpretive bias is one of the dangers of hypothesis generating research. One of the best safeguards against such bias is presenting enough data so that the reader joins in the interpretive exploration.

Sondra Perl (1979) and Brian Monahan (1984) conducted studies in which they had students 'compose aloud' as they created their compositions. Composing aloud has become a very useful technique for making inferences about some of the underlying mental processes involved in composing. The subjects say aloud, usually into a tape recorder, everything that comes to mind as they are engaging in the process of composing a text. The resulting 'protocol' then can be analyzed for patterns of planning, drafting, revising, and editing.

Perl and Monahan selected older students: basic (sometimes called remedial) college writers in the former, and basic and competent high school writers in the latter. They assigned 'school-type' writing tasks. As the students proceeded to organize, draft, and review their work, the researchers recorded the students' behaviors and later interviewed them about their decisions.

Perl developed an elaborate coding scheme to analyze the behaviors of the writers she studied. The writers produced texts that were badly marred by various surface feature errors. Unlike previous analyses of such writers which had tended to interpret their performance as the result of ignorance or the lack of stable composing processes, Perl presents persuasive data to support hypotheses that her students' problems stemmed from an overriding and premature concern for correctness. Just as importantly, she showed that they, indeed, did have stable processes of composing, but their worry about being correct truncated their thought processes. Ironically, this resulted in texts which were both incoherent and error filled.

In addition to her careful description of her processes of data collection and analysis, which make this study a useful model for other researchers, Perl also showed how the intensive analysis of a small number of subjects can substantially change our understanding of a large group of writers. Even though her results are presented tentatively, the depth of analysis she provided made it clear that we could no longer make statements like, 'basic writers are the same as beginners in that they lack control of a composing process'.

Monahan compared the revising strategies of 'basic' and 'competent' student writers. His results led to the hypothesis that they shared the same concern for organizational and thematic revision. His analysis further showed that those writers who were labelled competent were more likely to display this capacity for large-scale revision strategies and displayed it more frequently.

Thus, by intensively studying these students, as they engage in writing, the researchers were able to formulate descriptions of their composing processes. These descriptions were expressed in the form of tentative hypotheses which need to be further verified through other studies. Such questions as whether these processes are characteristic of other similar students, whether there is a difference in students' processes when writing independently or in class, or when doing 'real' writing in contrast to 'school' writing are among the issues in need of further exploration. Classroom teachers are ideally situated to conduct such studies.

An ethnographic study of the functions of elementary school writing was conducted by Florio and Clark (1982). They focussed on how writing was used in a first grade classroom. Students used writing for four functions: to participate in the community; to know oneself and others; to occupy free time; and to demonstrate academic competence. Only the last is systematically evaluated or responded to in class (as noted in figure 9.4).

The findings of this study evolved from videotapes of daily activities in the classroom. One of the striking features of this study was the active participation of the classroom teacher in analyzing the writing of the children and its purposes within the classroom context. Since activities often serve multiple purposes, the collaboration between teacher and researchers in this case, made the analysis far more comprehensive and thus, more persuasive.

The categories in figure 9.4 provide a useful model for the analysis of writing in any classroom. If we find, for example, that we are evaluating all the writing that our students do or that all of the writing is directed to us as the audience, then we may be able to recognize that we are limiting the opportunities for genuine writing in our classrooms. Such an analysis would not require a tremendous amount of data collection, but could be done by reviewing our lesson plans for a marking period to see what kinds of writing has occurred, who it was written for, and what was done with it after completion.

Figure 9.4: The functions of writing in room 12

Function type	Sample activity		Distinctive Features					
		Initiator	Composer	Writer/speaker	Audience	Format	Fate	Evaluation
Type I: Writing to participate in community	classroom rule-setting	teacher	teacher & students	teacher	student	by teacher and students: drafted on chalkboard; printed in colored marker on large white paper	posted: referred to when rules are broken	no
Type II: Writing to know oneself and others	diaries	teacher	student	student	student	by teacher: written or printed on lined paper in student-made booklets	locked in teacher's file cabinet or kept in student desk; occasionally shared with teacher, other students, or family	no
Type III: Writing to occupy free time	letters and cards	student	student	student	other (parents, friends, family)	by student: printed or drawn on lined or construction paper	kept; may be given as gift to parents or friend	no
Type IV: Writing to demonstrate academic competence	science lab booklets	teacher	publisher	publisher & student(s)	teacher	by publisher: printed in commercial booklet	checked by teacher; filed for later use by student; pages sent home to parents by teacher	yes

(Florio and Clark, 1982)

Reading and Interpreting Texts

English language arts teachers are committed to developing their students' understanding of literature, particularly as a basis for understanding life and the human condition. All teachers are concerned with improving their students' abilities to interpret texts. We have an example of this process in Alice's discussion with Tweedledum:

> 'I like the Walrus best because you see, he was a *little* sorry for the poor oysters.'
>
> 'He ate more than the Carpenter, though', said Tweedledee. 'You see, he held his handkerchief in front so that the carpenter couldn't count how many he took; contrariwise.'
>
> 'That was mean!' Alice said indignantly. 'Then I like the Carpenter best — if he didn't eat so many as the Walrus.'
>
> 'But he ate as many as he could get', said Tweedledum.
>
> This was a puzzler. After a pause, Alice began, 'Well! They were *both* very unpleasant characters.' (p. 164)

The interchange of ideas among Alice, Tweedledee, and Tweedledum provided the opportunity for each to consider different interpretations thereby enriching their ultimate understanding. This is reminiscent of lively classroom discussions. Fortunately, the time-consuming nature of analyzing individual's interpretations of literary texts has not stopped several researchers from conducting such inquiries.

Lee Galda (1982) conducted a study of three fifth grade students' responses to two novels. She interviewed them individually and observed their interactive group discussion. Her findings suggested specific aspects of change or development in the girls' responses. The primary response mode was evaluative with three distinct differences identified:

> Emily was subjective and reality bound, uncertain of the rationale behind her responses. Charlotte was more objective but still limited by her dependence on real life as a measure. She used her objective stance to regulate her response to the texts. Ann analyzed both the text and her own responses as she sought explanations for both literary and real life experiences. (p. 17)

In addition, Galda hypothesized differences in both the students' focus and their perceptions of the author's role. Ann, in particular, was able to recognize that the events of each story were under the control of the author and could have been different had the author so decided. The other two, Emily and Charlotte, were so tied to their conception of the way people actually behave in the real world, that they judged the book to be deficient when it didn't correspond to their sense of the way it really is. Galda concluded by hypothesizing that 'evaluative style, perception of author's role, and focus influenced the ability to assume and maintain a spectator stance. Differences in this ability ... may be a function of development' (p. 1).

Galda's study could be replicated by classroom teachers to understand the individual nature of student responses and how these responses are influenced by participation in small group discussions. Since a teacher is responsible for much larger groups of students, it would probably by practical to suggest the selection of students who represent a range of proficiencies in the class. The hypotheses developed from looking at some of the students' responses, then, could be used in planning, implementing and evaluating instruction with a larger segment of the class.

Few materials are required: an audio-taperecorder with sufficient tapes to store the discussions for repeated playback, copies of materials to be read, and a quiet, comfortable place to talk. While a person is participating in a discussion it is impossible to take the observer's role and simultaneously analyze the data. Thus, taping such discussions is essential. Through replaying segments and transcribing verbatim contributions, the pattern of individual responses becomes apparent. This process permits generalizations to be formulated and hypotheses to be generated.

As a teaching device, these discussions may be listened to by other students. This will provide additional perspectives and interpretations to be considered in discussing a literary work. Groups could attempt to influence each other's stances through the exchange of these tapes, much like local community groups use tapes of televised 'roundtable discussions' on news events and other current issues.

Vocabulary Studies

In addition to the development of reading and writing abilities, teachers are also concerned with the continued development of the oral language proficiencies of their students. Talking to learn, for example, has been widely recognized in recent years as a valuable and under-utilized resource for student learning. Some of the most careful and insightful analyses of how this can happen in student-led discussion groups has been done in England by Douglas Barnes (1971 and 1976). Barnes' work presents transcripts of both whole class and small group interchanges which he then perceptively analyzes to reveal the patterns of learning they contain. In his examples of whole class teaching, he shows that teachers very frequently dominate the class both by doing most of the talking and by controlling the vocabulary employed. He shows that what often passes for student learning is the student repetition of teacher terminology which they rarely show any real command of, and are unable to use independently.

In small groups, in contrast, when the teacher is not present, the students fumble linguistically, but do so with purpose and eventual understanding of the concepts being discussed. The small group work can be most accurately characterized as using talk to build a bridge between linguistic and conceptual resources that the children bring to the task and the concepts embodied in the curriculum. In the large group work, this process is often short-circuited with the repetition of a verbal label substituting for real comprehension.

Teachers who tape record their own classes and/or small groups within their classes, and then look at them collaboratively with another colleague or with their students will frequently be shocked by both the limits we place on student learning and the resourcefulness our students demonstrate when they operate independently. One of the most straightforward ways to begin hypothesis generating research in our own classrooms can be to tape record them and try to see patterns in our own and our students' language.

Conclusion

Despite centuries of research, observations and theory building, learning and teaching remain remarkably complex and mysterious processes. One of the most exciting, although sometimes frustrating aspects of teaching is that no matter how experienced we are there are always new challenges to meet. This year's class is never quite the same as last year's and sometimes even our formerly most successful lessons fall flat.

Professional teachers are constantly asking themselves WHY? The suggestions given here on how to conduct hypothesis generating research provide some avenues down which we can travel in our quest to understand WHY?

References

BARNES, D. (1971) 'Language in the secondary classroom' in BARNES, D., BRITTON, J. and ROSEN, H. (Eds) *Language, the Learner and the Schools*, Baltimore, MD, Penguin.

BARNES, D. (1976) *From Communication to Curriculum*, New York, Penguin.

BISSEX, G. (1980) *GNYS at WRK*, Cambridge, MA, Harvard University Press.

BRAUSE, R.S. (forthcoming) *Enduring Schools*, Lewes, Falmer Press.

BRAUSE, R.S. and MAYHER, J.S. (1982) 'Teachers, students and classroom organization', *Research in the Teaching of English*, 16, 2.

BRAUSE, R.S. and MAYHER, J.S. (1983) 'Classroom teacher as researcher', *Language Arts*, 60, 6.

BRAUSE, R.S., MAYHER, J.S. and BRUNO, J. (1985) *An Investigation into Bilingual Students' Classroom Communicative Competence. Final Report to the National Institute of Education*, Rosslyn, VA, Clearinghouse on Bilingual Education.

BRIGGS, C. (1987) *Learning How to Ask*, New York, Cambridge University Press.

COCHRAN-SMITH, M. (1984) *The Making of a Reader*, Norwood, NJ, Ablex.

DONMOYER, R. (1985) 'The rescue from relativism: Two failed attempts and an alternative strategy', *Educational Researcher*, 14, 10.

ELIOT, J. (1980) 'Implications of classroom research for professional development' in HOYLE, E. and MEGARRY, J. (Eds) *World Yearbook of Education 1980: Professional Development of Teachers*, New York, Nichols.

FLORIO, S. and CLARK, C. (1982) 'The functions of writing in an elementary classroom', *Research in the Teaching of English*, 16, 2.

FREEDMAN, S. (1990) *Small Victories: The Real World of a Teacher, Her Students and Their High School*, New York, Harper and Row.

GALDA, S.L. (1982) 'Assuming the spectator stance: An examination of the responses of three young readers', *Research in the Teaching of English*, 16, 1.

GLASER, B. and STRAUSS, A.L. (1967) *The Discovery of Grounded Theory: Strategies for Qualitative Research*, New York, Aldine.

GOETZ, J.P. and LeCOMPTE, M.D. (1984) *Ethnography and Qualitative Design in Educational Research*, Orlando, FL, Academic Press.

GRAVES, D.H. (1975) 'An examination of the writing process of seven year old children', *Research in the Teaching of English*, 9, 3.

GRIFFIN, P. and SHUY, R. (Eds) (1978) *The Study of Children's Functional Language and Education in the Early Years*, Final Report to the Carnegie Corporation, New York.

HEATH, S.B. (1985) *Ways With Words*, New York, Cambridge University Press.

Rita S. Brause

MAYHER, J.S. (1990) *Uncommon Sense: Theoretical Practice in Language Education*. Portsmouth, NH, Boynton/Cook.

MAYHER, J.S. and BRAUSE, R.S. (1984) 'Learning through teaching: Asking the right questions', *Language Arts*, 61, 5.

MAYHER, J.S. and BRAUSE R.S. (1985) 'Learning through teaching: Adele Fiderer reflects with her fifth graders', *Language Arts*, 62, 3.

MAYHER, J.S. and BRAUSE R.S. (1986) 'Learning through teaching: Is testing crippling language education?, *Language Arts*, 63, 4.

McLAREN, P. (1989) *Life in Schools*, New York, Longman.

MEHAN, H. (1979) *Learning Lessons*, Cambridge, MA, Harvard University Press.

MISHLER, E. (1987) *The Research Interview*, Cambridge, MA, Harvard University Press.

MONAHAN, B. (1984) 'Revision strategies of basic and competent writers as they write for different audiences', *Research in the Teaching of English*, 18, 3.

PERL, S. (1979) 'The composing processes of unskilled college writers', *Research in the Teaching of English*, 13, 4.

ROSENBLATT, L.M. (1978) *The Reader, the Text, the Poem*, Carbondale, IL, Southern Illinois University Press.

SCHÖN, D. (1987) *Educating the Reflective Practitioner*, San Francisco, CA, Jossey Bass.

STRAUSS, A. (1987) *Qualitative Analysis for Social Scientists*, New York, Cambridge University Press.

TAYLOR, D. (1983) *Family Literacy*, Portsmouth, NH, Heinemann.

VYGOTSKY, L.S. (1978) *Mind in Society*, Cambridge, MA, Harvard University Press.

WELLS, G. (1986) *The Meaning Makers*, Portsmouth, NH, Heinemann.

Chapter 10

Concluding and Beginning

John S. Mayher and Rita S. Brause

This book as a whole has had several complementary purposes: to help teachers understand the importance of being perpetual learners; to help teachers read and understand relevant published research studies; and to help teachers begin the process of becoming teacher-researchers in their own classrooms. We see these three ideals as mutually inter-dependent because we are convinced that teachers who continue to grow are essential to the profession and that such growth requires all three capacities: to be able to examine one's own theoretical/practical assumptions; to be able to use the professional/theoretical research literature as an aid to those reflections; and to be able to inquire into our own classrooms by making them the locus of teacher-research.

We have tried to show throughout that each of these activities is intimately dependent on the other two. Teacher research, for example, which is attempted without either a process for examining our assumptions or of familiarizing ourselves with the current state of knowledge in our field, will be a sterile activity indeed. Similarly, merely reflecting on our assumptions without either being aware of what others have done or inquiring into our practice will be unlikely to produce change. Finally, research on classrooms which does not take into account either the assumptions of practitioners or their intentions in their classrooms rarely speaks to the real world concerns of teachers and learners.

We hope that these chapters have helped not only to demystify the processes and products of research but to encourage each teacher-reader to join the community of inquiry. While this book and others like it may be useful in getting the process started, the value that will come for all of our students will depend on our actions as well as our understandings.

John S. Mayher and Rita S. Brause

Benefits of Teacher-Research

As researching teachers ourselves, we have seen the benefits of teacher-research in our own classrooms. We believe we have become more effective as teachers by taking on the stance of teacher-researchers. We talk less, but our students learn more because they are becoming increasingly responsible for their own learning. More important, as an incentive for joining us, we can promise you that it's simply more fun to teach when we are continually reflecting on our practice.

In addition to the self-satisfaction that teacher research can bring, we can see many benefits of teacher research to the profession, the individual teacher and above all, to all of our students which we enumerate in figure 10.1.

Figure 10.1: Benefits of Teacher Research

TO THE PROFESSION	By conducting research on the teaching-learning process we increase the knowledge base for professional practice which can influence our effectiveness not only in our own classrooms, but in current and future classrooms of our colleagues locally and nationally.
	Teacher-researchers are at the forefront of educational reform, collaborating in the establishment of local policies at the decision-making level, including participating in school-based management teams, as knowledgeable, informed educators with clear perspectives, if not in possession of all the answers to improve educational practice.
TO EACH TEACHER	We get to know and understand our students better, making us more sensitive to their specific needs. We increase our effectiveness as teachers because we are able to design and institute practices which are sensitive to the needs of our individual students.
	We garner respect from our professional colleagues similarly involved in perpetual learning. This respect leads to increased professional autonomy, essential in promoting professional change. We share with colleagues our concerns, insights, and practices, foregoing the isolation typically associated with teaching.
	We sustain our initial professional idealism, never becoming stagnant or burning-out since there are always new questions which become apparent once others are researched.
TO ALL OF OUR STUDENTS	Our students learn about learning from witnessing adults in the process of learning from which they see the ultimate effects of persistence and become aware of an abundance of resources which contribute to our learning.
	Our students become known to us as individuals, allowing us to challenge all of our students and promote their individual progress. Thus students in researching teachers' rooms are more empowered and have greater awareness both of their essential role in their learning as well as the ways to help society progress.

Characteristics of Effective Teacher-Research

It may also be useful to briefly reflect as a kind of summary, on those qualities that make for effective and productive teacher-research.

(i)   The teacher takes an inquiring, reflective stance, questioning and researching traditions and assumptions about learning inherent in his/her classroom practices.

(ii) These questions and the research which is conducted to answer the questions are identified from working with our students in our classrooms.

(iii) The research is structured to obtain clear understandings of the learning processes of individual students in our classrooms, sampling student products over an extended time period thereby getting to understand more about all students as learners.

(iv) The research questions and processes draw on the teacher's knowledge base which is derived from a combination of working with these particular students and reading extensively in our professional literature.

(v)   The teacher-researcher interprets findings and plans activities to ensure the academic success of students while exciting them to become perpetual learners.

(vi) Teacher-researchers share outcomes in professional contexts.

All of these benefits are achieved only with significant commitment to our professional responsibilities. No one who understands the complexity of teaching ever said teaching was easy — but we strongly urge you to make this commitment for its rewards are awe-inspiring.

One final bit of advice as you begin the journey through the looking-glass: Be on the lookout for fellow travellers! The community of inquirers is steadily growing. Local, regional and national professional organizations are sponsoring more and more forums where such inquiries are shared both in person and in print. Further, many of these organizations are offering small grants to defray some of the expenses involved.

Most important, however, will be to find colleagues within your school district or region who will share this process with you as you share yours with them. Don't exclude in your search for colleagues researchers who work in different contexts including those of us who teach at universities who are often lonely and would love to have you drop by for a chat or to have you invite us to be another pair of eyes in your classroom.

Gook luck in your journey. We look forward to meeting you somewhere down the road.

Notes on Contributors

All of the contributors are active members of the Conference on English Education and the National Council of Teachers of English and served together as members of the NCTE Standing Committee on Research. (In addition, all are active researchers in their own classrooms.)

Rita S. Brause is Professor of Education at Fordham University where she teaches courses in literacy, applied linguistics, learning and research. A former member of the Executive Committee of the Conference on English Education of the NCTE, she has chaired its committees on the Richard Meade Award for Research in English Education and the James Britton Award for Teacher Research in English Language Arts Education. She is the author of the forthcoming *Enduring Schools* (Falmer Press, 1991) and from 1983 was co-author with John Mayher of a column in *Language Arts*, 'Learning through teaching'.

James L. Collins is Associate Professor in the Graduate School of Education at the State University of New York at Buffalo. He edited *Teaching All the Children to Write* for the New York State English Council and is currently editing *Vital Signs*, a series for Heinemann Boynton/Cook. The first volume in the series is *Bringing Together Reading and Writing* and the second is *Teaching and Learning Language Collaboratively*. He co-edited *Writing on Line: Using Computers in the Teaching of Writing* with Elizabeth A. Sommers for Boynton/Cook.

Ken Kantor is Professor in the National College of Education of National-Louis University. He directs the doctoral program in Instructional Leadership, and teaches courses in writing, linguistics, curriculum theory and development, and qualitative research. His publications include a number of chapters in books and articles in *English Education*, *Research in the Teaching of English*, *Language Arts*, *English Journal*, *Theory into Practice*, and the *Journal of Curriculum Theorizing*.

John S. Mayher is Professor of English Education at New York University where he teaches courses in educational linguistics and research methodology and directs the doctoral program. He is Chair (1990–92) of the Conference on English Education of the NCTE. He is the author of *Uncommon Sense: Theoretical Practice in Language Education* (Boynton/Cook, 1990) and co-author with Nancy Lester and Gordon Pradl of *Learning to Write/Writing to Learn* (Boynton/Cook, 1983). From 1983 to 1986 he was the co-author with Rita Brause of a column in *Language Arts* entitled 'Learning through teaching'.

William L. Smith is Professor of English and English Education at the University of Pittsburgh where he is the Director of the Writing Workshop, Director of Testing, and Coordinator of Computers-in-Composition. He has published numerous articles and is a frequent presenter at national and state conferences.

Index

Alice in Wonderland 3, 4, 6–7, 8–9, 181
ANOVA (Analysis of Variance) 173–7

Beach, R. 160
behaviorism 49
bibliographies 88–9
Birnbaum, J.C. 97, 100, 101, 102, 103, 104, 105, 106
Bissex, Glenda 197–9
Brause, Rita S. 54, 98, 100, 102, 103, 106, 107, 109, 118, 138, 187
Bridwell, L.S. 98, 100, 101, 103, 105, 106, 109
Briggs, C. 187
Britton, J.N. 139, 145, 146, 147, 154
Bronfenbrenner, U. 103
Bruner, J.S. 153

case studies 183–5
Childers, N.M. 98–9, 100, 101, 102, 103, 104, 106, 107
chi-square test 81
Clark, C.M. 98, 100, 102, 103, 104, 105, 107, 108, 109, 200
classroom studies 131–4
colleagues 29–32
Collins, James L. 69, 160
commonsense 5, 6–9
conceptual development 153–5
constructs 4
    Teaching Act Model 25–8
control groups 67–8, 169

Cook, T.D. 92
Cooper, C.R. 160
correctness 16–18
correlational analysis 161–3
critical ethnographies 183
cross-sectional research 67
Cuban, Larry 31
curricular decisions 118–19

data analysis 80–1, 95–6, 104–8, 135–6, 188–9
    data reduction or discovery process 189–93
    findings as abstractions from specific data 137–8, 193–4
    qualitative analysis 137
    quantitative analysis 136–7
    teacher-researcher vocabulary study 140–7
    transcript on synonyms 148–53
    verification and validation process 193
data bases 71
data collection 64–5, 66, 79–80, 94–5, 102–4, 128, 186–7
    classroom studies 131–4
    quantity of data 134–5
    teacher-researcher vocabulary study 138–9
    transcript on synonyms 147–8
data presentation 82–5
data reduction 189–93
Diderich, F. 49

Dillon, D. 98, 100, 101, 102, 106,
  107, 108
Dixon, J. 154
Donmoyer, R. 188

English teaching 9, 12–13 *see also*
  literature, reading, writing skills
ERIC 71
ethics 174
ethnographic studies 183
experimental research 66

Fiderer, Adele 33–4, 36, 37, 39, 40
fieldnotes 187
figures 83–5 *see also* statistics
Florio, S. 98, 100, 102, 103, 104, 105,
  107, 108, 109, 200
Frye, Northrop 14
F test 173

Galda, Lee 98, 100, 101, 102, 103,
  105, 106, 108, 202–3
Goetz, J.P. 193
grammar 16, 17, 18
Graves, Donald 34, 99, 102, 196–7
Griffin, W.J. 83
grounded theory 96–7, 108–9, 194
grouping 24

Hawthorne Effect 174
Hickman, J. 98, 100, 102, 106, 107,
  109
Hill, J. 49
Hogan, Robert 91
Hunt, K.W. 72, 88
hypothesis generating 91–2, 181–2
  see also under research
  case studies 183–5
  characteristics 92
  criteria for selecting participants
    and settings 94, 101–2, 186
  data analysis 95–6, 104–8, 188–9
    data reduction or discovery
      process 189–93
    findings 193–4
    verification and validation
      process 193
  data collection 94–5, 102–4,
    186–7

ethnographic studies 183
grounded theory and implications
  96–7, 108–9, 194
initial questions and objectives
  93–4, 100–1, 186
procedures 188
research design 121–6
sample studies 195–6
how children learn concepts 153–5
  reading and interpreting texts
    202–3
  vocabulary studies 203–4
  writing studies 196–201
teacher-researchers 194–5
theoretical and research
  background 93, 99–100, 185
hypothesis testing 63, 165–7 *see also*
under research
characteristics of research reports
  64–5
descriptive phase 159–65
identifying variables and measures
  167–70
interpreting findings 177–8
quantitative analysis 157–9
reading research reports 68–70
  author 71–2
  discussion and implications
    86–8
  figures 83–5
  measures used 78
  methods used to analyze data
    80–1
  methods used to collect data
    79–80
  procedures 74–5
  rationale and review of
    literature 72–3, 164–5
  references 88–9
  results 81–2
  statement of purpose 73–4
  subjects used 75–8
  tables 82–3
  title 70–1
research design 117–18, 170–1
sampling 171–3
statistical testing 173–7
types of research 65–8

independent variable 167, 173–4
interviews 187

Kantor, Ken 184
Kelly, George 4, 46, 57
key words 71
Kroll, Barry 70, 71, 72–3, 74, 75, 76,
    77, 78, 80, 81, 82, 87, 89

Lamme, L.L. 98–9, 100, 101, 102,
    103, 104, 106, 107
language acquisition 153–5
    synonyms 147–53
    vocabulary development 10–12
    data collection and analysis 138–47
    hypothesis generating studies
        203–4
learning concepts 153–5
LeCompte, M.D. 193
Lester, N.B. 41
Levine, Denise 138–41, 144–7, 155
literature 9, 12–15
    reading and interpreting texts
        202–3
literature review 72–3, 164–5
Loban, Walter 70, 71, 72, 73, 74, 75,
    76, 77, 78, 80, 81, 82, 83, 85, 87,
    88, 89
longitudinal research 66–7

Martin, Nancy 21
Mayher, John S. 24, 25, 51, 54, 98,
    100, 102, 103, 106, 107, 109, 118,
    138, 147, 153, 187, 191
Mishler, E. 187
Monahan, Brian 199, 200
Murray, Donald M. 34, 37, 109

Norris, R.C. 83
North, S.M. 48
null hypothesis 163, 173, 174, 175,
    176, 177

O'Donnell, R.C. 83, 88
Onore, C.S. 41

participant-observers 188
Pearson product-moment correlation
    161–2

Perl, Sondra 16, 17, 91, 99, 101, 102,
    103, 105, 106, 107, 160, 199
Pettigrew, J. 99, 100, 101, 102, 103,
    105, 106, 107, 108, 109
Piaget, Jean 76
piloting 133–4
professional isolation 29–30
punctuation 16, 20

qualitative analysis 137
quantitative analysis 136–7, 157–9

Rakosi, Carl 60
random sampling 77, 171
reading 12–15
    interpreting texts 202–3
references 88–9
Reichardt, C.S. 92
research
    definition 46–7
    ethics 174
    hypothesis generating and testing
        51–4 *see also*
        hypothesis generating,
            hypothesis testing
    context 59
    distinction 54–6
    outcomes 59–60
    perspectives 60–1
    research processes 58–9
    scientific origins 57–8
    objectives 47–51
    teacher-research 194–5
        benefits 208
        characteristics of effective
            teacher-research 209–10
    use of findings by teachers 45–6
research design 115–16
    finding research questions 116–17
        context of curricular decisions
            118–19
        planning, doing and evaluating
            instruction 119–21
        research which generates theory
            121–6
        research which tests theories
            117–21
    framing researchable questions

accessible information 128
population 127–8
representative data 128
resources available 129
sample questions 129–30
Rist, R.C. 102
Rosenblatt, Louise 13

sampling 77–8, 171–3
Schön, Donald 5–6, 25, 46
Searle, D. 98, 100, 101, 102, 106, 107, 108
self-assessment 33–4
semantic abbreviation 69
Shaughnessy, M.P. 160
Shaw, R.A. 99, 100, 101, 102, 103, 105, 106, 107, 108, 109
Singleton, C. 49
Sizer, Ted 31
Smith, F. 153
spelling 16, 17
statistical analysis 64, 81, 158–9, 160–3, 173–7
status research 66
stratified sampling 77, 172
student-centered teaching 24–5
learning concepts 153–5
students writing for younger students 34–40
synonyms 147–53

tables 82–3
teachers
as researchers 194–5 *see also* research
benefits of teacher-research 208
characteristics of effective teacher-research 209–10
financial rewards 31
growth 23
formulating and reformulating questions 28–9
observation and reflection 35–7
seeking out colleagues 29–32
self-assessment and reflection 33–4
using literature and colleagues 34–5

professional isolation 29–30
student-centered teaching 24–5
learning concepts 153–5
students writing for younger students 34–40
use of research findings 45–6
Teaching Act Model 25–8, 117, 118, 121
Terry, Ann 70, 71, 72, 73, 74, 75, 76, 77, 78, 79, 81, 82, 83, 87, 89
theory based perceptions 4–6
commonsense versus uncommonsense 6–9
research objectives *see* research
Teaching Act Model 25–8
Thomson, Jack 15
transactional theory of fiction 13
transcripts 148–53, 187
triangulation 193
t-test 81, 173

uncommonsense 5, 6–9

validation 193
Van Nostrand, A.D. 99, 100, 101, 102, 103, 105, 106, 107, 108, 109
Van Tassell, Frances 34
variables 167–9
verbal transcripts 148–53, 187
verification 193
Vine, H.A. 25
vocabulary development 10–12
data collection and analysis 138–47
hypothesis generating studies 203–4
Vygotsky, L.S. 56, 147, 154

Watts, A.F. 72
Wells, G. 155
writing skills
correctness 16–18
hypothesis generating studies 196–201
power in writing 18–21
revising texts for fuller meaning 157, 160–1, 163, 165–6, 168–9, 172, 177–8
students writing for younger students 34–40